The Feeling Intellect

In *The Feeling Intellect*, Steven Groarke explores the overlap between psychoanalysis and philosophy in order to provide the first critical evaluation of the Independent tradition in British and American psychoanalysis.

The book focuses on the formation of Independent object-relations theory as an original mid- to late-twentieth-century development in post-Freudian psychoanalysis, focusing on contributions by Fairbairn, Winnicott, Loewald, and others to add to our understanding of what the author terms the dependence relationship: the earliest relationship between mother and infant. The theory of acts and relations provides the basic framework for more detailed discussions of the psychoanalysis of time, including, Loewald's idea of the inner future and the role of re-descriptive memory as a type of reclamation.

This book is aimed at a readership intent on exploring the philosophical aspects of contemporary psychoanalysis in more detail. It will be of great value to psychoanalysts, psychotherapists, and students studying psychology.

Steven Groarke is professor emeritus at Roehampton University, a member of the British Psychoanalytic Society, author of *Managed Lives: Psychoanalysis, Inner Security and the Social Order* (Routledge, 2014), and a practicing adult psychoanalyst.

'This erudite and lucid study of "object relations" is an interesting perspective on the convergences and divergences of the British Independent tradition and the contributions of American relational psychoanalysis. Psychoanalysis needs its theoreticians – for it to grow and develop – and readers have much to gain from diving into this text from a leading theoretician in the British Psychoanalytical Society'.

Christopher Bollas, *psychoanalyst and writer*

'With so much literature competing for the analyst's attention, my hope is that enough readers will register the importance of this remarkable book. With an unostentatious mastery, it offers a boldly ambitious and rigorous reconceptualization of the fundamentals of metapsychology from an Independent psychoanalytic perspective. Its contribution to such basic concepts as the drive, the object, time and memory is wholly original and brilliantly stimulating. This is a book to be read and debated for decades to come'.

Josh Cohen, *Psychoanalyst and Fellow of British Psychoanalytical Society and Professor of Literary Theory, Goldsmiths University of London*

The Feeling Intellect

An Essay on the Independent Tradition in British and American Psychoanalysis

Steven Groarke

Routledge
Taylor & Francis Group
LONDON AND NEW YORK

Cover image: Luke Groarke aged 2 years

First published 2022
by Routledge
4 Park Square, Milton Park, Abingdon, Oxon OX14 4RN

and by Routledge
605 Third Avenue, New York, NY 10158

Routledge is an imprint of the Taylor & Francis Group, an informa business

Library of Congress Cataloguing-in-Publication Data
Names: Groarke, Steven, author.
Title: The feeling intellect : an essay on the independent tradition in British and American psychoanalysis / Steven Groarke.
Description: 1 Edition. | New York, NY : Routledge, 2022. | Includes bibliographical references and index. | Summary: "In The Feeling Intellect, Steven Groarke explores the overlap between psychoanalysis and philosophy in order to provide the first critical evaluation of the Independent tradition in British and American psychoanalysis"-- Provided by publisher.
Identifiers: LCCN 2021055671 | ISBN 9781138241091 (hardback) | ISBN 9781138241237 (paperback) | ISBN 9781315280899 (ebook)
Subjects: LCSH: Psychoanalysis–Great Britain. | Psychoanalysis–United States. | Social sciences--Philosophy.
Classification: LCC BF173 .G7196 2022 | DDC 150.19/5--dc23/eng/20220203
LC record available at https://lccn.loc.gov/2021055671

ISBN: 978-1-138-24109-1 (hbk)
ISBN: 978-1-138-24123-7 (pbk)
ISBN: 978-1-315-28089-9 (ebk)

DOI: 10.4324/9781315280899

Typeset in Times New Roman
by MPS Limited, Dehradun

in memoriam
Mary Groarke 2 May 1935 to 16 May 1935

for my bereaved grandparents
and those among their generation in want of consolation
for the mercy of their hands in the diaspora of migrant labour

Contents

And he whose soul has risen
Up to the height of feeling intellect
Shall want no humbler tenderness, his heart
Be tender as a nursing mother's heart.
Wordsworth, The Prelude, 1805, Book XIII, ll. 204–7

Acknowledgements

Parts of this book, in earlier versions, have been previously published and are used here with permission: 'Reflections on the psychoanalysis of hope', Steven Groarke, *Psychoanalysis, Culture & Society*, 23 (4): 365–383, 2018, Springer Nature; 'Freud and the remembered past', Steven Groarke, *American Imago*, 77 (2): 277–308, 2020, John Hopkins University Press; 'The sense of the past: theoretical and clinical aspects of deferred action', Steven Groarke, *International Journal of Psychoanalysis*, 102 (6): 1097–1115, 2021, copyright © Institute of Psychoanalysis reprinted by permission of Taylor & Francis Ltd on behalf of Institute of Psychoanalysis.

Introduction

I

This book explores a series of theoretical and clinical developments in mid- to late-twentieth-century post-Freudian thought. It is a study in the remarkable ability of psychoanalysis to renew and enlarge itself on its own terms, in accordance with its intrinsic value and cogency, and by means of its internal resources and system of metapsychology.[1] Independent psychoanalysis, which is my topic, developed under the tutelage of the classical Freudian interpretation, although this is not a straightforward matter: what is handed down to us from the past may be understood in one of two ways. On the one hand, Freud's legacy is transmitted in the form of received or established doctrines. As with any fixed system of knowledge, the Freudian *doxa* forms part of the authority of the past, where precedent is taken as the principal criterion of action. We act the way we do because that is how Freud acted. As the history of psychoanalysis demonstrates, new orthodoxies are established on similar grounds, often in the mantle of the innovator. In which case the replication of bodies of doctrine and an apotheosis of method ensure that the familiar structure of obedience and conformity remains intact.

On the other hand, legacies tend to run ahead of us, which means that we cannot simply delegate the question of meaning to tradition. The modifications and revisions, as well as the more far-reaching alterations, breakthroughs, and new directions in the history of psychoanalysis, demonstrate the role of tradition as an active, propulsive force. The transmission of the 'living past', conceived as a construct of the historical imagination, involves the *use* of tradition, rather than its conservation. Freud's purposes are not necessarily ours. Indeed, a pragmatic, action-based conception of tradition allows us to distance ourselves from tradition with the express purpose of augmenting its available reach. As a result, we are in a position to gather and use a past with which we are not adhesively identified. I am not suggesting that history simply mimics the present. Nevertheless, in my view a tradition is realised, with due respect to 'the authority of the dead and the charisma of the

DOI: 10.4324/9781315280899-1

ancestors' (Harrison 2003: 94), only by the contributions that one makes to it. As such, one's actions remain indebted and guided without being validated by compliance.

The mere ratification of authority weakens the meaning of tradition and truncates its reach; whereas the strong version of tradition consists in finding ways to make use of it, invariably, in the name of the dead. The *modernity* of Freudian thought rests on the active use of tradition, that is to say, on the idea that the past leads into, animates, and is animated by the present. We set about creating meaning in relation to our forebears, as a result of which 'the sedimented history of assembled meanings' is reclaimed in the form of 'a new semantic aim' (Ricoeur 1978: 298). My study is based on the assumption that the speculative horizon of the Freudian interpretation acts as 'an inductive principle capable of guiding semantic innovation' (1978: 298). What psychoanalysis needs, as Loewald (1978a: 193) noted, is 'not a "new language" but a less inhibited, less pedantic and narrow understanding and interpretation of its current language, leading to elaborations and transformations of the meanings of concepts, theoretical formulations, or definitions that may or may not have been envisaged by Freud'.

Loewald's view rules against the idea that anything goes. Freudian discourse has its necessity in itself. In making a case for the active transmission of psychoanalysis, I am not presenting the Independent perspective as yet one more *alternative* to classical theory. The (oedipal) wish to diminish or do away with Freud is an all too familiar feature of the contemporary scene; whereas Independent psychoanalysis, at its best, credits the possibilities germinal in Freud's thought. This book is an inquiry into some of those possibilities. It aims to trace the points at which Freudianism pushes against the limits of its own thinking; hence my focus on things that are simultaneously announced and occluded by Freud, the openings and closures in his thinking. In this respect, much of what I have to say in this book is implicit in Freud's own formulations and hypotheses. The main part of my work consists in critical reconstruction, with the aim of building on Freud's hypotheses from an Independent object-relations perspective. Starting with a strong version of tradition as a means of semantic innovation, I assume that the future of psychoanalysis depends on reinterpretations of what Freud anticipated and envisaged but did not necessarily formulate himself, or formulated only partially.

It is not a case of finding out more about the same things so much as realising further possibilities by inventing new problems; when we refer to a legacy there is the straightforward sense of a bequest, but, as Lear (1996: 123) notes, 'there is also a sense of a legacy as that which a person did *not* hand down (but should have)'. I believe Winnicott (1969: 241) exemplified this approach by drawing attention to the fact that Freud 'has left us to carry on with the researches that his invention of psychoanalysis makes possible, and yet he cannot participate when we make a step forward'. In a spirit of restoration *and* innovation, Independent thought crosses Freud's heritage – the theory of instinctual drive – with the deep meanings of early development and developmental needs. I take Mitchell's (1988) point that Freud's drive theory and the interactive, relational model are *not* discretely dichotomous, which is why it makes no sense to say that the Freudian interpretation has been 'outgrown'. Innovations in psychoanalysis, theoretical and clinical, often rely on the tendency towards excess in Freud's own thinking. The characteristic tendency of Freud's thought to overrun itself suggests that the full import of the Freudian interpretation has yet to reach us, that we are advancing towards Freud, towards a thought that is always a beginning (Pontalis 1993). I doubt that I am alone in feeling myself grow into Freud, an experience of inner weathering that has continued for almost half a century in my case, further proof of which (for better or worse) may be found in this essay.

Let me add two provisos at this point. A comprehensive account of how Independent psychoanalysis came into existence is not my topic. A cultural history of the Independent tradition and its relation to twentieth-century English intellectual life remains to be written. The highly selective nature of my essay will be self-evident. In reflecting on the Independent dialogue with Freud, I engage with preferred voices: Fairbairn, Winnicott, and Loewald. These are undoubtedly remarkable figures, who may be counted among the most original thinkers in post-Freudian psychoanalysis. Yet my discussion of their work focuses unapologetically on topics that are of interest to me – the acting person, the dependence relationship, and the intrigues of time. These are the principal themes of my study. There is nothing idiosyncratic about these choices, which allow me to address what I believe is distinctive about Independent psychoanalytic thought.

While developments in Independent psychoanalysis testify to the integrity of Freudianism as an expanding field of inquiry, matters do not and cannot rest with psychoanalysis alone. The dialogue with Freud, insofar as it concerns what is decisive for thought, is necessarily wide-ranging. Freudianism forms part of our discursive tradition, and I intend to keep the larger context of twentieth-century thought in view. It is not part of my argument that psychoanalysis can replace philosophy, extend the reach of the phenomenological insight, or succeed in solving problems posed by philosophy.[2] Rather, I aim to detail the *overlap* between psychoanalysis and philosophy, particularly with reference to Heidegger's analysis of temporality as the meaning of *Dasein*; Levinas's 'intentional analyses' of the self (*l'ipséité*) and its responsibility for the other; Wojtyła's analysis of the person-action relation; and Ricoeur's hermeneutics of action. The extended philosophical passages in the following chapters, in which the authors are often profoundly at odds with one another, provide a manifold frame for my study of psychoanalytic thought.

2

Language is an obvious starting point for my inquiry. I. A. Richards (1955: 224) was surely not mistaken in judging that 'there is no study which is not a language study'. It seems likely therefore that any study involves 'reliving the ... language-game we find ourselves playing' (Rorty 1980: 34). The narcissism of small differences prevails in local skirmishes. Yet the history of analytic practice, more broadly conceived, amounts to what analysts have been able to agree on, the shared meanings belonging to otherwise disparate schools of thought and diverse perspectives. As such, a study of post-Freudian thought historically considered concentrates on the choice of words in analytic theory, the language (the metaphors) in which psychoanalysis emerged and continues to hold sway.[3] I approach my topic along these lines, firstly, with reference to the analytic context in which concepts acquire meaning and, secondly, in terms of the creative use that individual analysts make of available meanings.

Classical Freudian science prevailed (roughly) from 1900 to 1940 as a type of 'grand narrative' (Lyotard 1984), a modern *Weltanschauung* with the capacity to legitimate and unify its own claims as a coherent system of scientific knowledge.[4] But insofar as psychoanalysis calls into question its own inaugural gesture, Freudianism is repeatedly played out in the deferred realisation of its own thought. Admittedly, the 'arrival' of psychoanalysis, understood in terms of the phylogenetic needs of human beings (Bollas 2007), adds to our available stock of knowledge; but also, more significantly, the 'Freudian moment' represents an ever-increasing plurality of views and emergent possibilities. Freudianism arrived as a propulsive force within the culture, an open-ended *praxis* of interpretation and innovation that allows us to make more of ourselves through new habits of action. The fact that psychoanalytic thought still has a future, or is 'still entirely to come' (Derrida 1964: 79), suggests that the 'moment' has yet to reach us.[5]

The mid-twentieth-century counts as a pivotal occasion in the ongoing renewal of the Freudian interpretation, an occasion for a specific series of innovations. Independent psychoanalysis was shaped in this context not only under a new set of clinical and technical conditions but also in a world where the norms and conditions of thinking as such could no longer be taken for granted. The recourse to irony, skepticism, and various kinds of relativism may be understood in this context; nor has psychoanalysis been slow to exploit these cultural attitudes. How far the Independent tradition has assimilated these views is a moot point. The term 'Independent' was not used in British psychoanalysis until around the middle of the twentieth century – at the original suggestion of Paula Heimann (King 1989: 8). The tradition, however, goes back to the early part of the century. As with any new scientific endeavour, the English school of psychoanalysis originated from a disparate intellectual background – ranging from the institutional efforts of Ernest Jones and his colleagues in founding the British Psycho-Analytical Society in 1919 (Jones 1959) to the more loosely defined 'flurry of activity' centred around the likes of Arthur Tansley and W. H. R. Rivers in Cambridge (Forrester and Cameron 2017). Given the delays, false starts, and heterogenous points of departure, one cannot refer meaningfully to *the* birth of English Freudianism.

Aside from the question of origins, Independent psychoanalysis, operating under this newly acquired classificatory designation, assumed a more coherent form in the late 1940s and 1950s as a distinct postwar phenomenon. Following the 'controversial discussions', which took place in the British Psycho-Analytical Society in the wake of Freud's death in 1939, English Freudianism underwent a significant reorganisation.[6] Due to historical circumstances, the English school occupied the strongest position in postwar European psychoanalysis, where it effectively became the cardinal site of the movement (with the Freuds in residence after 1938). Independent psychoanalysis emerged as a coherent theoretical and clinical formation under these conditions, and the disputatious circumstances, which were hardly incidental for its emergence and early formation, have left their mark.

It seems fair to say that no debate of comparable significance or quality has taken place in the discipline since the controversial discussions. The deeply argued positions of the British Society during the years 1940 to 1946 amount to a pivotal moment in the history of psychoanalysis. For Green (2005: 10) the 'controversies' count as 'the most important document in post-Freudian psychoanalysis'. I am broadly in agreement with this estimation. Nevertheless, I wish to make a more precise point – namely, that the 'controversies' constitute the groundwork of Independent psychoanalytic thought. This was not evident at the time, given that the debate was focused explicitly on Melanie Klein's contribution. Alongside Edward Glover, Melitta and Walter Schmideberg, and other members of the British Society, Anna Freud together with her colleagues and supporters – Dorothy Burlingham, Barbara Lantos, Kate Friedlander, and Barbara Low – were intent on challenging what they saw as a heresy. The critical argument was levelled at Klein and her followers – including, Susan Isaacs, Joan Riviere, Paula Heimann, John Rickman, and Donald Winnicott. It seems much clearer, in retrospect, that the 'controversies' have proved to be most significant for the Independent tradition.

Freud (1912: 111) set the parameters for the discussion of analytic integrity in terms of personal autonomy rather than group identity: 'The technical rules which I am putting forward here have been arrived at from my own experience in the course of many years ... I must make it clear, however, that what I am asserting is that this technique is the only one suited to my individuality; I do not venture to deny that a physician quite differently constituted might find himself driven to adopt a different attitude to his patients and to the task before him'. Freud's statement represents something of a touchstone for Independent analysis. One is wary of endorsing the stereotype of a so-called 'English analyst'; nevertheless, historically considered, there has always been a place for determined individualists as well as a more temperate, principled sensibility in the English school. In fact, the Independent approach goes beyond the settlement of institutes and professional societies, beyond clearly delineated national boundaries, and may be thought of as a 'school' only in the loose sense of the word.

Despite a degree of conflict between the different groups in the British Society, the history of postwar English psychoanalysis is not one of tripartite evolution along strictly delineated lines. This is a familiar but oversimplified view of the situation in the British Society. It would be more accurate to describe the situation as one of intense and lively discussion, with a focus not only on matters of psychoanalytic theory but also on the related issues of technique and transmission. In this interfluent, manifestly volatile context, we can discern common Independent characteristics, including: a commitment to the classic tenet that what is well-conceived may be expressed clearly and distinctly; an adherence to the criterion of ordinary language as well as the art of 'saying it well'; a sceptical attitude towards general assumptions, rigid preoccupations, and prescriptive systems of thought; a willingness to adapt to the uniqueness of each patient, to credit the particular (the patient's individuality); and an overriding 'elasticity' (to borrow Ella Sharpe's term) of psychic orientation.[7]

It is no surprise to discover that teaching has been at the centre of these debates. Despite the important caveat that I have just issued regarding the tripartite view of postwar British psychoanalysis, the reorganisation of training arrangements in the wake of the 'controversies' was indicative of the levels of disagreement within the British Society. Training has inevitably been a major issue in the history of psychoanalytic thought.[8] In the event of a general stalemate, a compromise was reached in 1946 involving two parallel streams of training, one organised as formerly, in which teachers were drawn from all the groups in the Society but with a strong Kleinian element, and a second course organised according to the teachings of Anna Freud and her colleagues – courses 'A' and 'B', respectively. The supervisor for the first of the two-training cases was drawn from the candidate's own group; the second supervisor for candidates in analysis with either a Kleinian or a member of the 'B Group' had to be selected from those who were independent of both – that is, from among the nonaffiliated members of the 'A Group'.

The 'Middle Group' first emerged in these circumstances and included those analysts who chose not to align themselves with either the Kleinians or Anna Freud and her colleagues. A relatively small number of analysts within the British Society have continued to exercise this choice. Again, without overstating the nature of these discriminations, the Society's future was nonetheless set on the model of three groups for administrative and training purposes. The requirement for a nonaffiliated supervisor (for the second case) was subsequently set aside in the face of persistent disagreement, followed by the formation of a specifically Kleinian group in place of the 'A Group'. As I have been at pains to point out, it would be a mistake to overstate the lines of demarcation. Nevertheless, in a context where each candidate was able to select his or her own course of study from the curriculum, the institutional arrangements supported the development of a *loosely* tripartite group structure: Kleinian, Contemporary Freudian – as the 'B Group' came to be called – and Independent. Over the course of time, a different relationship to orthodoxy and the Freudian legacy became increasingly apparent in each of the three groups.[9]

3

My book is not intended as a summary overview of the Independent tradition. Eric Rayner attempted something along these lines, more than 30 years ago, with felicitous results. *The Independent Mind in British Psychoanalysis* (1990) remains the standard reference text in the field, the most informative account available of the development of British Independent psychoanalysis.[10] More than a system of knowledge, Rayner presents an ethos of clinical thinking, an Independent psychoanalytic 'mind', characterised by creativity, tolerance, and an 'avowed openness to learning from any psychoanalytic theories' (1991: 4).[11] In addition to Rayner's readable survey, Kohon edited a collection of papers, *The British School of Psychoanalysis* (1986), with contributions from senior and (at the time) less well-established members of the Independent Group, most of whom have subsequently gone on to assume positions of seniority in the group. Kohon subsequently reissued a revised version of his original collection. *British Psychoanalysis: New Perspectives in the Independent Tradition* (2018) includes a revised selection of papers; it does not include any additional papers but includes new introductory chapters from a younger generation of psychoanalysts. In a more loosely conceived edited collection entitled *Independent Psychoanalysis Today* (2012), Williams, Keene, and Dermen attempt to update readers on the current state of play in Independent thinking. The contributors to this volume are, to a greater or lesser extent, intent on drawing attention to Freud's 'underdeveloped assumption' concerning the environmental conditions of primitive emotional development.[12]

Further to these compendious collections and overviews (useful as they are), my study is conceived quite differently. I intend to concentrate on a number of related themes. My exploration of action, object-relations, and time is based on a reading of key Independent texts. I aim to get at something more essential than 'group mentality', following Symington's (2007: 202) critical point that 'projection of the self into a group mentality [is] a central feature of narcissism'. Symington was, arguably, the leading

Independent object-relations thinker of his generation – and yet his pre-eminence from the 1980s until his death in 2019 was not based on group affiliation. In fact, Symington (2007: 202) explains how he achieved a singular independence only after withdrawing from his 'projection' initially into his analyst, John Klauber, and into the Independent Group, and subsequently into the Klein group. Similarly, Parsons (2014b: 187) notes that 'the Independent tradition does not coincide with the Independent Group'; that being an Independent analyst is not 'linked intrinsically to membership of the Independent Group'. In fact, the three figures that I single out for detailed consideration (Fairbairn, Winnicott, and Loewald) were manifestly unsuited to group membership and did not belong to any school.

I trust that the inevitable limits imposed by my approach, most notably on systematicity and generalisability, are compensated for by the gain in remaining open to the 'work within us [that] makes us think' (Widlöcher 2012: 248). In fact, the hermeneutic nature of the analytic task means that the validity of one approach cannot be called into question in the language of an alternative approach (Hayman 2013: 60). Strachey (1943; quoted in King and Steiner 1991: 607) attempted to establish this principle, during the 'controversies', by shifting the grounds of debate from veridical discourse, or the realm of inference and theory, to 'valid technique': 'I suggest that the essential criterion of whether a person is fit to conduct a training analysis [or for that matter any analysis at all] is not whether his views on aetiology or theory are true, but whether his technique is valid'.

The more 'fundamental validity' that Strachey referred to privileges the sort of person the analyst is, the 'way in which the analyst behaves', rather than 'the knowledge he possesses' (1943; quoted in King and Steiner 1991: 608). The message of Strachey's Memorandum remains undiminished, no doubt each of us could do with being 'even a little sceptical about [our] own conclusions and a little ready to consider other people's' (1943; quoted in King and Steiner 1991: 609). Pronouncing on 'right' and 'wrong' applications discredits psychoanalysis as an interpretative science. In a field of inquiry characterised essentially by its 'dialogic' nature, it would be anomalous to present oneself as an advocate of a particular school of thought, intent on garnering a system of beliefs, or conversely as an adversary of so-called 'opposing' schools. Among the increasingly large number of contemporary schools of thought, none has 'exclusive rights of descent' (Mitchell 1988: 12).

There is nonetheless a degree of common ground, with respect to the various ways in which psychoanalysis is practiced. In particular, one lives as an analyst with the rule of 'saying what comes to mind' on the understanding that 'the fundamental technical rule' (Freud 1923a: 237–38) does not become an endpoint. Evocative rather than instructive (Hayman 2013: 60–62), the free play of associative construction is *the* Freudian legacy (Bollas 2009; Roussillon 2011; Donnet 2016; Parsons 2017). A 'rule' that we carry towards the future, indeed, as an *act* of freedom (Widlöcher 2012), free association is therefore an opportunity to do justice to play *as the universal* (Winnicott 1971b; 1971c). It allows for the language of affect as well as the spoken word; for the inextricability of primary and secondary processes (Loewald 1978a); for the irreducible mystery of things as well as a reliable framework for creative thinking (Bollas 1999); and for the conjunction of the basic psycho-physical situation and metaphorical expression (Sharpe 1940).

The sense of inner freedom that allows us to think and speak in this unique and peculiar way is twofold. Free association comprises the *freedom to* think associatively; hence the associative chains, or network of associated activities (sensations, affects, affect-representations, dreams, memories, mental images) that characterise the communicative nature of the analytic encounter. Experienced over the course of time within a particular setting, 'these associations instantiate the patient's own idiom of thinking'; *speech acts* thus 'provide the basis upon which the patient can appreciate the value of the self's unconscious creativity' (Bollas 2009: 45). Similarly, for Roussillon (2011: 190) 'psychoanalysis is predicated on the idea that the progressive freeing of associative liberty will make regulation possible by means of becoming conscious through psychic reflexivity'. On the other hand, our thinking is neither sufficiently free nor properly independent so long as we reify one-sided expressions of action. In this case, free association denotes *freedom from* certain individual and collective constraints. Our patients rely on psychoanalysis for the experience of freedom from in-struction, a negative freedom which, in conjunction with *freedom to*, defines the action of the analytic encounter.

Notes

1 Freud first used the term 'metapsychology' in a letter to Fliess in 1896, where he refers to his preoccupation with psychology – 'really *meta*psychology' (1985: 172). Writing to Fliess again in December 1896, he described his preoccupation with metapsychology as no more than an 'ideal and woebegone child' (1985: 216). However, by 1915 Freud was in a position to propose, in a letter to Abraham, a definitive statement under the title *Preparatory Essays for Metapsychology*. He wrote to Abraham in May 1915, telling him that he had five essays prepared: 'Instincts and their Vicissitudes'; 'Repression'; 'The Unconscious'; 'A Metapsychological Supplement to the Theory of Dreams'; and 'Mourning and Melancholia'. The letter went on to explain that he hoped 'to get together about a dozen such papers and in quieter times to offer them to the ignorant world ... I think on the whole [the book] will represent progress' (Falzeder 2002: 309). In the event, he became increasingly dissatisfied with the aim of providing a comprehensive overview along these lines, and while the first three papers were published in 1915, followed by two further papers in 1917, it would appear that Freud destroyed the remainder of the original papers, although one of the unpublished papers, 'A Phylogenetic Fantasy: Overview of the Transference Neuroses', was discovered among Ferenczi's papers in 1983 and subsequently published (Freud 1987).

 2 Rorty's (1980: 165 n 1) point about the 'naturalisation' of epistemology by psychology is well made: 'Psychology was born out of philosophy in the confused hope that we might get back behind Kant and recapture Lockean innocence. Ever since, psychologists have vainly protested their neglect by neo-Kantian philosophers (of both the analytic and the phenomenological sorts)'.
 3 See Hayman (2013) for a series of essays, written from an Independent standpoint, on some of the ways in which psychoanalysts use words.
 4 Psychoanalysis is the absent presence in Lyotard's examination of the 'postmodern condition'.
 5 See Hutchinson (2016) for the belatedness of modernity in European literary culture. I contend that psychoanalysis occupies a comparable position in the post-Romantic context of our modernity.
 6 See King and Steiner (1991) for a comprehensive record of the 'controversies', including, the four main papers presented at Scientific Meetings of the British Society between 1943 and 1944, together with the memoranda on technique and related correspondence.
 7 See Sharpe (1943; quoted in King and Steiner 1991: 641) for the original formulation of these criteria as the basis of a 'favourable atmosphere' in the analytic encounter. On each count, psychoanalysis proves inimical to standardisation and clinical 'examples'; the 'atmosphere' in the room pertains to the treatment of *this* or *that* patient. An Independent theory of clinical technique reminds us it is the individual that is to be treated, that the patient comes before psychoanalysis. We inherit the principle from Aristotle, as set out in the *Metaphysica* (A 981 a 15): 'experience is knowledge of individuals … actions and production are all concerned with the individual; for the physician does not cure *man*, except in an incidental way, but Callias or Socrates or some other called by some such individual name, who happens to be a man'. Rooted in the tradition of Ella Sharpe, this principle has remained *the* defining attitude of Independent thought.
 8 See Parsons (2014) for the role of psychoanalytic training in the formation of an analytic identity. Parsons takes up two questions under the heading of training, first what it means to *be* an analyst, and second what is involved in *becoming* one.
 9 See Grosskurth (1985), Kohon (1986), and Hughes (1989) for further discussion of these developments.
10 The book was republished with a new foreword from Maurice Whelan in 2020.
11 Compare Freud's (1910b; 1912; 1913a; 1915d) contributions on the technique of psychoanalytic therapy.
12 Giannakoulas (2010) provides a contemporary account of Independent psychoanalysis from a vantage point outside the English school. More recently, Chodorow (2020) has introduced the idea of an American Independent school, what she calls 'intersubjective ego-psychology', co-founded by Erikson and Loewald, with its roots in ego-psychology (Hartmann) and interpersonal psychoanalysis (Sullivan).

Chapter 1

Acts and relations

The object-relation and the acting person are the pivotal reference points of my study. And both the theory of object-relations and the analysis of the interrelation between the person and the action may be worked out logically from the Freudian interpretation. This is the position that I mean to defend in chapters 1 and 2 with regards to the vicissitudes of the dependence relationship, before turning in chapters 3 and 4 to the psychoanalysis of time. Throughout the book, I approach my main topic on the grounds that there is a significant degree of overlap between British object-relations theory and the Independent tradition. They are evidently different formations of theoretical and clinical thinking – and yet the fact that they represent confluent developments in post-Freudian thought is clear from their common findings, principally, that the dependence relationship is the irreducible *datum*, and that our being together with one another *is* our experience of life. I shall begin with some general comments on the theoretical significance of these findings.

Further to these introductory remarks and a clarification of the term and concept 'acting person', I turn in the second part of the chapter to a discussion of drives and action. The limitations of the classical model are well-documented and will not be reviewed here. The question will instead be taken up in terms of drives *and* action on the grounds (a) that Freud's drive model need not be confined to the theory of libidinal and aggressive drives and (b) that the model provides the basis for a general theory of meaningful human action. Schafer (1976) has taken this line of inquiry as far it goes in one direction. The approach adopted in my study is based on the hermeneutics of action broadly defined (Ricoeur 1991a); it entails building on Freudian hypotheses from the perspective of the acting person. In the third and final part of the chapter, I elaborate on Freud's contribution to object-relations through a close reading of 'Mourning and Melancholia', with special reference to the concept of identification. I discuss the paper at some length not only as a transitional work in Freud's own intellectual itinerary, but also as a landmark contribution to psychoanalysis. Moreover, with the

DOI: 10.4324/9781315280899-2

emphasis on internalisation and identification, the paper may be seen as part of the groundwork of object-relations theory (Ogden 2002).

Living together

Husserl's fifth *Cartesianische Meditationen* (the work was written in 1929, but was only published in German in 1950) is the philosophical *locus classicus* for the primordial world of simultaneous coexistence, where phenomenal 'pairing' *(Paarung)* gives rise to 'a living mutual awakening and an overlaying of each with the objective sense of the other' (1950: 113). The thrust of my argument is set against the background of Husserl's phenomenology of 'intersubjectivity' (*Intersubjektivität*), which, in many respects, anticipates the principal findings of Independent object-relations theory. Husserl's view encompasses the body-ego and the object-world: 'The other organism, as appearing in my primordial sphere, is first of all a body in my primordial Nature, which is a synthetic unity belonging to me and therefore, as a determining part included in my own essence, inseparable from me myself' (1950: 121). Husserl (1950: 139) notes that living-with 'involves being a plurality of monads that constitutes in itself an Objective world and that spatializes, temporalizes, realizes itself – psychologically and, in particular, as human beings – within that world'. I return to the primordial condition of 'empathy' (*Einfühlung*) throughout the book, although I treat the empathic relation between 'me' and 'not-me' (Husserl's topic) as an elaboration of a more primitive emotional tie between the infant and the primary carer, what I call the dependence relationship.

Husserl continued to grapple with the fundamental problem of the other, the problem of intersubjectivity, formulating the matter more explicitly in his last work, *Die Krisis der europäischen Wissenschaften und die transzendentale Phänomenologie*, as a problem of the 'life-world' (*Lebenswelt*). Husserl's analysis of the life-world, conceived as the prescientific world of experience, represents 'a radicalisation of his analysis of intersubjectivity, insofar as concepts like *historicity*, *generativity*, *tradition*, and *normality* are given a central transcendental-philosophical significance' (Zahavi 2003: 125). In this respect, *empathy* is essentially reframed in terms of our existence through *living together*:

> in whatever way we may be conscious of the world as universal horizon, as coherent universe of existing objects, we, each "I-the-man" and all of us together, belong to the world as living with one another in the world, and the world is our world, valid for our consciousness as existing precisely through this "living together" …here we also find ourselves, we who always and inevitably belong to the affective sphere, always functioning as subjects of acts [ego-subjects] … this is true not only for me, the individual ego; rather we, in living together, have the world

pregiven in this "together", as the world valid as existing for us and to which we, together, belong, the world as world for all, pregiven with this ontic meaning. Constantly functioning in wakeful life, we also function together, in the manifold ways of considering, together, planning acting together.

(Husserl 1970b: 108–09)

The elaboration of 'empathy' as existing and acting together does not necessarily meet the criticism levelled at Husserl's constituting ego. Levinas (1974), most notably, found Husserl's notion of constitution problematic, and proposed instead that the ego of the person is constituted by the encounter with the other. I shall come back to Levinas in the following chapter. Suffice it to note here that the philosophical framework of my study effectively retraces the trajectory from Husserl to Levinas. In my analyses of dependence and relational being, of *taking part in a meeting*, I aim to apply, where appropriate, some of the seminal and ongoing debates in phenomenology to Independent psychoanalytic thought. Karol Wojtyła has made an outstanding contribution to these debates. The idea that 'participation' is a distinct feature of the person, that to be a person means to be capable of participation, represents a major advance in phenomenological inquiry. Essentially, the idea is that being and acting together-with-others discloses a fundamental dimension of oneself *as a person*. I consider Wojtyła's analysis of the person-action relation in the following section. The basic insight that the reality of our existing 'together-with-others' is a consequence of human reality itself augments the phenomenological insight as a whole. It also illuminates some of the more radical advances in post-Freudian thought, as I demonstrate in my analyses of Fairbairn and Winnicott in the following chapter.

My central thesis is that our understanding of the person, that is, of the person as it manifests itself in actions, is based on his or her *relations* to other persons (Spitz 1957). The person discloses himself through action only insofar as the personal unfolds in relations. Relations signify primordially who a person is and how he or she exists. The actions of the person, and the fulfilment of the person in the action, are rooted in and mediated by relationships. Infantile dependence emerges on these grounds as *the* defining preoccupation of Independent object-relations theory. Aside from the inevitable attempts to restrict the hypotheses of relationality and relational being to the classical Freudian model: the interconnected interpretation of the Oedipus complex, the repressed unconscious, the castration complex, the concept of penis envy, and so on, there is no evidence of a purely personalistic view in any of the major exponents of Independent thought. Accordingly, the equiprimordiality of human coexistence and dependence, exemplified in Fairbairn's description of the 'suckling-situation' and Winnicott's concept of 'holding', is the standing premise of my inquiry.

Stephen Mitchell (1988) provides a comprehensive account of the 'object-relational matrix' that underpins the English school. The principal findings of the Independent object-relations tradition of Fairbairn and Winnicott – i.e. the equiprimordiality of psychological dependence and human coexistence – are highlighted in Mitchell's (1988) broadly conceived 'relational model' of intersubjectivity. Mitchell eschews the idea of universal and inherent psychological meanings. Instead, 'bodily experiences and events are understood as evoked potentials which derive meaning from the way they become patterned in interaction with others. From [the relational] viewpoint *what is inherent is not necessarily formative*; it does not push and shape experience, but is itself shaped by the relational context ... the underlying structure of experience and its deeper meanings, derive from relational patterns' (1988: 4; emphasis in the original). This describes a being whose existence is always and irreducibly relational; being-there is in each case mine but only insofar as it is related to the existence of someone; being-there *is* co-being.

Fairbairn and Winnicott laid the foundations for this perspective in Independent psychoanalytic thought. Fairbairn (1940: 10–11) proposed that the 'first social relationship established by the individual is that between himself and his mother; and the focus of this relationship is the suckling situation, in which his mother's breast provides the focal point of his libidinal object, and his mouth the focal point of his own libidinal attitude'. Looked at from the point of view of object-relationship psychology, dependency is perceived not as an end in itself but as a means to yet more life. Starting with the early oral situation, the dependent infant is fundamentally helpless but, at the same time, has the makings of an active person. This discovery is evident in Fairbairn's (1946: 141) idea that the object to be found has first to be made, an idea that Winnicott developed in terms of 'primary creativity' and the 'spontaneous gesture'. I shall come back to Winnicott's theory of spontaneity below.

In a comprehensive theory of worldmaking, the instinctual reach for life, understood as an expression of the 'mouth ego', rests on the child being assured, firstly, 'that he is genuinely loved as a person by his parents', and secondly, 'that his parents genuinely accept his love' (Fairbairn 1941: 39). The 'good' object is thus 'both satisfying and amenable from the infant's point of view' (Fairbairn 1944: 111). Fairbairn (1944: 93 n 1) maintained that the full potentiality of the self ('central ego'), or the individual *as a person*, is realised only in relation to a mother ('ideal object') who meets her child's developmental needs, whose milk proves 'sufficient to satisfy [the child's] incorporative needs'. Conversely, individuals displaying schizoid features, according to Fairbairn (1940: 23), 'gained the conviction, whether through apparent indifference or through apparent possessiveness on the part of their mothers, that their mother did not really love and value them as persons in their own right'. Fairbairn's (1940: 13) singular insight is that the type of mother who is likely to provoke a regression to schizoid states is 'the mother who fails to convince her child by spontaneous and genuine expressions of affection that she herself loves him as a person'. The child is therefore left with 'a sense of lack of love, and indeed emotional *rejection* on his mother's part' (Fairbairn 1944: 113–14; emphasis in the original).

Fairbairn (1940: 11) argued further that 'in proportion as disturbances in the [mother-infant] relationship occur, the breast itself tends to assume the role of libidinal object; i.e. the libidinal object tends to assume the form of a bodily organ or *partial object* (in contrast to that of a person or whole object)'. For Fairbairn, part-objects (exciting and rejecting) emerge only where the child is faced with a more or less traumatic situation, excessively and cumulatively frustrated by an unreliable or uncaring mother. Assuming, however, that the child cannot survive childhood psychically without a 'good' object, and that it proves insufferable for the child 'to have a good object which is also bad', Fairbairn (1944: 110) proposed that the child 'seeks to alleviate the situation by splitting the figure of his mother into two objects'. The mother who satisfies her child libidinally is experienced as a 'good' object; the mother who fails to satisfy her child libidinally, as a 'bad' object. The internal 'bad' object, in turn, is split into two objects – namely, 'the needed or exciting object' and 'the frustrating or rejecting object' (1944: 111). The role of 'ultimate cause' is assigned to the phenomenon of infantile dependence, rather than the explanatory concept of the Oedipus situation in the Freudian interpretation. In accounting for the origins of repression and the structuration of psyche, priority is assigned to the 'problem of adjustment', that is to say, those 'measures adopted by the child in an attempt to cope with the difficulties inherent in the ambivalent situation which develops during his infancy in his relationship with his mother as his original object' (1944: 120).

As a theory of dynamic psychical structure, Fairbairn's position is unambiguous: firstly, it is maternal deprivation, the breakdown of maternal capacity, that necessitates the defence mechanism of splitting in the child; and, secondly, the split-off self-states and part-object structures characteristic of the deprived child reveal the defensive and pathological nature of 'differentiation' at the beginning of life (Rubens 1984). Consider the following statements by Freud: 'love strives after objects' (1930 [1929]: 117); for the ego 'living means the same as being loved' (1923a: 58). This is essentially Fairbairn's point: human beings *become* human beings on account of their dependency needs being met by an appropriate response of love and care at the beginning of life, what Freud called the 'function of protecting and saving'. Freud, of course, situated object-seeking and the function of mother as a protective shield within an instinct-based, drive/structure model; whereas Fairbairn addressed the satisfying object, the mother in her capacity of a good object, in the primary context of the dependence relationship. The main point here is that 'it is only ego structures that can seek relationships with objects' (Fairbairn 1944: 88). This accounts for the hate and destructiveness of the antilibidinal ego, which Fairbairn (1940: 24) treated as the outcome of failed object-relationships – including, not only an unloving environment but also the mother's failure to 'appreciate and accept [the child's] love as good'. As a result, the world comprises what Fairbairn (1940: 26) described as the two 'great tragedies' to which persons with a schizoid tendency are liable: (a) the child's feeling that his love is 'destructive of those he loves' and (b) his becoming subject to 'a compulsion to hate and be hated, while all the time he longs deep down to love and to be loved'.

My aim in this book is to open up the dialogue between Independent object-relations theory and the Freudian tradition. I discuss the object-relation in post-Freudian thought in the following chapter. In this chapter, I focus on the problem of the object in Freud – including, the extent to which Freudian drive theory was 'a *kind* of object-relations theory' (Mitchell 2000: ix), as well as a general theory of human action. In a similar vein, Pine (1990: x) proposes that 'transference and the oedipal constellations are as much object relations concepts as they are drive concepts'. I shall keep this proposal in view throughout the book, while at the same time considering the challenge posed by the Independent tradition to the Freudian interpretation, most notably, in the work of Fairbairn, Winnicott, and Loewald. Suffice it to note in these introductory remarks the basic terms of the debate.[1] Fairbairn (1944: 126) provided the basic insight that 'although Freud's whole system of thought was concerned with object-relationships, he adhered theoretically to the principle that libido is primarily pleasure-seeking, i.e. that it is directionless'. By contrast, Fairbairn (1941: 47) singled out infantile dependence as *the* defining feature of the human situation and, furthermore, identified the 'unconditional character' of dependency as its most prominent feature: 'The infant is completely dependent upon his object ... the very helplessness of the child is sufficient to render him dependent in an unconditional sense'.

Consequently, far from an explanation of non-directional 'equilibrium-seeking' activity, the concept of 'libido' was systematically and irrevocably decoupled from the Freudian theory of sexual and aggressive drives. Fairbairn (1941: 31) turned classic libido theory into 'a theory of development based essentially upon object-relationships ... The ultimate goal of libido is the object'. The relational matrix is conceived from the standpoint of dependency and, on these grounds, constitutes an innate 'drive' towards relationship: 'libido is primarily object-seeking, i.e. it has direction' (Fairbairn 1944: 126). Moreover, with respect to the relational field, erotogenic zones are conceived as 'channels' through which libido flows in its reach for life, or, what amount to the same thing, in its search for the object. Object-seeking is effectively a life-seeking impulse, which Fairbairn discussed under the heading of self-preservation and psychological survival.

The problem of infantile dependence was central for Winnicott as well as Fairbairn, although they approached the problem from different vantage points. For Fairbairn infantile dependence is the major determinant of psychic life; whereas Winnicott proposed that need is overdetermined from the beginning by spontaneity, that maternity meets or fails to meet the infant's primary (psychic) creativity. The identification of 'primary creativity' (Winnicott 1971a: 11) – indeed, as the groundwork of the intermediate area prior to objective perception – gives full rein to potentiality at the origin. This is indicative of the significant differences between Fairbairn and Winnicott, which I discuss at greater length in the following chapter. Nevertheless, following Fairbairn's lead, Winnicott established the 'vital importance' of object-relationships in terms of the earliest relationship between the baby and the mother. It is the mother (a) who 'makes real' the baby's innate potential, (b) who gives the baby 'the idea' of what the baby is reaching for, and (c) who enables the constitutive process of worldmaking. Thus, allowing that 'the baby created the breast', Winnicott (1968a:101) adds that it 'could not have done so had not the mother come along with the breast just at that moment'. Worldmaking issues from the baby *as a relational event*.

Importantly, for Winnicott (1952: 98), as for Fairbairn, the baby-mother relationship 'antedates instinct experience, as well as running concurrently with it, and getting mixed up with it'. The drive/object-relations debate is one of the central parameters of post-Freudian thought, and the idea that the earliest relationship is not a derivation of instinctual experience – that living an experience together (Winnicott 1945: 145) and, thereby, creating the world, precedes drive aims – brings the Independent dialogue with Freudianism sharply into focus. In recent decades, the idea that relationships precede drives has become more familiar and less contentious; contemporary thinking allows for Fairbairn's (1944: 88) fundamental insight that 'the ego [is] the source of impulse-tension from the beginning'. And yet the following theoretical presuppositions warrant further attention: (a) that drives are simply forms of energy at the disposal of ego structures; and (b) that experience and experiential needs give shape to the drives. I am concerned in this essay, largely, with the implications of these presuppositions, starting with the idea that Independent psychoanalytic thought is predicated on the notion of experiential determinants in infancy.

The shift from endogenous needs and the constitution of objects by drives, on the one hand, to the structuration of drives by the meeting of primitive developmental needs within a relational field, on the other, places the Freudian development on an entirely new footing. Alongside the inaugural contributions of Fairbairn and Winnicott, Loewald (1970: 291) formulated the revised view with characteristic rigour: 'instinctual drives, as psychic forces, are processes taking place within a field – the mother-infant matrix'. The shift in analytic focus from the preexperiential nature of drive to the unintegrated manifold of preoedipal relations redefined the problem of the object in psychoanalysis. For Loewald (1971b: 130) 'the object does not become "assigned" to the instinct (understood as a psychic force) but contributes crucially to the organization of instincts *qua* instincts, just as instinctual forces crucially contribute to the organization of objects *qua* objects ... the object is no less an original element of the instinct than its pressure, aim, or source'. Loewald argued explicitly for the integration of experience into the structure of the drive. This stands in marked contrast to Freud's (1905: 148) defining move, namely, to 'loosen the bond' between the sexual instinct and its object on the grounds that initially the former is 'independent' of the latter, that 'the sexual instinct and the sexual object are merely soldered together'.

The person-action relation

I want to come back now to the basic intuition of the person as it manifests itself in action and, before turning to a discussion of the drives, to clarify my understanding of the 'acting person'. The Freudian interpretation provides a starting point. Freud (1925c: 236–37) elaborated on *actus humanus* as a function of judgement, an act of decision along the axes of 'affirmation' and 'disaffirmation'. Experiences are thus judged agreeable or disagreeable from the point of view of the 'original' pleasure-ego: 'The attribute to be decided about may originally have been good or bad, useful or harmful. Expressed in the language of the oldest – the oral – instinctual impulses, the judgement is: "I should like to eat this", or "I should like to spit it out"; and, put more generally: "I should like to take this into myself and to keep that out". That is to say: "It shall be inside me" or "it shall be outside me"'. The function of judgement, one's spontaneous ability to feel values in the way that Freud described matters, represents a basic element of the feeling intellect.

In addition, Freud (1925c: 237) identified an act of decision concerning the judgement of the reality-ego: 'It is now no longer a question of whether what has been perceived (a thing) shall be taken into the ego or not, but of whether something which is in the ego as a presentation can be rediscovered in perception (reality) as well ... What is unreal, merely a presentation and subjective, is only internal; what is real is also there *outside* ... it is there in the external world'. Further to the 'subjective' investment of the object with a value, the 'objective' distinction between inside and outside represents an additional development in mental structure. The feeling intellect thus becomes an integral part of the reality function. It is possible to extrapolate the practical implications of this function in terms of the evaluation and distinction of what is true what is not. For Freud, our capacity to grasp the truth and to distinguish it from illusion, to adhere to truth in judging as well as in acting, allows for the broadest possible contacts with reality.[2] Nevertheless, the impulse, or the reach for life, is active before it becomes a judgement. The criterion of truthfulness, in the first instance, is a function of the body-ego. The reality of the good emanates from living-there, even as the experience of conviction, or a more certain truth is derived from an older, more primitive 'language'.[3] It is the recourse, in the Freudian schema, to 'the oldest instinctual impulses' that prevents the want-to-be-good from degenerating into superficiality or hypocrisy. The sense of conviction is binding all the way down, an arrangement that is in full accord with the maturity of the person.

We can approach the human experience from the point of view of meaningful action, specifically, in terms of the movement from the act of nourishment, our experience of the nutritive value of food, to the act of object-cathexis and the concomitant sense of reality. Instinctive activity, broadly defined, extends from basic needs to object-cathexes or object-interest. For Freud, the appetitive nature of the former corresponds to activity determined by the pleasure principle; whereas the judgement of the reality-ego adheres to the reality principle.[4] This rudimentary arrangement takes the form of a dialectic: on the one hand, the combined forces of appetitive (agreeable/disagreeable) and interactive (real/unreal) judgements situate the dynamic correlation of the action with the person in the context of interiority/exteriority. On the other hand, an increasingly coherent sense of 'inside' and 'outside' emerges, precisely from the experience of the person in action. Freud provides the basis for an appetitive-interactive frame of reference on biological and psychological grounds. The existential implications of meaningful action were worked out in-depth by Wojtyła (1979) in his study of what takes place or goes on in the person, on the one hand, and, on the other, the person's dynamism in action, namely, having the experience of being the actor.[5] For Wojtyła (1979: 178) the basic intuition of the person as it manifests itself in action comprises the fundamental experiences of 'something happens in man' and 'man acts'.

Appetite and the apprehension of the world are equiprimordially determined: for Wojtyła, as for Freud, action (the act of decision) may be seen (a) as a 'root factor' in the original dependence relationship and (b) as a type of reality-testing, or *modus operandi* in the object-world. Wojtyła thus allows us to draw out the existential-ontological reach of the Freudian interpretation, with reference to the interrelation between the person and the action. For Wojtyła the human being is 'revealed' *as a person* in the very enactment of his or her existence; action is conceived as a 'special moment' of apprehending the person. On this view, the human act is not limited to the cognitive action of the intellect but, rather, extends via the primordial activity of appetitive and interactive tendencies to the feeling intellect of the human being as a whole. It is not the cognitive presentation of objects that elicits 'the act of will'; if such were the case, then 'motivation would amount to determinism' (Wojtyła 1979: 140), and this would undermine the originality of worldmaking, the personal originality of primary creativity.

Wojtyła demonstrates the transcendence that distinguishes the person from a mere individual, precisely, the person's transcendence *in the action* (see 1979, Part II). Transcendence is seen as the shape of human life itself and, as such, the analysis of the transcendence of the person in the action allows for the human person's dynamism as a whole. In a Thomistic elaboration of personalism, Wojtyła distinguishes between (a) the dynamism at the level of the person, a dynamism that is dependent on the ego, and (b) the dynamism at the level of nature, the dynamism that has 'instinct' as its integrating factor. The assumption is that the 'dynamic transcendence of the person' as freedom (the act of freedom) is absent in the 'causation of nature' within which there are no constituted egos: 'In the dynamism at the level of nature there is no self-determination to serve as the basis from which acting itself as well as its direction and purpose are derived. The dynamism at the level of nature lacks that special dependence on the ego which is the characteristic mark of the specific dynamism of the person' (1979: 117). The 'spirituality of man' is described in light of this distinction: 'the mode itself of existence and acting that reveals and crystallizes [the spiritual] element or, to put it differently, that liberates this element in man is … the mode of existence and acting not of nature as such but of the person … personal freedom repudiates the necessity peculiar to nature … if we are to speak of the nature of the person, we can do so only in terms expressing the need to act freely' (1979: 182–83). The spiritual element therefore is seen as the source of the dynamism of the person.

Conjointly with transcendence, integration is presented as the other aspect of being a person. Wojtyła refers here to the two poles of personal dynamism, and proposes that the integration of the person in action complements the transcendence of the person in action. Transcendence and integration, in other words, are seen as 'complementary aspects of the same dynamic person-action reality' (1979: 194). Wojtyła accounts for the person's transcendence in the action as manifest in 'self-determination' and 'efficacy'; whereas the person's integration in the action, including the dynamism of both the human soma and the human psyche, is seen as subject to the will: 'every human action is due not only to the transcendence of the person acquired in self-determination and efficacy but also to the control exercised over the dynamic subjective ego by self-determination and efficacy' (1979: 220).

Wojtyła draws a number of important conclusions from the hypothesis of the integration of the acting person. I singled out here the propositions that are especially relevant for my study: firstly, the personalistic problem of integration concerns the irreducible 'complexity' of somatic and psychical dynamism: 'The psyche and the soma are distinctive with respect to each other even though they form a mutually conditioned unity in man' (1979: 220). Secondly, integration plays its own role in shaping the structure of the human being; indeed, Wojtyła maintains that it is the notion of integration that provides the key to the interpretation and the understanding of the 'complex manifold unity' of the psyche and the soma. Thirdly, the view of the human being as a psycho-somatic entity presupposes the intrinsic unity of action and person; the person-action 'unity' has precedence over the psycho-somatic 'complexity': 'ultimately man owes his psycho-somatic unity to the integration as well as the transcendence of the person in the action ... it is in action that the whole psycho-somatic complexity develops into the specific person-action unity ... the dynamisms of the psyche and the soma take an active part in integration, not at their own levels but *at the level of the person*' (1979: 196–98: emphasis in the original). The psychical integrity of the person, together with the somatic constitution of human nature, constitutes the basis of the integration of the person in the action.

I contend that the dynamic person-action conjunction, including, the transcendence and the integration of the person in the action, provides a phenomenological frame for Freud's concept of the drive. Wojtyła appears to be only tangentially concerned with Freudian psychoanalysis. In fact, he is overtly critical of Freud's central concepts, including, the pleasure principle and the unconscious, understood purely as 'a negation of consciousness' (1979: 308 n 34). The pleasure principle is seen as indicative of a 'purely subjectivistic vision of man'. The critique is aimed at the libidinal interpretation insofar as it posits libido as 'the primary end of the sexual drive and even the whole urge-related life in man – the end *per se* ... In this understanding, the person remains only a subject that is "exteriorly" sensitized to sensory-sexual stimuli, which evoke the lived-experience of delight [*libido*]' (Wojtyla 2013: 46–47). Wojtyla (2013: 47) posited an alternative interpretation in which the sexual drive is conceived as an existential phenomenon, rather than a purely libidinal function: 'A subject equipped with "interiority" as man is, a subject that is a person, cannot leave to instinct [*instynkt*] the whole responsibility for the drive [*popęd*], disposing himself only towards delight [*libido*], but he must take up full responsibility for the way he uses the sexual drive'. I draw on this line of inquiry, concerning the drive aspect of impulse, in my attempt to situate Freud's drive model as a general theory of human action, distinct from a purely libidinal interpretation.

Despite the view that the unconscious seems to denote nothing that would form part of the real structure of the human subject, Wojtyła cites the following passage from *The Ego and the Id* in support of his speculations on the 'continuous relation' between conscious and unconscious:

There are two paths by which the contents of the id can penetrate into the ego. The one is direct, the other leads by way of the ego ideal; which of these two paths they take may, for some mental activities, be of decisive importance. The ego develops from perceiving instincts to controlling them, from obeying instincts to inhibiting them. In this achievement a large share is taken by the ego ideal, which indeed is partly a reaction-formation against the instinctual impulses of the id.

(Freud 1923b: 55–56)

The idea of the 'potentiality of man', understood as 'the source that is inherent and that ceaselessly pulsates in the subject' (1979: 88), underpins the principal claim of this chapter that excitation is inherently relational. To understand 'human nature' from the point of view of the person's potentiality confirms the view that one becomes active by reaching for life, or 'turning towards objects'. For Wojtyła (1979: 154) the potentiality that remains below the level of consciousness is further confirmation that '[e]very being that must strive to attain its own fullness, and that is subjected to actualization, appears indeed to be contingent', even as the 'turning toward ...' may be done exclusively by the person.

The Freudian drives

Do we have to make a choice between the alternatives of drive theory and object theory? Clinical diversity is meritorious in principle but raises a number of questions. For Pine (1985: 65), who exemplifies the pluralistic approach in contemporary psychoanalysis, 'an emphasis on moments of experience, varying in their prime content, impact, and subsequent organization, permits reconciliation of the competing demands of drive, ego, and object-relations theories upon the child's developmental time'. Drive theory and object theory are seen as complementary *perspectives* on psychic reality. More precisely, Pine aims to combine four psychoanalytic theories (conceptually separable, but not separate) corresponding to four discrete *personal* psychologies – namely, drives, ego functioning, the object-relation, and self-experience.[6] The 'four psychologies' of psychoanalysis refer not only to clinical models but also to psychic phenomena, or actual formations of psyche, with characteristic developmental lines and core motivational aspects. For Pine (1989: 57) 'there are moments in the lives of every infant and child that are particularly significant, particularly formative, for the phenomena addressed in the perspectives of each of the psychologies'. Pine (1989: 31–32) is concerned primarily with the relevance of the 'four psychologies' in the clinical situation: 'My interest in these psychologies, and specifically as a differentiable yet interconnected foursome, has come about through the help they offer in clinical work'. Clearly, Pine (1988) is intent on referring to psychic phenomena, or different aspects of mind, in the analytic encounter, rather than foregrounding the larger theoretical *systems* of Freud's drive psychology, the ego psychology of Hartmann, the object-relations theory of Fairbairn, or Kohut's self-psychology.

The integration of the 'four psychologies' is seen as a developmental outcome, insofar as each of the psychologies achieve motivational status through the maturational processes. Pine (1989: 57) notes that 'we each develop personal hierarchies of the phenomena and motives of the four psychologies'. The approach to personality organisation, as well as motivation, is unequivocally developmental, the focus is on what happens developmentally among the sets of phenomena addressed by the 'four psychologies': how motivations emerge and how the personality becomes organised in the course of human development. In this respect, the idea of 'integration in the person', indeed, based on 'the developmental actualities of the child's life' (Pine 1985: 65), represents a significant advance in clinical thinking, not least of all, by cautioning against the reification of bits of the person. The applied nature of Pine's contribution notwithstanding, his non-reductive, integrative approach to the 'four psychologies' raises important theoretical questions. These questions are especially relevant to my analysis of post-Freudian thought. Further to my discussion of the person-action relation, we can see important points of overlap between Pine's (1990: 217) 'theories of persons' and the phenomenology of *actus humanus*.

The following points are particularly pertinent for the formulation of a non-reductionist relational drive model, which may be found in some, but by no means all of the Independent analysts discussed in this essay. Firstly, Pine is primarily interested in the developmental transformation of innate motivational tendencies. Thus, assuming that the phenomena of each of the 'four psychologies' achieve motivational status, Pine (1989: 35) presents a broadly-defined theory of motivation along developmental lines: 'there are motivations specific to the domains of each of the four psychologies, and one cannot render a comprehensive account of mental life without taking each of them into account'. Moreover, for Pine (1989: 36) core human motives are formed in the course of development rather than existing fully formed at birth: 'All human motives have a developmental history. Whatever the nature of their initial biological base, the final forms of motivation are the result of complex shaping processes that take time to occur ... the relevant question is how motivational status is achieved over time'. The emphasis is clearly on the development of an *active* motive. The active expressions of an achieved life, according to Pine (1989: 56), have 'a particular history and a place in the personal drive, ego, object-relations, and self-psychologies, and can be addressed from the conceptual perspectives of those same four psychologies'.

Secondly, turning more specifically to motivation theory as applied to the domain of object-relations psychology, the argument is essentially twofold: (a) 'we begin with a primal readiness for connection to the other' and (b) evolve tendencies in the course of development 'to repeat old, now internalized, object relations in efforts after mastery' (Pine 1989: 51). As for the perennial question of origin, Pine (1989: 37) admits that even if we could ascertain which comes first: drive gratification or object interconnection (the 'good' and 'bad' internal objects constituted by the *mode of connection* in the earliest relationship), 'it is clear that from very early on they are each already present and are *en route* on a complex developmental path, intertwined with one another, so that nothing significant about human functioning can be described without reference to both'. In addition, while internal object-relations are understood to be formed out of 'experiences with the primary objects of childhood', nonetheless, they are not seen as 'veridical representations of those relationships'. On the contrary, Pine (1988: 573; emphasis in the original) maintains that 'the object relation *as experienced* by the child is what is laid down in memory and repeated, and this experience is a function of the affect and wishes active in the child at the moment of the experience'.

Thirdly, in terms of the drive psychology of the individual, particularly the motivational aspect of the sexual and aggressive drives, Pine (1989: 51) proposes that in each case motivation is not confined to drive gratification, insofar as the drive itself 'serves functions' within the other psychologies (ego, object, self) as well. In particular, Pine (1989: 49) argues that 'while cyclicity, peremptoriness, and potential pleasure may account for the primary motivational aspect of sexuality, the omnipresence of the search for sensual pleasure requires recognition of the functions it serves within the spheres of ego, object relations, and self-experience as well'. The point is that sensual pleasure (touch, rocking, warmth) serves many functions besides the attainment of pleasure in itself: 'Sexual drives include the biological givens of bodily sensation, but include also a record of personal history embodied in cognitions (wishes, fantasies, goals) that guide the form of arousal and satisfaction; they are not simply urges automatically played out' (Pine 1989: 48). The sexual drive is indissociable from its relational context. Similar considerations are also applied to the aggressive drive. Given the unavoidable nature of frustration, interference of one kind or another, and narcissistic injury, 'reactive aggression' is seen as ubiquitous. On the other hand, the self-producing and cyclic aspects of 'proactive aggression' are considered less central. Most importantly, Pine (1989: 51) maintains that 'reactive aggression' becomes a drive and, as such, achieves motivational status, only by being held over a period of time; the force of the drive may begin reactively but 'its object, immediate source, and mode of expression reflect developmental achievements'. As such, aggressive drive, like sexuality, can be 'sustained, displaced, expressed symbolically, defended against'. In the domain of drive, Pine (1989: 52) concludes that the various ways in which the infant attempts to reach for life '(a) become tied to specific objects and fantasies as those urges achieve cognitive representation and elaboration over time; (b) come to serve functions in relation to self-experience, ego functioning, and object relations; and (c) in the case of aggression, come to include reactive forms which achieve ongoing status as the capacity to hold the offending other in mind matures (object constancy)'.

Pine (1988: 595) contends that the 'four psychologies' provide 'a fuller approximation' to the analysing situation and personal human development than any one or two alone. This seems to be a reasonable proposition, although inevitably there is a risk of eclecticism in the recourse to hybrid or mixed models. The argument in favour of the complementarity of object theory and drive theory is in danger of glossing over irreconcilable theoretical and technical differences. As well as a lack of coherence and conceptual focus, there is a danger with eclecticism that the most compelling features of any given perspective inevitably become less conspicuous, if not entirely hidden. Mitchell (1988: 92) notes that drive theory and object theory 'cannot be juxtaposed or mixed without radically changing one or both of them'. At the same time, he points to what he calls 'developmental tilt' as one of the ways in which 'accommodation has been accomplished, leading to pervasive implications for the way object-relations concepts have been shaped'. The manoeuvre 'postulates that Freud was correct in understanding the mind of conflicts among drives *and* that object-relations are also important, but *earlier*' (1988: 136; emphasis in the original). We can see something of this manoeuvre at play in Pine's 'four psychologies' model.

On the other hand, rejecting the idea of drive entirely courts alternative problems and potential limitations. Reducing things to a choice between Freud and object-relations theory, as if psychoanalysis divides at this point into two branches or alternative pathways, effectively shuts down any further debate on a topic of paramount importance for the theoretical and clinical development of the discipline. Cross-fertilisation and a certain degree of open-mindedness are ruled out by this more black-and-white approach. It seems clear, for example, that the social determination of behaviour, taken to its logical conclusion, rules out the possibility of meaningful dialogue with the Freudian interpretation. Ultimately, everything comes down on the side of what actually happened. This makes sense (in principle, at least) in disciplines like history or sociology but is hardly a credible model for psychoanalytic inquiry. Drive theory was the main part of Freud's contribution, and to simply dismiss classical structural theory (and the drive model it incorporates) in favour of relational patterns, developmental pathways, attachment behaviour, interpersonal relations, self-experience, and so on undermines the interpretative rationale of Freudian psychoanalysis.

Hartmann (1948) consolidated the view of the drive concept as a prerequisite for the motivational system of psychoanalysis, a view we find expressed some 40-odd years later in Greenberg's (1991) summary overview of key developments in drive theory within and beyond the classical psychoanalytic tradition. Unconvinced by the viability of (especially) Fairbairn's and Kohut's attempts to come up with a drive-free theory of human experience, Greenberg (1991: 88–89) concludes that '[w]hether theorists are explicit about it or not, they are always working with some pre-experiential tendency that gives shape to relational experience'. As well as righting wrongs, the positive aspect of Greenberg's critique consists in redefining drive not as something that accumulates and therefore requires discharge, but rather, as directedness (intentionality) that orients human action. Greenberg's (1991: 118) approach 'focusses analytic attention on the endogenous elements of behaviour and experience without giving priority to bodily stimuli' or psychosomatic phenomena.

This tallies with the view that the major innovation of Freud's final theory of the drives – namely, the concept of the life drive – may be more fully integrated into contemporary psychoanalytic thought through object theory.[7] Despite our divergent views about Fairbairn and Loewald, my approach to Independent Freudianism has a good deal in common with Greenberg's critical assessment. The approach adopted throughout this book rests on the foundational composite of human directedness and human relatedness. Moreover, I agree that we need a concept of motivation in psychoanalysis, although I suggest that object-related motives and *a priori* 'feeling states' (Sandler 1972) provide a better option than a biologically based energy model of tension and discharge.

In focusing, then, on the drive/object-relations debate, I have two aims in mind: firstly, to situate Freud's drive model as a general theory of human action. Secondly, to acknowledge Freud's own attempts from 'Formulations on the Two Principles of Mental Functioning' (1911b) onwards, to integrate 'relational concepts into the established structure of the drive model' (Greenberg and Mitchel 1983: 25). The attempt to fit the notion of primary identification – 'a direct and immediate identification [that] takes place earlier than any object-cathexis' (Freud 1923b: 31) – into the economic model, and to retain the explanation of identifications as 'abandoned object-cathexes', remains unresolved in a series of key texts written during this period (Mitchell 1988). This is evident, most notably, in '*On Narcissism*' (1914b), '*Mourning and Melancholia*' (1917b), *Group Psychology and the Analysis of the Ego* (1921), and *The Ego and the Id* (1923b).

The idea of primary object-relatedness is effectively side-lined in classical theory by drive economics. There are nonetheless any number of attempts, extending across the entire range of post-Freudian thought, to broaden the interpretative focus of the drive model.[8] I propose that in terms of Independent object-relations theory, the integration of human-erotic relations into post-Freudian thought is based on the person-action relation, the experience of the person living together with others. Human life becomes living in and through the reach for life. The earliest phase of infancy admits no differentiation; the pure immanence of life is manifest rather in the auto-affection of affectivity. At this stage, the 'individual's object constitutes not only his world, but also himself' (Fairbairn 1941: 47).

Jacobson (1964: 13–14) advanced a comparable hypothesis, regarding, the 'undifferentiated psychophysiological energy' of affective phenomena; according to this view, undifferentiated energy denotes an inner life force intrinsically open to experience: 'at the very beginning of life, the instinctual energy is still in an undifferentiated state ... from birth on it develops into two kinds of psychic drives with different qualities under the influence of external stimulations, of psychic growth and the opening up and increasing maturation of pathways for outside discharge'. Loewald, in turn, took the hypothesis a good deal further by assigning object-relations a determining role in the origination and shaping of the drives themselves. As we shall see, for Loewald there is a relationship before there is a drive and, as such the nature of the relationship, to a greater or lesser extent, shapes the character of the drives.

Freud famously admitted that '[t]he theory of the instincts [*Trieblehre*] is so to speak our mythology':

> Instincts [*Triben*] are mythical entities, magnificent in their indefiniteness. In our work we cannot for a moment disregard them, yet we are never sure that we are seeing them clearly. You know how popular thinking deals with the instincts [*Triben*]. People assume as many and as various instincts as they happen to need at the moment – a self-assertive instinct, an imitative instinct, an instinct of play, a gregarious instinct and many others like them. People take them up, as it were, make each of them do its particular job, and then drop them again. We have always been moved by a suspicion that behind all these little *ad hoc* instincts there lay concealed something serious and powerful which we should like to approach cautiously.
>
> (Freud 1933: 95)

Throughout his work (from early to late), Freud took up what he sensed was behind the *ad hoc* compendium of drive activity. The metapsychological concept of the drive and the analysis of sexuality thus became 'closely intertwined in the fabric of classical psychoanalytic theory' (Mitchell 1988: 67). In terms of the history of the Freudian interpretation, the sexual aetiology of the neuroses predates the combination of sexuality and drive. But with the publication of *Three Essays on the Theory of Sexuality* (1905), Mitchell (1988: 67) notes that drive theory provided a 'solution' to the problem of the 'excess of stimulation fuelling neurotic symptomatology'. This marks a historic shift in Freud's interpretative focus, that is to say, from the role of the object in the theory of infantile seduction to the perspective of internal pressure. Interaction with external objects is increasingly displaced in Freud's interpretation by spontaneously arising, endogenous physiological pressures demanding discharge. The sexual instinct is thus conceived as 'the psychical representative of an endosomatic, continuously flowing source of stimulation, as contrasted with a "stimulus", which is set up by *single* excitations coming from *without*' (Freud 1905: 168).

The shift from the object to internal pressure in *Three Essays* was consistent with Freud's earlier hypotheses, although, as we shall see, the change of position was far from clear-cut, the object-relation was not simply displaced. Nevertheless, by the time of *Three Essays* certain key principles of mental activity were already in place – including, principles derived from the notions of 'quantity' (Q) and 'neurones' as set out in the *Project for a Scientific Psychology* (1895). The quantitative conception posits the basic principle of 'neuronal activity' – namely, that neurones tend to reduce tension or divest themselves of energy.[9] Freud sought to explain the structure and function of neurones on these grounds, particularly, with reference to the principle of 'neuronal inertia', or what he later described as the 'principle of constancy'. Basically, the idea is that organisms tend to rid themselves of tensions brought about by an increase in either external or internal stimuli. The principle accounts for the aim to eliminate excitation and, thereby, release tension. In the event, the aim of removing an increase in stimulus through 'discharge' (*Entlastung*) keeps the energy circulating within the neuronal system or apparatus at as low a level as possible. Freud (1895: 296) identified the pattern of the reflex arc as the simplest form of the tension/discharge model, and argued that the principle of inertia 'provides the motive for the reflex movement'.

Freud consistently viewed the psyche as a system or apparatus designed to reduce 'stimulus tension' (unpleasurable stimulation) and, in the first two editions of *Three Essays* at least, the sexual organs interact with stimuli from the outside world; the psyche is acted upon by the object: 'We can distinguish in them [the component instincts] (in addition to an "instinct" which is not itself sexual and which has its source in motor impulses) a contribution from an organ capable of receiving stimuli (e.g. the skin, the mucous membrane or a sense organ). An organ of this kind will be described in this connection as an "erotogenic zone" – as being the organ whose excitation lends the instinct a sexual character' (Freud 1905: 168n).[10] In the case of stimuli originating outside the organism, the principle of inertia describes a 'cessation' or 'flight from stimulus'; whereas in more complex organisms this 'giving-off' of energy applies to stimuli originating from 'the somatic element itself'. Freud (1895: 296) held that even in the case of external stimuli it may be necessary to 'retain' the 'paths of discharge' that keep the organism free from tension.

This arrangement clearly applies in the case of endogenous stimuli, understood as precursors of the drives, which 'have their origin in the cells of the body and give rise to the major needs: hunger, respiration, sexuality' (1895: 297). In the case of endogenously driven mental activity, 'the organism cannot withdraw as it does from external stimuli'; the level of tension can be reduced only under particular conditions, which 'must be realised in the external world'. Freud takes the act of nourishment as an exemplar of the interior situation of quantitative activity. The organism accomplishes this 'action', according to Freud (1895: 297), by abandoning its 'original trend to inertia' and, instead, finding a way to retain a store of energy 'sufficient to meet the demand for a specific action'. The systemic tendency of 'giving-off' is nonetheless upheld under these conditions insofar as levels of energy are kept as 'low as possible' and, at the same time, the system continues to 'guard itself against any increase' of energy.

It is immediately apparent that a general theory of action, if not the integration of the person in the action, is implicit in the most basic principles of Freud's economic model. Far from a clear-cut distinction between the object and internal pressure, in Freud's earliest writings the purpose (*Vorsatz*) attributed to the acting person involves taking the external world into account.[11] In a psychical arrangement that depends on both the libidinal cathexes of objects and the availability of those objects for the satisfaction of need (*Bedürfnis*), the effects of the excitatory process are discernible in the cathected objects themselves. The economic hypothesis thus posits object-situated action in conjunction with the distribution of quantities of excitation along associative (neuronal, psychical) pathways. Object usage instantiates the flow of energy between endogenously driven needs and external objects, linking the cathected object and the satisfying object. To restate this in more general terms: action translates instinct into external existence as part of the coevolution of psyche-soma and world. Again, if we take the act of nourishment as our exemplar, it is evident that mental activity cannot be conceived of as a context-independent (neuronal) system. The conception of 'neuronal excitation as quantity in a state of flow' (1895: 296) is integral to a more broadly defined action frame of reference oriented to the dynamic correlation of the action with the person. Indeed, the *Project* implies that human mental activity is actually a *function* of the object-world rather than an intrinsically determined intracerebral system or structure.

The fact that the conditions of action pertaining to our 'major needs' (hunger, respiration, sexuality) are realised only in the object-world means that the 'economic' situation itself is exogenously as well as endogenously driven. One cannot fail to see from the economic point of view that our minds are in the world. This clears the ground for the more far-reaching claim that the personal is inherently and irreducibly interpersonal. In effect, Freud advanced an object-situated perspective from the beginning: mind and world do not stand in relation to one another as separate entities but are reciprocally constructive, mutually dependent the one upon the other for their realisation. The economic viewpoint has not typically been viewed in this light. Yet starting from the tendency to discharge (*Entlastung*), the human nervous system (*Nervensystem*) is considered functionally incomplete. The implication is that 'apparatus' (neuronal, psychical) and 'world' are not externally connected but intrinsically linked, in accordance with the realisation of endogenously/exogenously driven needs as vital acts of human existence. Life exerts a pressure towards more life. The vitalisation of action and the generalisation of drive energy are different ways of describing the same event. Despite Freud's (1905: 148) aim to 'loosen the bond' between the instinct and the object, it seems clear that starting with the interactive matrix of mother and baby, the *person in action* is inherently relational. As such, the person's dynamism in action figures centrally in the defining statements of classical drive theory, namely: (a) an instinct is 'a measure of the demand made upon the mind for work' (Freud 1905: 168); and (b) instincts are 'the ultimate cause of all activity' (Freud 1940a: 148).

Vital activity

It is incumbent on me now to substantiate my main contention concerning the general theory of meaningful action in the Freudian interpretation. The idea that conflict is integral to life underpins Freud's theory of action, with respect to (a) the feeling of satisfaction; (b) the dialectic of discharge and generativity; and (c) the conflictive nature of living-there. I shall discuss each of these in turn, before presenting a more detailed discussion of the conflict in melancholia.

The activity of taking nourishment (cited as paradigmatic in the *Project*) demonstrates the extent to which a theory of action, based on the interrelation between the ego of the person and the action, is already implicit in the quantitative conception. It also raises questions about the form and function of major needs and their satisfaction or aims. In his initial formulation, Freud opposed the 'instincts of self-preservation' (*Selbsterhaltungstriebe*) – indeed, modelled on hunger – to the 'sexual instinct' (*Sexualtrieb*). The economic hypothesis was applied more pointedly to the latter – that is, to the force of libido seen as active throughout the alternations of the sexual instinct. The opposition itself is implicit in *Three Essays*, where, focusing systematically on the active sources of sexuality, Freud (1905: 232) proposed that the infant's sexual excitation arises from 'a multiplicity of forces' and, moreover, that infants 'already enjoy sexual satisfaction when they begin to take nourishment'. The theory of 'vital activity' is set out here in terms of the developmental bifurcation of basic needs: 'The satisfaction of the erotogenic zone is associated, in the first instance, with the satisfaction of the need for nourishment. To begin with, sexual activity attaches itself to functions serving the purpose of self-preservation and does not become independent of them until later' (1905: 181–82).

I shall come back to the conflict between these two types of drive activity. Meanwhile, in the case of infantile drive activity, satisfaction, arising 'first and foremost from the appropriate sensory excitation of ... erotogenic zones' (1905: 233), is realised in the external world through an irreducible combination of action and (libidinal) force-relations. The argument is not altogether consistent, however. Freud (1905: 212) maintained that pleasure and sexual tension are not coterminous and can only be connected in an 'indirect manner'. On the other hand, he (1905: 201) admitted that 'the concepts of "sexual excitation" and "satisfaction" can to a great extent be used without distinction'. The inconsistency is instructive. It introduces a theory of vital activity in which satisfaction does not consist in the elimination of excitation but, rather, in the pleasurable sensations that the infant experiences *as* excitation. The pursuit of excitation presupposes an active first principle, a dynamic human reality, whereby life becomes more life in the very act of living. Phenomenologically, the principle applies to the realisation of the 'purpose' (*Vorsatz*) of being as action (the power of action), rather than inactivity or quiescence. As distinct from the process of tension/discharge, the vitalism of the drives is predicated on the grounds that the sensation of sexual tension and the feeling of satisfaction are existentially coincident.

Starting, then, with *Three Essays* and the inextricable link between the theory of infantile sexuality and the metapsychological conception of drive, Freud adumbrated (a) the active nature of the drives, (b) the variability of aim, and (c) the contingency of the object. Set out explicitly in terms of what satisfies the drives, the argument is based, firstly, on the idea that 'an instinct is always active even when it has a passive aim in view' (1905: 219 n1). Secondly, in the case of infantile sexuality the aim 'consists in replacing the projected sensation of stimulation in the erotogenic zone by an external stimulus which removes that sensation by producing a feeling of satisfaction' (1905: 184). Thirdly, the object likewise is conceived in terms of this feeling of satisfaction: 'A child's intercourse with anyone responsible for his care affords him an unending source of sexual excitation and satisfaction from his erotogenic zone' (1905: 223). Freud (1905: 148) may well have felt that he overestimated the 'object's attractions' in the theory of infantile seduction. Nevertheless, looked at from the point of view of satisfaction, it is evident that the contingency of the environment-individual setup, conceived as an object-source of the drive, remains irreducible to the necessity of 'neuronal inertia'.

The argument that every instinct is 'a piece of activity' is elaborated further in 'Instincts and their Vicissitudes' (1915a). In the most extensive treatment of his first instinct theory, Freud reconceptualised the elimination of excitation, expressly, in terms of a drive/structure model. The nervous system (*Nervensystem*), once again, is conceived as functionally incomplete. The system itself is assigned the task of 'mastering stimuli' (*Reizbewältigung*): in the case of external stimuli, the task consists in 'withdrawal'; whereas instinctual stimuli originating from within place 'far higher demands' on the system, necessitating 'involved and interconnected activities' in order to achieve a feeling of satisfaction. Accordingly, Freud (1915a: 122) postulated the concept of 'instinct' – based on the *activity* of the system or apparatus – 'on the frontier between the mental and the somatic, as the psychical representative [*Repräsentant*] of the stimuli originating from within the organism and reaching the mind, as a measure of the demand made upon the mind for work in consequence of its connection with the body'. We find the postulate consistently restated throughout, for example, in Freud (1911a: 74): 'We regard the instinct as being the concept on the frontier-line between the somatic and the mental ... Further, we accept the popular distinction between ego-instincts and a sexual instinct'. Again, there appears to be an inconsistency in the argument, although, in his editorial note, Strachey attributes this to the frontier status of the concept itself. Strachey's reading is persuasive. The drive is understood as the 'psychical representative' (*Triebrepräsentanz*) of somatic impulses or force-relations on the one hand and, on the other, as a nonpsychical element distinct from the idea that affords it representation. As such, drive theory articulates an intermediate region of human action.

The reality of the acting person, indeed, living together with others, comes to the fore in psychoanalytical theory, initially, on the conceptual 'frontier' of the Freudian *Trieb*. The demand for work, identified as a dynamic phenomenon at the level of psyche-soma, articulates the connection between the action and the life drive. Moreover, elaborating on the idea that living itself is at once a dynamic phenomenon and a thoroughly practical matter, Freud described the threefold movement of desire, work, and satisfaction in terms of the basic constituents of the drives.[12] The dynamic process that Freud (1915a: 122) described at the heart of psychic life consists in a 'pressure' (*Drang*) that makes the drive active; hence the push (*Trieben*) for more life as 'the amount of force or the measure of the demand for work which [the stimulus originating from within] represents'. The characteristic of 'exercising pressure' is seen as the 'essence' of drive activity; it defines the inner distinctive nature of life-as-action. The 'aim' (*Ziel*) of each instinct, in turn, is defined in terms of the reach for life, understood as the obtainment of satisfaction by the removal or reduction of 'the state of stimulation at the source of the instinct'. As the reach for instinctual satisfaction, the aim remains 'unchangeable', although the pathways to this end admit 'variability' as a defining characteristic of drive activity.

The extent to which drive activity is contingent on the environment-individual setup becomes apparent at the level of the object-source of the drive. For Freud (1905: 148) the problem of the 'object' emerges, specifically, with reference to the variability of the object in sexual drive activity. The idea is that 'the sexual instinct is in the first instance independent of the object'. The main bone of contention for critics of drive theory concerns the reduction of the object to the role of drive satisfaction, where satisfaction is conceived in conformity with the pleasure-unpleasure principle. Nevertheless, an appreciation of contingency at the level of the object confirms the functional incompleteness of the nervous system and the concomitant mobility of drive activity. The idea that the efficacious participation of the human being is realised in relation to the object of the drive suggests another way of reading the wish to 'loosen the bond' between the instinct and the object. Freud established that the object is not inherent in the drive but remains contingent. The object is thus 'assigned' (*zugeordnet*) to the drive in such a way as to yield a feeling of satisfaction. Despite the fact that the status of the object-mother (environment) remains largely untheorised, the value of the object and of the environment surrounding the infant is nonetheless discernible in its use. The feeling of satisfaction comes about through an object the use of which 'may be changed any number of times in the course of the vicissitudes which the instinct undergoes during its existence' (1915a: 122–23). In principle, at least, so long as it is not seen as part and parcel of the instinct, the object is more not less available for use.

Primal generative tension

Together with the 'frontier' status of drive as an economic concept, the four basic elements of drive activity reveal a constitutive antagonism between the principle of discharge (the release of force-relations) on the one hand and, on the other, the coincidence of tension and the sense of satisfaction, or the pleasurable increase of tension. The somatic and psychical dynamism of the person, including, the personal fulfilment of the ego through action, extends beyond the work of mastering stimuli and becomes a more expansive use of tension. The latter may be seen as an irreducibly generative process. The acting person is engaged in *pressing* the tension further rather than simply eliminating it, 'holding it in a larger structure and discovering new tensions at that level which in turn will generate further fruitful crises' (Williams 2014: 130). The notion of generative tension, which is taken from Margaret Masterman (1957), provides support for an original theory of pressure. For example, Williams applies the theory to the phenomenology of religious utterance on the grounds that ordinary language appears far less ordinary, the intentions of ordinary language experiences are 'liable to rupture and strangeness', precisely, at those points where language comes 'under pressure'.

The idea of generative tension throws new light on the conflictual nature of human reality; in particular, it indicates the extent to which being is subject to the conflicting demands of more life. As a result, the hypothesis of the 'death drive' is not required in order to account for the elemental re-lationship of forces at the heart of life itself. It is not the negative so much as what cannot be mastered that disrupts the 'nervous system' and renders it functionally incomplete, even as it disrupts the very efficacy of the person-action conjugate. Thus, by situating the dynamic reality of the acting person in terms of a life 'under pressure', it is possible to link the 'essence' of drive activity to *a way of life*. The act of nourishment fits this comprehensive description of life 'under pressure', in which the elimination of excitation and the generativity of force-relations are equiprimordially existent. The pursuit of pleasure in the object and the pursuit of excitation – satisfaction and desire – proceed in tandem, with respect to the appetite of hunger. We can take the act of nourishment then as an exemplar of primal generative tensions or 'need-tensions' (*Bedürfnisspannungen*) in which, starting with the potentiality of the infant's first feed, eating satisfies the 'demand for work' as a creative act of being, a way of going-on-being.

The appetite of hunger and the act of nourishment are inextricably linked to the primordial drive to 'cling' (Hermann 1976), or what I call the reach for life, understood as object-seeking. The nursing baby simultaneously feeds and *reaches for* the mother. He begins to take in the object that is found/invented in the act of nourishment not only by latching on to the breast, but also by holding the mother's gaze – 'breast and face are experienced as one and indivisible' (Spitz 1955: 219). Together, the sucking reflex and the urge to cling drive meaningful human activity at the beginning of life. Need (*Bedürfnis*) drives the act, in this case, where the existential 'frontier' passes not only between the psyche and the soma but also between the modalities of formative illusion – namely, the readiness to eat well (*bien manger*) and the instantiation of the impulse to do so as a vital function of the personal ego. Generating what grows, the act of nourishment presupposes participation, expectancy, and a 'personal contribution' on the part of the acting person. Need prompts life from the beginning in accordance with specific appetites. Fairbairn was the first to work out in detail the extent to which 'the various "aims" of the libido described by Freud are determined by specific appetitive tendencies belonging to the innate endowment of man' (1930: 156). Winnicott (1988: 100), in turn, developed this line of inquiry in terms of 'primary creativity', which may be seen as a means of '*developing* instinct tension' at the level of the emergent ego of the person.

Freud (1905: 2029) acknowledged the difficulty of combining 'unpleasurable tension' with the 'feeling of pleasure'; while at the same time, providing the possibility for doing so. If, for example, we take up the argument in *Beyond the Pleasure Principle*, it is possible to extrapolate a principle of primal generativity (an *active* first principle) from the formulation of the 'principle of constancy'. Freud (1920: 9) states that 'the mental apparatus endeavours to keep the quantity of excitation present in it as low as possible or at least to keep it constant' (1920: 9). The statement allows that not all tension is unpleasurable. Thus, while an increase in excitation that 'deviates from complete stability' is equated with unpleasure; on the other hand, constancy, understood as 'stability' under pressure, may be seen as consistent with pleasurable tension. The latter designates the irreducible conjuncture of spontaneous action and environmental provision, where life is sufficiently provoked but not to the point of impingement, nor yet by drive activity exterior to life.

The disruptive nature of life

Freud's second dual-drive theory brings us back to the distinction between the self-preservative functions and the sexual drives. We have seen the extent to which Freud (1905: 181–82) described the pleasurable sensation that the infant derives from its 'first and most vital activity' as a flowing together of nutritional and sexual drives: 'The satisfaction of the erotogenic zone is associated, in the first instance, with the satisfaction of the need for nourishment'. The formative confluence of human activity leaves its mark on the act of nourishment as well as the satisfying object (subsequent types of object-choice), even as the sexual instincts become autonomous in the course of development. Freud emphasised the conflicted nature of the developmental distinction; further to the original libidinal/self-preservative drive he posited an 'opposition' between the two kinds of instinct – namely, 'the instincts which subserve sexuality ... and those other instincts, which have as their aim the self-preservation of the individual – the ego-instincts' (1910c: 214). Freud seized the opportunity this antithesis afforded him to distinguish his drive theory from attempts by others, most notably Jung, to generalise the instinctual force-relations of libido.

We can admit the opposition of sex and hunger without denying the formative confluence of the drives. In fact, Freud demonstrated the extent to which the psychic legacy of the latter – the erotic *flowing together* of living-there – is active in the very antagonism between self-preservative and sexual drives. It is the infant's libidinal relation with the mother that brings this situation to life. The earliest relationship is animated by relations of forces, where, in the first dual-drive theory, antagonism is presented as an active first principle. Vitalism thus pertains without recourse to monism. Confirmation of this view follows with the new instinctual dualism in *Beyond the Pleasure Principle* in which Freud contrasts life instincts and death instincts. With the revision of the Freudian interpretation from 1920 onwards, the fate of the self-preservative instincts, once again, is reckoned on the basis of generative tension. In fact, the vital antagonism that persists from the first to the second instinctual dualism becomes more explicit in the revised version. This was not immediately evident to Freud. He hesitated before deciding to drop the option of classifying the self-preservative instincts among the death instincts. Initially, he defined them as 'component instincts whose function it is to assure that the organism shall follow its own path to death' (1920: 39). In the event, he was not convinced by this hypothesis.

We can discern a variant line here in Freud's thinking: on the one hand, psychic reality hinges for Freud on the explicit opposition between the life instincts and the death instincts. On the other hand, Freud (1920: 41) postulated an antagonism *within* the life instincts that he reckoned, now, was active from the beginning: 'the instincts which were later to be described as sexual may have been in operation from the very first, and it may not be true that it was only at a later time that they started upon their work of opposing the activities of the "ego-instincts"'. Eros itself admits a destructive element, or 'demonic' dimension, which is far from 'correlative with the ego' (Laplanche 2015: 170). This is a familiar argument and, at the same time, a radically new formulation concerning the disruptive or unsettling nature of life itself. A 'starting-point for the study of further problems', the conflictive nature of life remains something of an 'insoluble problem' in the classical Freudian interpretation. With the assimilation in the final instinct theory of the self-preservative instincts (sucking reflex, urge to cling) and the sexual instincts (infantile sexuality) into the category of the life drive or Eros, Freud (1930: 118 n 2) identified the 'opposition between the ceaseless trend by Eros towards extension [more life] and the general conservative nature of the instincts'.

In the articulation of 'extension' and 'conservation' Eros appears as an expression of life under pressure, which, broadly speaking, is another way of expressing the conflictive nature of meaningful action. Freud (1920: 42–43) described this situation in terms of 'the efforts of Eros to combine organic substances into ever larger unities'. The efforts of the life drive should not be viewed from the restrictive vantage point of ego psychology. On the contrary, placed under the heading of Eros, the conflictive nature of life is evident as a series of opposing forces, ranging from the tendency towards the preservation and the state of primary participatory belonging (prior to any subject-object correlation) to the pleasurable experience of tension and the more organised activity of living together with others (object-cathexis).

Active life is conceptualised in the new instinctual dualism, specifically, with respect to the work of binding and the fusion of the drives, neither of which is necessarily dependent on the hypothesis of the 'death drive'. Freud accounts for what Eros *does* in terms of the 'demand for work' – namely, the developmental efforts of Eros not only to join living substance into ever-larger units but also to construct, to conserve, and to tie or bind these vital unities as an ongoing project. We can identify the trend of Eros towards increasing tension with living-there as the pressure for more life. In this respect, uniting and binding may be seen at work in the interstices of life, rather than primarily in opposition to the 'unbinding' (*Entbindung*) of the death instincts, the removal of 'internal tension due to stimuli' (1920: 55–56), and, ultimately, the aim of bringing vital unities 'back to their primaeval, inorganic state' (1930: 118–19). The dynamism of the acting person is not defined in opposition to the constancy or Nirvana principle but is essentially generative and consists in the creation of new tensions. For Freud (1923b: 45) this takes place through the work of 'binding' (*Bindung*), understood as the defining characteristic or 'main purpose' of Eros.

In a further elaboration of the erotic forces constitutive of the person-action totality, Freud maintained that it is in the nature of Eros to seek union with something else. The problem of the object, therefore, arises as integral to the vital antagonism of erotic drive activity. On the one hand, 'instincts are directed towards objects', that is, as purposive expressions of Eros; on the other hand, 'objects can only be of significance if the individual has some drive to relate to them' (Rycroft 1995: 83–84). It is not necessary, therefore, to make a case for a formal distinction between instincts and their vicissitudes on the one hand and, on the other, the object-relation. Drives are situated in an erotically related object-world from the beginning of life and, as such, remain integral to the creation of meaningful relations, both loving and destructive. The person as it manifests itself in action reveals the extent to which life disrupts itself.

The articulation of instinct theory and object theory applies to the whole of psychic life. For Freud (1930: 121 n 1) 'libido has a share in every instinctual manifestation', a view that he advanced on the grounds of instinctual fusion. Introduced as part of the final instinct theory, the 'fusion of instincts' (*Triebmischung*) accounts for the relations between the life instincts and the death instincts, although it is important not to confuse the 'destructive drive' (*Destruktionstrieb*) and the 'death drive' (*Todestrieb*). It is the becoming active of the so-called 'death drive' through destructive forces, or demonic Eros, that animates the ego of the person. Combined with the life drives, destructive forces are therefore actively oriented towards object-relating rather than the annulment or dissolution of vitality. Indeed, the entropic tendency of *Todestrieb* does not cover the more active manifestations of destructiveness, compulsive repetition, and negative therapeutic reactions. Combined with erotic force-relations, the latter may be seen as symptomatic expressions of the acting person's need to relate to objects. This applies even under the most severe conditions – that is, where the subject appears *actively* disorganised.[13] The ubiquity of drive *activity*, however, the idea that Eros is the vital force in 'every instinctual manifestation', amounts to more than a description of structural combinations. The inclusion of human destructiveness within an active first principle presupposes a general theory of human action as distinct from an instinctual dualism. Destruction of the object, understood as a condition of its use (Winnicott 1971d), is no less a manifestation of the pressure for more life than the play of erotic force-relations.

To summarise, the person-action relation figures in Freud's drive theory in terms of (a) the coincidence of satisfaction and excitation (satisfactory and exciting objects), (b) the force-relations of generative tension, and (c) the disruptive nature of life itself. The Freudian interpretation was replete with a theory of action from the beginning. Yet even at its most capacious, the classical view admits the psychic reality of objects only insofar as they prove efficacious (in principle) in satisfying basic bodily-*based* needs, experienced as pleasure. For Freud instinctual sexuality remains an expression of the pursuit of pleasure in the object, where the object is viewed merely as an opportunity for satisfying this pursuit. It was possible to advance the theory of human action only so far from the point of view of desire-satisfaction and the second topography. In answer to the question 'Why is there something rather than nothing?' Freud (1940a: 148) remained committed to the idea that instincts are 'the ultimate cause of all activity'. He left us to elaborate on human action – including, 'environmental activity' and the 'demonic' force-relations of Eros – as a problem of our being together with one another in the world. Mitchell (1997: 2–3) succinctly contextualised the problem: 'There has been a largely unacknowledged feature at the heart of clinical psychoanalysis from its very inception, a feature that has been difficult to come to terms with, to integrate with other analytic principles ... This central, largely unacknowledged feature of psychoanalysis is its fundamentally *interactive* nature'. In taking up the challenge of the Freudian legacy, object-relations theory casts doubt on a purely desire-driven conception of human beings. On the positive side, the integration of human-erotic relations into the life-world sets the agenda for Independent Freudian thought at its most far-reaching.

The shadow of the object

Let us now turn to 'Mourning and Melancholia' (1917b), which, alongside the recourse to drive economics, advances the Freudian interpretation as a theory of action *and* relations. Replete with insights on introjection and identification, the paper is a masterpiece of psychoanalytic thinking. It is also an indispensable link in the history of object-relations theory.[14] Freud completed the final version of the paper in May 1915 as one of twelve contributions to metapsychology. As we have noted above, all twelve papers were scheduled for publication under the heading *Zur Vorbereitung einer Metapsychologie*; in the event, Freud published only five of the twelve papers. A copy of the 12th (unpublished) paper, 'A Phylogenetic Fantasy: Overview of the Transference Neuroses', was discovered among Ferenczi's papers in 1983 and subsequently published (Freud 1987).

Before turning to the final published version of the paper, let me begin with its gestation.[15] Freud completed what was in effect a preliminary sketch for 'Mourning and Melancholia' in February 1915, a copy of which he sent in a letter to Ferenczi, asking him to forward it to Abraham (Falzeder, Brabant, and Giampieri-Deutsche 1996: 47–49). Abraham received the sketch from Ferenczi at the beginning of March and replied to Freud at the end of the month (Falzeder 2002: 303–306). In the draft, Freud elaborated on the aetiology of depression in terms of self-criticism and delusional moral inferiority, which he saw as an unconscious reproachful attitude towards the object. The principal discovery of the final version of the paper is already set out in the draft – namely, the mechanism of introjection. The fundamental insight in the paper concerns the formation of the object as a separate entity in the inner world through the process of oral introjection, which, in the case of depressive illness, is combined with (a) a regression from object-love to narcissism and (b) a turning back upon oneself the hate and aggressiveness originally aimed at the object. Freud maintained this view in subsequent contributions on the topic of melancholia; meanwhile, the prevailing emotional atmosphere of melancholia is clearly acknowledged in the draft – including, the intense hostility and hatred directed towards the ego in identification with the object, and the ego's giving itself up (unloved) for dead.

In the letter to Ferenczi on 7 February 1915, Freud identified the mechanism of melancholia as 'the beginning of an understanding of the *narcissistic* neuroses'. The argument is set out as follows. Firstly, melancholia is situated in relation to the so-called 'normal model' of mourning – including, the painful work of libidinal detachment. It remained incomprehensible to Freud why 'the detachment of the libido hurts so much', nonetheless, he maintained this view throughout his writings on the topic. Secondly, the observing ego remains 'intact' in depression, even under the most violent circumstances. Thirdly, the central manoeuvre of melancholia is set out in terms of these violent self-reproaches. Fourthly, Freud compares hysterical and narcissistic types of identification: in hysteria the object cathexis is not 'shut down'; whereas in the narcissistic identification of melancholia the object cathexis is 'removed'. The identification in both cases, however, is seen as a symptomatic expression of 'being in love'. Finally, the outline concludes with a difficult question concerning the 'preponderance of narcissistic object choice', and an admission that 'mania' is not explained by the mechanism of melancholia.

Despite a shared theoretical vocabulary, Freud and Abraham did not come to the same conclusions in their respective accounts of manic-depressive disorders. In the draft as well as the final version of Freud's paper, depression is defined as a 'narcissistic neurosis' in which the libido regresses to the cannibalistic oral phase of development – that is, where the ego incorporates the object into itself by devouring it. These radically new insights into the narcissistic relation between the self and the object-world were based on an account of the withdrawal of libidinal object cathexis and the deformation of the ego. For Freud the object is taken in through the mechanism of narcissistic identification as part of the ego ('loving' the object at this primitive level entails 'being' the object); and in the melancholic state, the ego takes upon itself the reproaches directed against the object. The ego is suffering while 'being' the object.

Abraham came to somewhat different conclusions. In a previously published paper, 'Notes on the Psycho-Analytical Investigation and Treatment of Manic-Depressive Insanity and Allied Conditions' (1911), Abraham emphasised the conflict in melancholia due to ambivalence characterised by 'an attitude of the libido in which hatred predominates'. This attitude is expressed in the statement 'I cannot love people; I have to hate them'. Abraham (1911: 145) thus treats the marked 'feelings of inadequacy' in melancholia in terms of the 'discomforting internal perception' of one's inability to love and, consequently, one's feeling unlovable: 'If the content of the perception is repressed and projected externally, the patient gets the idea that he is not loved by his environment but hated by it … This idea is detached from its primary causal connection with his own attitude of hate, and is brought into association with other … deficiencies'. Abraham concludes that 'feelings of inferiority' favour the formation of depressive illness.

He subsequently elaborated on these views in his seminal paper 'The First Pregenital Stage of Libido' (1916), which set out in detail his own theory of depression. Essentially, for Abraham the depressive patient reproaches himself for his oral-sadistic wish to devour the object.

In his letter to Freud on 31 March 1915, Abraham recapitulated his theory of depression; inevitably, the correspondence touched on their respective views of psychic functioning in general. The letter begins with the question of why melancholia develops in one case and obsession in another. To repeat, based on his reading of the case study of the Rat Man (Freud 1909b) and the centrality of sadism and anal erotism, Abraham (Falzeder 2002: 303) 'deduced depression from a perception of one's inability to love'. Similarly, he assumed that the self-reproaches in melancholia indicate repressed hostile feelings. For Abraham depressive patients demonstrate an inability to love due to the violent nature of their sadistic fantasies, a situation that pertains equally in melancholia and manic states. But Abraham had his own ideas about the role of self-reproaches in melancholia, which allowed him to differentiate the latter from obsessional neurosis:

> it appears to me as if the melancholic, incapable of loving as he is, desperately tries to get possession of a love-object. In my experience, he does in fact identify with his love-object, cannot tolerate its loss, and is hyper-sensitive to the slightest unfriendliness, etc., from that side. He often allows himself to be tormented by the loved person in masochistic self-punishment. He reproaches himself for this instead of reproaching the loved person because unconsciously he has done far greater harm to that person (omnipotence of thought).
>
> (Falzeder 2002: 304)

What does Abraham mean by psychic damage? He turns for an explanation to the third edition of the *Three Essays on the Theory of Sexuality*, which appeared in October 1914, where Freud (1905: 198; emphasis in the original) introduced for the first time the concept of an 'oral' or 'cannibalistic pregenital' organisation of the libido: 'sexual activity has not yet been separated from the ingestion of food; nor are opposite currents within the activity differentiated. The *object* of both activities is the same; the sexual *aim* consists in the incorporation of the object – the prototype of a process which, in the form of identification, is later to play such an important psychological part'.[16] Abraham adopts Freud's account of the 'preliminary stages of love' as an explanation for depression: 'I have strong reason to suspect that such cannibalistic tendencies exist in the melancholic's identification' (Falzeder 2002: 304). Consequently, he proposed that sadism and oral eroticism be added to Freud's account of narcissistic identification and the regression of the ego.[17]

Furthermore, as evidence of this view, Abraham (Falzeder 2002: 305) identified the following symptoms: 'the melancholic's fear of starvation'; 'the refusal of food'; 'the delusion of being a werewolf and of having eaten men'; and 'the impoverishment of the ego'. In this respect, the ambivalent nature of the identification – 'a manifestation of love as well as destruction' – attests to the role of sadism in depression. However, unlike Freud, who attributed sadism to the anal-erotic stage and not to the oral or narcissistic stage, Abraham (Falzeder 2002: 305) maintained that 'the role played by the anal zone in obsessional neurosis is assigned to the mouth in melancholia'.

Freud and Abraham agreed, more or less, about the nature of the oral phase of the libido. Yet the record shows that Freud effectively dismissed Abraham's views concerning the role of 'incorporation' in the aetiology of depression. Similarly, he passed over Ferenczi's theory of 'introjection' – and the concomitant disturbance in the demarcation of the ego and the narcissistic ego, and of the narcissistic ego and the external world – in favour of the projection of the object onto the narcissistic ego (Falzeder, Barabant, and Giampieri-Deutsch 1996: 51). Freud's acknowledgement of the respective contributions of Ferenczi and Abraham to the theory of normal psychic development was not a *carte-blanche* endorsement of their views on depression. In fact, their views do not feature in the definitive formulations of 'Mourning and Melancholia'. Most importantly, in his reply to Abraham on 4 May 1915, Freud noted what he saw as Abraham's reduction of the ego to the drive: 'you do not bring out sufficiently the essential feature of the assumption, that is to say the topical element, the regression of the libido, and the abandonment of the unconscious object cathexis, but instead put into the foreground sadism and anal [oral?] erotism as explanatory motifs' (Falzeder 2002: 308–309).

The criticism is unambiguous. Freud (Falzeder 2002: 309) pointed out that while instinctual impulses, the Oedipus complex, castration anxiety, and so on are 'ubiquitous sources of excitation that have their part in *every* symptom … the explanation of the illness can be derived only from the mechanism'. In the case of depression, the explanation rests unequivocally on the mechanism of narcissistic identification. Instincts and their vicissitudes are viewed in a wider psychical context – including, an explicit emphasis on *alternations in the nature of the object-relationship*. Whereas Abraham was preoccupied with the trajectory of specific instinctual impulses, Freud (1917b: 252) continued to point out, both in the draft and in the final paper, that 'in regression from narcissistic object-choice the object has … been got rid of, but it has nonetheless proved more powerful than the ego itself'. It is the 'abandoned' object that continues to haunt the subject in narcissistic identification: 'The difference … between narcissistic and hysterical identification may be seen in this: that, whereas in the former the object-cathexis is abandoned [shut down], in the latter it persists and manifests its influence' (1917b: 250).

Internalisation

The conceptualisation of the narcissistic relation between ego and object effectively redefined the foundations of Freudian metapsychology. The existing theoretical framework could not accommodate Freud's clinical findings concerning libidinal and narcissistic types of object cathexis. It became necessary therefore to devise a new model or at least revise the current model. I shall attempt to tease out variations on the radical hypotheses that Freud presented in his analysis of the aetiology of depression, particularly in terms of narcissistic object choice and the narcissistic use of the object.

The concept of psychic pain modelled on the depressive patient's narcissistic identification with an object that is abandoned but cannot be lost (Chabert 2003), has wide-ranging implications for our understanding of the Freudian interpretation. Recourse to the pleasure-unpleasure principle gets us only so far here. The problem of object-relations is implicit in Freudianism more or less from the beginning. As Rycroft (1995: 83–84) points out: 'instincts are directed towards objects and objects can only be of significance if the individual has some drive to relate to them'. Formally speaking, the distinction between 'instinct theory' and 'object theory' does not stand up to scrutiny. But the *concept* of internal object-relations is not integrated into Freud's metapsychology until he turns to the treatment of self-hatred in melancholic and depressive states. There is a qualitative shift in Freud's thinking with the discovery that melancholia is based on the internalisation of an 'object-relationship' (Freud 1917b: 249). The theoretical and clinical implications of this finding are far-reaching and support the more general hypothesis that 'the character of the ego is a precipitate of abandoned object-cathexes and that it contains the history of those object-choices' (Freud 1923b: 29).

We have prepared the ground in the foregoing discussion of Freud's theory of action for an appreciation of his approach to the problem of object-relations. Consider the following statement from *Three Essays*: 'There are ... good reasons why a child sucking at his mother's breast has become the prototype of every relation of love. The finding of an object is in fact a refinding of it'. Similar claims may be found at various points throughout Freud's work, where pleasure points the way to the 're-finding' of an object, or to object-choice.[18] The vicissitudes of pleasure (*les destins du plaisir*) continue to delimit the form and function of the object. However, with the introduction in his study of Leonardo of the mechanism whereby an object-cathexis is replaced by an identification via the introjection of the object, Freud raised the question of how and why an external libidinal object becomes internalised in the first place:

> A mother's love for the infant she suckles and cares for is something far more profound than her later affection for the growing child. It is in the

nature of a completely satisfying love-relation, which not only fulfils every mental wish but also every physical need; and if it represents one of the forms of attainable human happiness, that is in no little measure due to the possibility it offers of satisfying, without reproach, wishful impulses which have long been repressed and which must be called perverse.

(Freud 1910a: 117)

Essentially, the object is internalised as a way of maintaining the vitality of the object-cathexis – in Leonardo's case, this involves an identification with the mother. At the same time, one takes as a love-object someone representing an aspect of oneself. Identification consists in drive gratification; but the influence of primitive object-ties is clearly evident in this arrangement. The question of pleasure and *its contexts* guides the amplification of Freudianism as a general theory of the person-action relation. Freud modelled the scene of human happiness, if not blissful communion, on the mother 'fondling' her baby at the breast. In this respect, at least, his description of the 'love-relation' brings the relationship between the cathected feeling of pleasure and the object-seeking infant sharply into focus.

It is not immediately clear from this point of view how we might conceptualise the zone-object schema. The classical model is one of drive satisfaction/frustration, where object-relations remain a function of drive. The emphasis on the instinctual roots of object-relations means that the object is seen as a consequence of the genital organisation of the component instincts and erotogenic zones. *Three Essays* (1905: 210) is a clear guide to Freud's views on these matters: 'If an erotogenic zone in a person who is not sexually excited (e.g. the skin of a woman's breast) is stimulated by touch, the contact produces a pleasurable feeling ... it is at the same time better calculated than anything to arouse a sexual excitation that demands an increase of pleasure'. In light of Freud's comments here about foreplay, the context of feeding includes the mother's eroticised pleasure as well as her emotional response to the baby's wishes and physical needs. The pleasurable affect and its somatic substrate – the 'quality of excitation' (Freud 1905: 209) – is an essential part of the embodied emotional arrangement in which the baby's needs are met or not met.

The zone-object schema challenges the distinction between the 'natural' (biological) and the 'sexual' body. It also allows for a more comprehensive account of meaningful human activity. The inherent complexity in the Freudian interpretation supports an extended definition of contexts in the plural, including: (a) the permanent potentiality pertaining to the sensorial datum of primary participatory belonging; (b) psychosexual erogenous zones; (c) the more elaborated and differentiated level of object-relations proper; and (d) extra-psychic formations (history and culture). Drive remains Freud's answer to the question of why there is something rather than nothing. Nevertheless, the problem of the object was reframed in accordance with Freud's revised model of the mind: from the first topographical model through the papers on metapsychology (1915–17) to the structural point of view set out in the *Ego and the Id* (1923b). Endogenously arising, biologically determined drives remained the underlying motivational principle for Freud. We cannot, in retrospect, foist an object-relations theory on the classical interpretation. There is nonetheless greater emphasis in the later work on early relationships, particularly with regards to the organisation and realisation of the multiple demands of the drives.

We can summarise Freud's developing views on how the mind operates under both normal and pathological conditions, with reference to the following conceptual series: (a) narcissism (Freud 1914b), the preliminary stages of love (Freud 1915a), and the defensive regression to narcissistic identification and the splitting of the ego in depression (Freud 1917b); (b) the compulsion to repeat and the conservatism of the instincts (Freud 1920); (c) the fusion of instincts in Freud's second dual-drive model; (d) the hypothesis of desexualised libido and instinctual sublimation; (e) the generalisation of identification as a normal phenomenon – an emotional tie with the object – in *Group Psychology and the Analysis of the Ego* (1921); and (f) the consolidation of the concept of primary identification as a type of primary object-relatedness, rather than a compensation for lost objects (Freud 1923b).

The capacity of the object to 'influence' the nature of psychic structure – particularly, the structure of the ego – comes increasingly to the fore in this theoretical series, in which 'Mourning and Melancholia' plays a pivotal role. Thus, further to the main points set out in the letter to Ferenczi in February 1915, the following passage from the final version of the paper crystallises Freud's radical views on the aetiology of depression:

> An object-choice, an attachment of the libido to a particular person, had at one time existed; then, owing to a real slight or disappointment coming from the loved person, the object-relationship was shattered ... the free libido was not displaced on to another object; it was withdrawn into the ego ... it was not employed in an unspecified way, but served to establish an *identification* of the ego with the abandoned object. Thus the shadow of the object fell upon the ego, and the latter could henceforth be judged by a special agency, as though it were an object, the forsaken object.
>
> (Freud 1917b: 248–49; emphasis in the original)

In his attempts to understand the nature of melancholia, Freud credits the role of unconscious internal object-relationships in conjunction with the impact of external reality. The problem is seen first and foremost as a 'disturbance of self-regard' which distinguishes the melancholic from the bereaved. A disappointment issuing in reality (or fantasy) from the loved-object shatters the tie to the internal object. At the same time, the experience degrades or belittles the melancholic, whose sense of self-love is consequently turned into 'distressing self-denigration' through narcissistic identification with the abandoned object. This is the meaning of the depressive's self-reproaches: that the melancholic takes the experienced (or imagined) rejection from the object upon himself by means of identification; he counts himself worthless even as he believes the object perceives him to be worthless. A state of melancholy is thus brought about by 'the disappointment in other persons who served as models for the narcissistic ego and the devaluation of whom also reveals one's own worthlessness' (Falzeder, Barabant, and Giampieri-Deutsch 1996: 51).

The individual debases himself without reserve; hence a seemingly hopeless and abject state of affairs that the patient can hardly cease from putting before others. Humiliating himself in this way satisfies a need not only for self-punishment but also for revenge aimed at the abandoning cruel object. Freud treats the melancholic as a self-avenger in the guise of the self-sentenced:

> The self-tormenting in melancholia, which is without doubt enjoyable, signifies, just like the corresponding phenomenon in obsessional neurosis, a satisfaction of trends of sadism and hate which relate to an object, and which have been turned round upon the subject's own self ... In both disorders the patients usually still succeed, by a circuitous path of self-punishment, in taking revenge on the original object and in tormenting their loved one through their illness, having resorted to it in order to avoid the need to express their hostility to him openly ... The melancholic's erotic cathexis in regard to his object has thus undergone a double vicissitude: part of it has regressed to [narcissistic] identification, but the other part, under the influence of the conflict due to ambivalence, has been carried back to the stage of sadism.
>
> (Freud 1917b: 251–52)

The process of identification that Freud described in 'Mourning and Melancholia' was subsequently generalised in *Group Psychology and the Analysis of the Ego* (1921), where it is understood as a phenomenon of normal psychology. Freud accorded greater explanatory value to object-relations and primitive object-ties in these later works, the developmental implications of which were set out explicitly in *The Ego and the Id* – that is, with reference to 'a setting up of the object inside the ego' (1923b: 29). The structuration of the ego and the superego thus depends on a series of object losses; accordingly, Freud (1923b: 29) announced and inaugurated the view that 'the character of the ego is a precipitate of abandoned object-cathexes and that it contains the history of those object-choices'. Structures replete with a developmental history, understood as relics of object-relationships, are included alongside constitutionally determined drives and their transformations.

Identification

Based on the mechanism of identification, Freud's analysis of depressive illness pointed to a thoroughgoing revision of his metapsychology. This is not to say that Freud formulated a coherent theory of object-relationships; he continued to treat objects from the perspective of the drives. For Freud, the libido/aggression theory made sense of depressive problems; or, to put it the other way around, the idea of identification as a consequence of object loss is entirely consistent with classical drive theory. But 'the basic problem of the psychodynamic origins and metapsychological status of identifications' (Mitchell 1988: 48) persists with the broadening of the concept of identification in 1921. Freud himself set the change in motion. By speculating on the hostile attitude of the melancholic towards a part of his own ego in identification with the object, Freud introduced the possibility of assigning early identifications, arising in the primitive oral phase, a primary place in human development and motivation. So long as identifications proceed from object loss, that is to say, as a consequence of abandoned object-cathexes, they meet the classical criterion of instinctual vicissitudes.[19] To this extent, the motive for the formation of internalised object-relations (Kernberg 1976) – including, the mechanisms of superego formation – falls within the interpretative range of classical drive theory. The scope of meaningful action, however, turns on the further possibility that identifications are primary and irreducible, that they operate beyond drive gratification and defence, amounting to more than a compensation for lost (loved) objects.

For Mitchell (1988: 49) the possibility of primary identification presupposes 'a relational-model premise positing some sort of primary object-relatedness'. One cannot account for primary identification within the existing drive-model framework; nor did Freud resolve to do so. The problem was effectively left open for further exploration: characterised by 'a direct and immediate identification [that] takes place earlier than any object-cathexis' (Freud 1923b: 31), primary participatory belonging calls for a new conception of psychic reality. Ogden (2002) takes up the challenge of the Freudian legacy in his attempt to draw out the radical implications of Freud's analysis of melancholia, firstly, with respect to the constitution of internal objects, and secondly, in terms of the nature of narcissistic disturbances – as distinct, that is, from neurotic problems and other types of psychosis. Freud formulated a fundamental distinction between narcissistic object-relations and libidinal object-relations. The disturbance of self-love (worthlessness), which consists in the humiliated and insulted subject singing the praises of his own abjection, points to the substitution of an unconscious internal object-relationship for an external one. In this respect, Freud (1914b) set out a basic distinction between neurosis and psychosis: the substitution of internal object-relationships for real ones in the case of the transference neuroses, sets up the possibility of libidinal relations in fantasy. By contrast, the psychotic withdraws his libido from human relations without replacing the relations in fantasy, except when it comes to his attempts at self-recovery through the reinvestment of the object-world. The basic point is already set out in the letter to Ferenczi, namely, in melancholia 'the object cathexis is *removed*, the ego takes on its constellation, and the ego censorship remains intact' (Falzeder, Barabant, and Giampieri-Deutsch 1996: 48).

An important question arises on the grounds of primary object-relatedness, regarding the fate of love in depressive illness. Abraham (1911: 139) explains the reduced 'capacity for love' in manic-depressive cases and, similarly, in severe cases of obsessional neurosis – namely, 'the repression of the originally over-strong sadistic component of [the patient's] libido'. Freud (1917b: 249), in turn, described how the libido is 'withdrawn into the ego' where it serves to 'establish an identification of the ego with the abandoned object'. For Freud this entails a regression to the cannibalistic oral phase in which the ego incorporates the object into itself by 'devouring' it. Depressive patients therefore reveal some fundamental things about love. The symptomatic specificity of melancholia throws light on 'the constitution of the human ego' – precisely, insofar as it demonstrates how 'one part of the ego sets itself over against the other, judges it critically, and, as it were, takes it as its object' (1917b: 247). Consequently, by approaching the problem in terms of narcissistic regression, the underlying internal object-relations and the narcissistic use of the object are brought more clearly into view.

Ogden (2002: 771) glosses the general implications of this insight, with regards to internal structuration and the constitution of the ego. The salient points in Freud's thesis are identified as follows: (a) the spitting of the ego; (b) the capacity of the split-off part of the ego to exercise independent thoughts, feelings and perceptions; (c) the prevalence of internal unconscious relationships between a split-off part of the ego and another part of the ego; and (d) the normal and pathological nature of these internal splits, identifications, and relations. The clinical nature of Freud's approach is clear. What is the meaning of the self-accusations of the psychotically depressed patient? Why consent willingly, if not eagerly, to one's own suffering? Why would anyone attempt to organise a life around self-criticism? These questions go to the heart of the depressive illness. For Freud, melancholia and mourning alike are characterised by depressive moods, loss of the capacity to love, withdrawal of interest in the outside world, and a general sense of lethargy and inaction. It is the further disturbance of self-love that differentiates the melancholic from the bereaved. Here, as elsewhere, the somatic origin of the drives and their vicissitudes is the main part of Freud's interpretation; melancholia instantiates repetitive enactments of conflicted desires. But it is what Freud (1917b: 244) makes of self-abnegation that proves decisive – including his analysis of states of self-revilement and abuse that culminate in 'a delusional expectation of punishment'.

The 'unconscious sense of guilt' turns out to be no less multi-layered than any other psychic phenomenon. In this respect, Freud's interpretation gives due credit to the semantic as well as the energic determinants; the interpretation covers not only the function of endogenous forces (the drivers of meaning) but also the lived experience of motivational states (conscious and unconscious meanings). A distinction between 'ego-libido' and 'object-libido', which was set out for the first time in the paper on narcissism, allowed Freud to account for the defensive regression to narcissistic identification in melancholia. At the same time, it furnished object-relations theory with the possibility of a more far-reaching theory of primary participatory belonging based on 'cases of simultaneous object-cathexis and identification' (Freud 1923b: 29). As Ogden (2002: 775) notes: 'The world of unconscious internal object relations is being viewed by Freud as a defensive regression to very early forms of object relatedness in response to psychological pain'. It is not only an identification with the hated part of an ambivalently loved lost object, but also a defence against catastrophic disillusionment, that casts the melancholic between grievance and affliction. This is essentially what differentiates the melancholic from the bereaved.

The ambivalence of love and hate, the coexistence of contradictory feelings in the relationship to the lost (loved) object (including, the hatred of the abandoning cruel object), reflects an ambivalent conflict that applies to the sense of living itself. Thus 'countless separate struggles are carried on over the object, in which hate and love contend with each other; the one seeks to detach the libido from the object, the other to maintain this position of the libido against the assault' (Freud 1917b: 256). Ogden (2002: 779) identifies a line of argument, here, that anticipates object-relations theory at it most profound, where 'unconscious internal object relations may have either a living and enlivening quality or a dead and deadening quality'. The concept of ambivalence and its qualitative reach adds to the richness and complexity of Freud's interpretative system. That 'life itself' may be the object of ambivalent states of mind is surely one of the most radical lines of thought opened up by Freud's theory of depression. The theory is not dependent on the hypothesis of the death drive, but rather, is indicative of the disruptive nature of life.

Notes

1 See Greenberg and Mitchell (1983) and Aron (1996) for authoritative accounts of the postwar shift from Freudian structural theory and ego-psychology to relational psychoanalysis; for a landmark collection of papers see Mitchell and Aron (1999); and see Pine (1990) for a more broadly conceived 'synthesis' in contemporary clinical thinking, although the emphasis here is on the use of 'multiple perspectives' in clinical practice, rather than the theories as such.

2 Ayer (1936) represents the alternative view in which values (a) have no real existence or (b) are not the object of cognition.

3 I discuss the notion of 'conviction' below in my analysis of psychoanalysis and memory.

4 See Rapaport's (1960: 865) theory of motives as 'appetitive internal forces', a theory that is fully consistent with the drive/structure model.

5 Translated as *The Acting Person*, the Polish title *Osoba i Czyn* means literally *Person and Act*. In an attempt to analyse 'the experience of the dynamic reality of the acting person' (1979: 196) as properly personal, Wojtyła elaborates a 'dynamic' perspective based on Aristotelian and Thomistic principles; see Schmitz (1994) for a discussion of Wojtyła's philosophy of the total experience of the human being in the frame of traditional philosophy, particularly in the broad tradition of Christian personalism. Wojtyła (2013: 25) formulated the basic principle of Christian personalism in *Love and Responsibility*, first published in 1960, what he termed 'the personalistic norm': 'As a principle formulated negatively, this norm states that the person is a kind of good that is incompatible with using, which may not be treated as an object of use and, in this sense, as a means to an end. Hand in hand with this goes the positive formulation of the personalistic norm: the person is a kind of good to which only love constitutes the proper and fully-mature [*pełnowartościowy*] relation ... this positive content of the personalistic norm is precisely what the commandment to love brings out'.

6 Hanley (1994) points out that the classical model already allows for the phenomena addressed by Pine's 'four psychologies, a view that seems to come as no surprise to Pine (1988: 574): 'I do not mean to suggest that psychoanalysis has heretofore ignored any of these several points of view'.

7 See Loewald (1973: 79) for the innovative nature of the life drive, as distinct from the recapitulation of the principle of discharge under the heading of the death drive: 'the death instinct is nothing new, but merely a new conceptualisation of the constancy principle. What is new in Freud's last instinct theory is the life instinct as a force or tendency *sui generis*, not reducible to the old pleasure-unpleasure principle ... The pleasure principle is newly defined as owing its reign to the power of Eros'.

8 See Greenberg (1991) and Mitchell (1988: 52): 'Much of the complex and multifaced history of psychoanalytic ideas can be understood as a series of alternative strategies for dealing with the central conceptual dilemma with which Freud was grappling in 1923 – the clash between clinical data saturated with relations with others and a conceptual framework which relegates personal relations to a mediating, secondary role'. I take up the problem of the object and its origins in post-Freudian thought in the following chapter.

9 For Freud's initial formulation of a structural model along mechanistic lines, see Amacher (1965), Pribram (1969), Pribram and Gill (1976), and Solms and Saling (1987).

10 This passage was subsequently excised following the revisions set out in 'Instincts and their Vicissitudes' (1915a).

11 I intend to underline the problematic of purposive action in the Freudian interpretation. However, despite the wish to promote the use of the term 'purpose' in the context of drive activity, the Standard Edition is nonetheless apt to confuse matters in those passages where Freud's *Tendenz* is rendered as 'purpose' rather than 'tendency'.

12 For the connection between *bios* and *praxis*, the idea that 'life *is* action', see Aristotle, *Politica*, Book I, chapter 2, 1254a7.

13 Loewald (1969: 324) credits the active nature of psychic 'disorganisation' in his revised theory of the negative therapeutic reaction, where he argues that severe cases of the latter are 'rooted in extreme pre-oedipal disturbances of primitive object-ties'.

14 Ogden (2002) demonstrates the Freudian origins of object-relations theory by tracing the theory of unconscious internal object-relations back to Freud.

15 See Paris (2000), Haynal and Falzeder (2002), and May (2019) for the background to 'Mourning and Melancholia'. I focus specifically on the correspondence between Freud and Abraham, although I should point out that the draft under discussion was discovered by Ernest Falzeder in the Freud Archives in 1991 and first published, in 1996, in *The Correspondence of Sigmund Freud and Sándor Ferenczi, Vol. 2, 1914–1919*.

16 See also the case history of the Wolf Man (1918), written in 1914, and 'Instincts and their Vicissitudes' (1915a) for further elaboration of the oral or cannibalistic phase of libidinal development. The ego's wish to 'devour' or 'incorporate' the object into itself is seen as part of the 'preliminary stages of love' – 'a type of love which is consistent with abolishing the object's separate existence and which may therefore be described as ambivalent' (1915a: 138).

17 Abraham (1924) consolidated his contribution to the theory of depression by postulating an oral-sadistic stage, as distinct from Freud's oral-cannibalistic stage; the oral-sadistic phase, as well as the early anal phase, are seen as fixation points of depression.

18 See for example Freud (1909a: 108; 1925c: 237–38).

19 Fenichel (1926: 97–101) summarises the classical drive model of identification: 'The motive force of identifications is always supplied by *drives* (or instincts). These, originating in somatic sources and imposing demands upon the ego, which controls motility, strive for *gratification*, that is, for an adequate alteration of the external world by means of which the tension at the source of the drive can finally be eliminated. This takes place through actions, which amount to a realization of an instinctual *aim* in regard to an instinctual *object* … It is thus plausible to describe identification too as an instinctual vicissitude. A change is made both in the object and the aim of the original objectual instinct which leads to the identificatory process … in the final analysis every identification is motivated by an economic factor, namely, the striving to find a substitute for lost gratification'.

Chapter 2

Dependence

Let me begin with a basic definition of the dependence relationship: human life becomes living, with the ongoing possibility of more life, only on condition of a loved and well cared for person. That it is he or she who is loved does not entail the infant being for the mother everything that *she* wants, or being what he or she is for the mother's love. Life becomes worth living only so long as the child is loved for what he or she is; at the same time, the child is capable of an act love, an act that predates the stage of concern (Winnicott 1954–55; 1963a). The need to be loved is inextricably linked with the need to love from the very beginning of life; whereas the capacity for concern applies at the level of relative dependence. In meeting the infant's needs the mother, amongst other things, meets the infant's need to love. Thus, living-*there* becomes living-*with* through primal acts of love in which mother and infant propose themselves in their whole being. It is the act of love that is constitutive. This is my understanding of primary love in the earliest relationship (Balint 1939): namely, acts of love are mediated by a gift-object comprising maternal preoccupation and the infant's spontaneous gesture as an expression of the 'creative centre' of his 'individual person' (Symington 1987: 61).

Broadly speaking, the condition of living and living-well, the condition of human flourishing (*eudaemonia* in Aristotelian ethics), is the topic of this chapter. Life itself lies at the origin of human beings. But it is only where needs are met, where the child is the focus of his or her parents' affection, that life comes into the full vigour of vital existence, the existence of living beings. The vital function thus precedes the virile function characteristic of the oedipal situation. The fact of birth announces its own possibility. But what is born (*natus*) has also yet to be born (*nascor*), or fully realised. Potentiality denotes something that already *is* but also *is not yet*. In the human situation, psychological birth calls for care and contact on the one hand and, on the other, accounts for the fact that the dynamic readiness of the new-born (the readiness to act or 'strive toward ...') exerts an absolute, ruthless claim on maternity. Taking care of the infant's tending-toward-living, his vital tendency and personal outgoing, defines the mother-infant

DOI: 10.4324/9781315280899-3

relationship at is most fundamental, which, in turn, defines being *qua* being. The psychoanalytical theory of dependence, in sum, comprises (a) a phenomenology of care, (b) an ethics of living, and (c) a theory of being. I present this theoretic manifold as a framework for the analysis of the inner structure of the life processes in the earliest relationship.

The mother-child relationship

I discuss Fairbairn and Winnicott in more detail below, but I shall begin with some introductory remarks on their respective contributions. Winnicott's notion of the psyche-soma continuity of being is a good place to start. Despite the fact that body needs and their being met (or not) precede the considerations of the object-world and object-relations proper, the provision for living-well goes beyond the physical sustenance a child needs to stay alive. By going 'beyond' I mean that flesh or the skin-ego accounts neither for the whole of the unintegrated manifold pertaining to dependence nor for the relatively independent aspects of the psyche-soma. The body has its own particular inwardness from the beginning.[1] In fact, the dependence relationship itself demonstrates that the life of a concrete person is not merely or essentially biological, even when it concerns the loving care of the infant's body. The reach for the inner needed 'object' is a proto-psychic event, rather than an instinct in the classical Freudian sense. Can we speak here of a *spiritual* ego? Do we require a metaphysical analysis to adequately address the meaning of the feeling intellect? No doubt, '[a] baby can be *fed* without love, but loveless or impersonal *management* cannot succeed in producing a new autonomous human child. Here where there is trust and reliability is a potential space, one that can become an infinite area of separation' (Winnicott 1971e: 108; emphasis in the original). The being of the person, the ontology of the personal ego, depends on this very 'infinity' inscribed within the concrete provision of maternal love and care.

Unless the mother 'can identify very closely with her infant at the beginning, she cannot "have a good breast", because just having the thing means nothing whatsoever to the infant' (Winnicott 1987: 96). The infant who thrives reaches for a mother who *is there*. Consequently, the care that animates the-want-to-be at the beginning, 'the actual dependability [of the mother] at the beginning' (Winnicott 1987: 159), enables the infant's innate potential. Indeed, for Winnicott (1960b: 54; emphasis in the original) the provision for living covers almost exactly the infant's dependency needs, a situation that he described as '*a live adaptation to the infant's needs*': with 'the care that it receives from its mother' each infant, therefore, is 'able to have a personal existence, and so begins to build up what might be called *a continuity of being*'. Based on the provision of an 'average expectable' environment the 'inherited potential' itself becomes 'a continuity of being' (1960b: 47). The mother's preoccupation with an infant who is prey to a need describes the horizon of intersubjectivity. The environmental mother thus facilitates the infant's natural love of life, animates the possibility of living well, and instigates the maturational processes even as she protects life itself.

The mother who provides for her infant is not seen as a 'perfect' mother, nor does her 'adaptation-to-need' denote a fully completed action. Winnicott (1987: 38) was nonetheless clear that the 'good enough' mother was an integral part of the human infant's situation; indeed, 'the word "enough" gradually (in favourable circumstances) widens in scope according to the infant's growing ability to deal with failure'. The theory of illusion-disillusionment (Winnicott 1971a: 13–14) is based on the idea that re-cognition of the mother's failure to adapt to the infant's needs is integral to the process of maturation; the mother who gradually fails her infant, the fallible mother, *is* the 'good enough' mother. Once again, in favourable circumstances, failure indicates neither a lack nor an environmental defi-ciency, but rather, a precondition of the infant's sense of being really and truly alive.

However, where there exists 'inadequate adaptation-to-need' (Winnicott 1954a: 261) in the first place; where the infant, in a state of absolute de-pendence or 'immature being', is forced to 'react' to an unreliable en-vironment (a mother who is not reliably present at the beginning); where '[m]aternal failures produce phases of reaction to impingement' (Winnicott 1956a: 303) – where this is the case, Winnicott (1960b: 47) noted that the reaction interrupts and annihilates 'personal being'. The continuity of the being of the person is broken, which may result clinically in more severe forms of psychopathology than psychoneurotic conflict.

An excess of reaction to the interruption of being, according to Winnicott (1956a: 303; emphasis in the original), 'produces not frustration but *a threat of annihilation*'. The latter is a type of primitive anxiety that is not felt as a maternal failure but, rather, acts as a threat to 'personal self-existence' – 'the feeling of real is absent and if there is not too much chaos the ultimate feeling is of futility. The inherent difficulties of life cannot be reached, let alone the satisfactions'; nor can the person eventually 'afford to sacrifice spontaneity, even to die' (1956a: 304–305). It is the world of the person that is at risk here. Thus, the breakdown in the mother-infant tie is not accounted for by the existence of an unsatisfying object, let alone a bad object; nor yet by the feeling of frustration in relation to the breast *qua* real object. Rather, the infant's sense of 'going on being' is threatened where, at the very be-ginning of life, mothers are unable 'to become preoccupied with their own infant to the exclusion of other interests, in a way that is normal and tem-porary' (1956a: 302). The happiness that accompanies the fulfilment of one's potential is replaced under adverse environmental conditions by despair or yet more persecutory states of mind.

Freud (1911b: 220 n 4) admitted the vital condition of infant care, allowing that the infant survives on account of 'the care it receives from its mother'. In the first dual-drive theory, the object of the ego instincts is the actual mother; it is the presence of the maternal object that cathects need. Moreover, Freud (1940a: 201) noted in a final assessment that 'we have repeatedly had to insist on the fact that the ego owes its origin as well as the most important of its acquired characteristics to its relation to the real external world. We are thus prepared to assume that the ego's pathological states, in which it most approximates once again to the id, are founded on a cessation or slackening of that relation to the external world'. Yet Freud continued to view the object essentially as a vehicle for the instinct's libidinal or aggressive aims, which trigger the acting person endogenously. By contrast, in the Winnicottian tradition human coexistence is conceived, explicitly, in terms of the early sensual interactions between the infant and the mother.

Winnicott (1952: 99) tried to come up with a more vital understanding than hitherto of what precedes the first object-relationship: 'I have had a long struggle with this problem. It started when I found myself saying in [a Scientific Meeting of the British Psycho-Analytical Society] ... and I said it rather excitedly and with heat: "*There is no such thing as a baby*" ... if you show me a baby you certainly show me also someone caring for the baby, or at least a pram with someone's eyes and ears glued to it'. The mother thus meets the infant's anticipation of meeting, the infant's innate expectation of 'live company' (Alvarez 1992), which enables the mother and the infant to go on and 'live an experience together' (Winnicott 1945: 152). Experience is an achievement that pertains to increasingly independent ego energies. Initially, however, living-there depends on a more primitive vital arrangement: 'the good-enough mother is able to meet the needs of her infant at the beginning, and to meet these needs so well that the infant, as emergence from the matrix of the infant-mother relationship takes places, is able to have a brief *experience of omnipotence*' (Winnicott 1962: 57; emphasis in the original).

The existential groundwork of human experience is simultaneously receptive and appropriative. As I mean to demonstrate in this chapter, in the Independent tradition the fundamental human situation is conceived along these two axes: (a) as a primordial feeling of *living-there* (the rhythm of safety); and (b) as a spontaneously arising movement on the infant's part towards *more life* (the reach for life).[2] The fundamental experience of the human infant is one of helplessness. Feeling safe and properly cared for are, therefore, basic needs; they provide the requisite experiential expressions of gratifying dependence. In favourable circumstances, primary distress is tempered by the facilitation of primary creativity. As such, the reach for life is expressed as omnipotence without compulsive pressure. In marked contrast to the repetitive patterns of neurotic misery that Freud associated with the intractability of the sexual impulse, the reach for life involves a primitive, spontaneous gesture that not only grasps what is within reach but also augments available reality in the very act of grasping or appropriating. The potential activity of this situated 'reach for ...' casts the 'pertinacity of early impressions' (Freud 1905: 242) – our attachments to primary objects and their long-lasting reach – in an entirely different light, that is to say, quite apart from the aetiology of the psychoneuroses.

Some of the more influential and far-reaching post-Freudian theories of the acting person have emerged as an attempt to reconfigure the 'driven' quality of infantile experience (conceived by Freud as the desire for plea-sure), explicitly, in terms of relational patterns and their vicissitudes. The critical revisions are aimed at the idea that libido and primary processes are regulated by the pleasure-unpleasure principle. The positive claim is that libido is object-seeking. Mitchell (2000: 105–106; emphasis in the original) illustrates the basic argument by comparing Freud and Fairbairn: 'For Freud, objects are sought for sexual and aggressive discharge'; whereas for Fairbairn 'objects are sought for the gratification of oral dependency ... Fairbairn was suggesting that object-seeking, in its most radical form, is not the vehicle for the satisfaction of a specific need, but is the expression of our very nature, the form through which we become specifically *human* beings'. The point is that we are not 'drawn into interaction' but 'embedded in an interactive matrix' or relational field from the beginning.

In a systematic break with classical drive theory, Fairbairn decoupled object-seeking from a discretely experienced need. Despite a commitment to certain basic Freudian hypotheses, Winnicott in turn augmented and re-worked the theory of dependence formulated by Fairbairn.[3] In particular, he (1939: 88) identified an urgent striving on the infant's part as a type of in-herent 'primary aggression', and proposed the terms 'greed' or 'mouth-love' to describe 'the original fusion of love and aggression' that is manifest at the beginning of life. On the further point of maternal deficiency, Winnicott was unequivocal: the mother who fails to convey the sense that she loves her infant as a person is the mother who fails to meet her infant's own needs. Winnicott's account thus came close to Fairbairn's (1944: 109) views on the mother of the schizoid type, with regards to the link between deprivation and aggression: 'whilst I regard aggression as a primary dynamic factor in that it does not appear capable of being resolved into libido ... at the same time I regard it as ultimately subordinate to libido ... I do not consider that the infant directs aggression spontaneously towards his libidinal object in the absence of some kind of frustration'. Aggression is not seen as a primary motivational factor; in fact, we can discern a similar developmental sequence in Winnicott and Fairbairn: libidinal frustration, experienced in affective terms as emotional rejection, or a sense of lack of love, and ag-gression towards the libidinal object, as a result of which the mother be-comes an ambivalent object. Winnicott thus followed Fairbairn's inaugural efforts to establish a deficit model in psychoanalysis. This has since become a hallmark of post-Freud thought, but Fairbairn was the first to introduce the deficit model.[4]

In a further elaboration that is evident throughout his work, Winnicott (1945: 154) postulated a 'primitive ruthlessness' where the mother satisfies the infant's needs by tolerating his 'ruthless *relation*' towards her.[5] The idea of primitive ruthlessness anticipates Winnicott's later theory of object-use, which further underlines and broadens the meaning of early interpersonal relations and emotional object ties. As such, the following statement crystallises an object-relations approach to the stage of absolute dependence: 'At first the infant (from our point of view) is ruthless; there is no concern yet as to results of instinctual love. This love is originally a form of impulse, gesture, contact, relationship, and it affords the infant the satisfaction of self-expression and release from instinct tension; more, it places the object outside the self' (1954–55: 265).

Fairbairn, on the other hand, formulated a comparable developmental sequence but without any reference whatsoever to the drive/structure model and the hypothesis of 'instinct tension'. The focus is solely on the maturation of different modes of relations with others, whereby 'infantile dependence' upon the object is gradually replaced by 'mature dependence' upon the object: 'This process of development is characterized (a) by the gradual abandonment of an original object-relationship based on primary identification [the infant's experience of merger with its mother], and (b) by gradual adoption of an object-relationship based upon differentiation of the object' (Fairbairn 1941: 34). The developmental trajectory is articulated by the transformations in *identification*: the more mature a dependent relationship is, the less it is characterised by primary identification. Libido theory is effectively subsumed by an object-relations model on the grounds that 'an original oral, sucking, incorporating and predominately "taking" [libidinal] aim comes to be replaced by a mature, non-incorporating and predominantly "giving" aim compatible with [but not reducible to] developed genital sexuality' (Fairbairn 1941: 35).

The Kleinian development

Accounting for the clinical significance of object-relations, according to Greenberg and Mitchell (1983: 4), 'has been the central conceptual problem within the history of psychoanalytic ideas. Every major psychoanalytic author has had to address himself to this issue, and his manner of resolving it determines the basic approach and sets the foundation for subsequent theorizing'. The problem of the object assumes increasing importance in psychoanalysis from the 1940s onwards, with a widespread shift from the drive/structure model to an object-relations model. In a thoroughgoing critical reconstruction of this momentous shift in Freudian thought, Greenberg and

Mitchell (1983: 4) identify two contrasting accounts of object-relations: 'one preserving the original drive model and the other replacing it with a fundamentally different model'. Clearly, the primary participatory belonging that characterises our living-there is variously conceived in post-Freudian psychoanalysis, although the common endeavour is evident in the following statements concerning the earliest relationship: (a) a state of 'infantile dependence' (corresponding to Abraham's earlier and later 'oral phases'), characterized by 'an absolute degree of identification and absence of differentiation' (Fairbairn 1941: 47); (b) an irreducible 'environment-individual set-up' (Winnicott 1952: 99); and (c) a type of 'primordial density' or 'unitary whole that differentiates into distinct parts' (Loewald 1949: 11). Variations on the basic model privilege maternity, the breast *qua* real object, as the basis of the 'primal psychical situation' (*psychische Ursituation*).

Fairbairn noted that initially, the person's object constitutes not only his world but also himself; it is not that the breast is felt to be mine but, rather, that there is no difference between myself and the breast. The stage of infantile dependence is thus characterised by the confluence of emotional identification and oral incorporation. The original arrangement presupposes a reach for life that Fairbairn (1941: 48) described in terms of 'the fundamental equivalence for the infant of being held in his mother's arms and incorporating the contents of her breast'. This account is in marked contrast (as we shall see in our more detailed discussion of Fairbairn in the next section) to the Kleinian view of a primitive relationship dominated by innate hostility towards the object. For Klein (1946: 4) Fairbairn failed to give due weight to the role of 'early anxiety and conflict'. To be clear, the oral instinctual impulses are conceived by Fairbairn in such a way that differentiated and purposive destruction plays no part at the beginning of life. Abolishing the object's separate existence is not seen as the motive of primary identification and incorporation; although it is considered integral to primitive object-ties, oral incorporation is not reduced to a state of angry possessiveness, or an oral-sadistic wish on the part of the ego to cannibalistically devour the object.

Following Fairbairn, Winnicott (1952: 99) went on to formulate the basic proposition of primary participatory belonging in relation to the real object: 'The capacity for a one-body relationship *follows* that of a two-body relationship, through the introjection of the object ... the unit is not the individual, the unit is an environment-individual set-up. The centre of gravity of the being does not start off in the individual. It is in the total set-up'. The original situation of absolute dependence constitutes the main frame of reference in Independent object-relations theory (Keene 2012: 8). Conceived as 'equivalent to oral dependence' (Fairbairn 1941: 47), the primitive object-tie emerged as a shared example in postwar British psychoanalysis. Klein laid the foundations for the basic model of object-relations. Taken together, her major papers 'A Contribution to the Psychogenesis of Manic-Depressive

States' (1935), 'Mourning and Its Relation to Manic-Depressive States' (1940), and 'Notes on Some Schizoid Mechanisms' (1946) established a new direction in psychoanalytic thought. The originality of Klein's contribution is evident in her principal claim that mental activities are directed upon objects from the beginning of life. It was possible from this starting point to elaborate on the intentionality of the acting person – 'the intentional action of human beings' (Symington 2002: 70) – as the central concern of psychoanalysis.

Klein revised the notion of psychic reality by reconceptualising the drives as purposive phenomena; she retained the classical notion of drives as the major motivation of human life but accorded them a larger degree of intentionality. Fairbairn took the 'directedness' of object-relationships to its logical conclusion and dispensed with the drive/structure model altogether. Klein pursued an alternative solution based on a rearticulation of drives and fantasy, in which the energetic referents of the Freudian interpretation, that is, not only libidinal desires but also destructive impulses and anxieties, were conceived from the point of view of unconscious fantasy. The latter became *the* mark of the mental in the Kleinian group. Susan Isaacs (1943: 276–77), in her contribution to the 'controversies', clarified Klein's emphasis on ideational content: 'unconscious phantasies are the primary content of all mental processes ... Phantasy is the mental corollary, the psychic representative of instinct. And there is no impulse, no instinctual urge, which is not experienced as (unconscious) phantasy'. Again, Klein and Fairbairn are evidently at variance in their respective views about the nature of fantasy: for Klein unconscious phantasy is a primary component of the drives and, as such, is seen as constitutive of psychic reality; whereas Fairbairn treated fantasy as substitutive, rather than primary.

The emphasis on the drives as purposive phenomena, the directedness of the infant's feelings of gratification towards the 'good' object and of persecution towards the 'bad' object, amounted to a far-reaching revision of the Freudian interpretation. The classical view posited energy detached from ego; whereas Klein (1935: 262) underlined the benign and evil *intent* of unconscious internal objects: 'The development of the infant is governed by the mechanisms of introjection and projection. From the beginning the ego introjects objects "good" and "bad", for both of which the mother's breast is the prototype ... it is because the baby projects its own aggression on to these objects that it feels them to be "bad" and not only in that they frustrate its desires'. Unlike Freud, Klein (1952a: 49) posited the existence of object-relations from the beginning of life: 'My use of the term "object-relations" is based on my contention that the infant has from the beginning of post-natal life a relation to the mother (although focusing primarily on her breast) which is imbued with the fundamental elements of an object-relation'. The latter was not seen simply, or primarily, as a relation to an external object:

[T]he processes of introjection and projection from the beginning of life lead to the institution inside ourselves of loved and hated objects, who are felt to be 'good' and 'bad', and who are interrelated with each other and with the self: that is to say, they constitute an inner world ... the phenomenon which was recognised by Freud, broadly speaking, as the voices and the influence of the actual parents established in the ego is, according to my findings, a complex object-world, which is felt by the individual, in deep layers of the unconscious, to be concretely inside himself, and for which I and some of my colleagues therefore use the term 'internalized objects' and an 'inner world'.

(Klein 1940: 362)

Klein's concept of internalised object fantasies provided the point of departure for British object-relations theory. The influence proved most significant in the case of Fairbairn's thoroughgoing revision of the Freudian interpretation, although, as we shall see, Klein and Fairbairn held diametrically opposed views about the origin of the internal object world. Nevertheless, the Freudian notion of internal objects (the theory of the superego) was substantially modified by the Kleinian interpretation; the structural properties of Freud's superego were accorded less importance than the 'inner world' of 'internalised objects'. Furthermore, the general shift of emphasis from structural entities to object-relations was combined with an amplification of psychic *content*, most notably, the violent fantasies that Klein identified with the earliest stages of development. Klein introduced an entirely new clinical domain, a new formation of clinical 'facts', comprising the child's fantasy of objects inside its own body as well as inside its mother's body.

In a radical reworking of the 'primal scene' (*Urszenen*), which Freud (1918 [1914]) himself treated under the heading of 'primal phantasies' (*Urphantasien*), Klein linked the oral-sadistic phase of development to the child's fantasies of its mother's body. For Klein (1930: 219) early oedipal conflict was ushered in by the anxiety-situations, and concomitant modes of defence, associated with the desire to devour the mother's breast: 'At the period of which I am speaking, the subject's dominant aim is to possess himself of the contents of the mother's body and destroy her by means of every weapon which sadism can command ... My whole argument depends on the fact that the Oedipus conflict begins at a period when sadism predominates'. The child's sadistic attacks, according to Klein (1930: 219), are focused on the mother's body, but they are aimed at both mother and father: 'The child expects to find within the mother (a) the father's penis, (b) excrement, and (c) children, and these things it equates with edible substances. According to the child's earliest phantasies (or "sexual theories") of parental coitus, the father's penis (or his whole body) becomes incorporated in the mother during the act. Thus, the child's sadistic attacks have for their object father and mother, who are in phantasy bitten, torn, cut or stamped to bits'. The anxiety that Klein (1930: 219) argues arises on account of these attacks 'becomes internalized in consequence of the oral-sadistic introjection of the objects and is thus already directed towards the early superego'.

The clinical scene was now set for a comprehensive interpretation of the inner world and its formation, together with the vicissitudes of internalised object-relations, anxieties, and the ego's earliest modes of defence. Klein depicted an all-encompassing internal world of nutritious and excremental encounters, out-and-out sadistic attacks (and the fear of retaliation), and the drive for reparation, in which urethral and anal sadism is coupled with oral and muscular sadism: 'In phantasy the excreta are transformed into dangerous weapons: wetting is regarded as cutting, stabbing, burning, drowning, while the faecal mass is equated with weapons and missiles. At a later stage of the phase which I have described, these violent modes of attack give place to hidden assaults by the most refined methods which sadism can devise, and the excreta are equated with poisonous substances' (1930: 219–20).

Despite the remarkable originality of her contributions, Klein's allegiance to classical drive theory continued in fundamental ways to guide her phenomenology of the inner world. Klein left intact some of the more basic premises of Freudian metapsychology. Unconscious internal objects were seen as an integral part of the primordial structure of human existence, which, for Klein, operate as such in conjunction with endogenous motivational forces. The idea that object-relations exist from birth onwards did not necessarily prove contentious in the wider context of post-Freudian thought. The major point of disagreement concerned Klein's emphasis on the child's innate aggression, understood as a projection arising from the death instinct. For Klein psychopathology is rooted in the drives, particularly the death drive, rather than maternal deprivation, environmental deficiency, or the disruptions in early relations; when considering the formation of specifically 'bad' objects, Klein invariably emphasised the extent to which the objects derived from the child's instinctual impulses. The implication is that drives generate their own objects. Klein (1946: 4) herself clarified the basic disagreement in her paper 'Notes on Some Schizoid Mechanisms', where she points out that Fairbairn not only rejected Freud's concept of 'primary instincts' but also underestimated 'the role which aggression and hatred play from the beginning of life ... he does not give enough weight to the importance of early anxiety and conflict and their dynamic effects on development'.

Klein's (1946: 3) account of 'schizoid mechanisms' appeared after Fairbairn's postulation of the 'schizoid position' and, indeed, she was keen to acknowledge her agreement with aspects of his formulation, particularly the idea that the schizoid position 'forms part of normal development and is the basis for adult schizoid and schizophrenic illness'. She also endorsed Fairbairn's view that 'the group of schizoid disorders' is far more extensive than had hitherto been acknowledged. Fairbairn, however, went further than Klein in positing the 'schizoid position' as the basis of an alternative structural model of purposive action, a theory of dynamic structure aimed at the interactive nature of psychic reality. Klein drew the line when it came to the revised theory of mental structure and instincts: 'Fairbairn's approach was largely from the angle of ego-development in relation to objects, while mine was predominantly from the angle of anxieties and their vicissitudes' (1946: 3).

Consequently, we can trace two contrasting lines of development within the British school of object-relations back to the founding figures of Klein and Fairbairn. The same holds for Klein as for Freud: oedipal relations and the genital phase, although situated at an earlier date in Klein's account, were nonetheless determined by sexual and aggressive instinctual impulses. Thus, in a deliberately circumscribed revision of metapsychology, the theory of internal objects was presented as a drive theory: 'good' and 'bad' objects were attributed with instinctually derived motives towards the subject. Undoubtedly, Klein's theory of internalised object-relations set the basic terms of reference for the British school of object-relations theory. However, in the event, the restrictions placed on relational psychoanalysis by the Kleinian development proved untenable for Independent-minded analysts. Mitchell and Black (2016: 113–14) note that the 'major figures in [the] middle group, W. R. D. Fairbairn, D. W. Winnicott, Michael Balint, John Bowlby, and Harry Guntrip, all built on Klein's vision of an infant wired for human interaction. Yet they also broke with Klein's premise of constitutional aggression deriving from the death instinct, promoting instead an infant wired for harmonious interaction and nontraumatic development but thwarted by inadequate parenting'. It will be helpful before discussing Fairbairn and Winnicott as the major architects of Independent object-relations theory, to consider Lacan's influential critique of these developments.

Lacan and the object-relation

Due in large part to Lacan's swingeing critique, including, a trenchant criticism of Fairbairn, the influence of object-relations theory in France was not immediately apparent or appreciated. Lacan's (1978: 248) sardonic dismissal of the attempts to 're-centre analysis on the object and on object-relations' adversely affected the reception not only of Fairbairn's work (Vermorel 2005) but also of object-relations theory in general. These criticisms warrant closer attention.

The criticism was aimed at the theoretical and clinical implications of Fairbairn's (1944) endopsychic schema. Theoretically, Lacan was intent on showing that Fairbairn's recourse to the Kleinian concept 'internal object' introduces a profound confusion between the real, the imaginary, and the symbolic. For Lacan (1978: 250) Fairbairn's notion of the object is predicated on a 'straightforward confusion' of these basic terms. He (1978: 253) rejected not only what he saw as the 'objectification' of the object but also 'the position chosen to objectify it, namely the [pre-oedipal] beginning of the subject's life'. Lacan's objection applies to object-relations theory *per se*. Fairbairn (1954: 28), however, explicitly reframed the concept of oedipal conflict in terms of object-relationships: 'whereas Freud's description of the psyche ... was framed in terms of the Oedipus conflict, my own concept of the basic endopsychic situation is framed in terms of the original relationship of the child to his mother and the ambivalence which develops out of it'. For Fairbairn, the oedipal situation does not depend on a castration complex, but rather, on a 'more basic situation' consisting of the actual mother's tendency to 'excite' or 'reject' the child.

The confusion of 'the imaginary value of the mother' and 'the value of her real character' was, according to Lacan (1978: 257), coupled with a failure to recognise that 'the symbolic relation is constituted as early as possible', that 'the imaginary experience is inscribed in the register of the symbolic' from the beginning of psychic life through the triad mother-child-phallus. Essentially, the imaginary relationship between the ego and the object, as Lacan construed it, 'misrecognises' the relationship of speech (the signifier and the signified) between the subject and *de l'Autre* (the capitalised Other). The criticism of Fairbairn, therefore, was levelled at the theory of primitive structuration, the structuration of the object by (imaginary) relations, and the idea that everything leads back to the mother, to the original frustration of the maternal object. Lacan (1978: 253) paraphrases Fairbairn's description of the difficulties that arise due to a breakdown of the natural inclination ('primitive harmony') between subject and object. I shall come back to Fairbairn's account of infantile frustration due to the want of a satisfying object. Suffice it to note here that Lacan singles out for critical comment the dilemma of an integral ego ('central ego') with an object that does not 'live up to expectations'.

The critique is based on certain assumptions. Firstly, the child's dependency ('the first wail and its cessation') – indeed, 'everything that happens in the order of the object relation' – is already operative in the symbolic order; it is already symbolised in terms of the threefold schema of mother, child, and phallus. Secondly, far from an encounter with obstacles in the early environment, or any kind of 'lived experience' for that matter, it is the infant's own 'sexual researches' which initially set things askew – that is, in terms of the ineradicable disjuncture between what the infant is looking for and what he finds. Lacan's views on these points are fundamentally at odds with contemporary developments, although he (1978: 253) admits that 'any valid notion of the *ego* must in effect put it into correlation with the objects'. Leaving aside the theoretical problems with the notion of 'correlation', the critical point concerns the object-relations model of internalisation. The critique has direct clinical implications. For Lacan the oversimplification ('objectification') of the process of internalisation in object-relations theory is played out, most importantly, in the analytic situation. The critique of the endopsychic schema thus extends to Lacan's (1978: 254) theorisation of analytic practice in the symbolic register: 'any theorisation of analysis organised around the object relation amounts in the end to advocating the recomposition of the subject's imaginary world according to the norm of the analyst's ego. The original introjection of the rejecting object, which has poisoned the exciting function of the said object, is corrected by the introjection of a correct ego, that of the analyst'.

Viewed by Lacan as a misguided conception of analytic experience, the idea of the *analyst as model* is conceived in wholly positive terms by Fairbairn, precisely as a relational phenomenon. Reflecting on the main factors involved in 'psychoanalytical cure', Fairbairn (1958a: 83) concludes that 'the really decisive factor is the relationship of the patient to the analyst ... it is upon this relationship that the other factors [insight, recollection and reconstruction of infantile memories, catharsis, and so on] depend not only for their effectiveness, but for their very existence'. Moreover, Fairbairn maintained that the 'personal relationship' pertaining between the patient and the analyst encompasses 'the relationship involved in the transference' but is not confined to the latter. Indeed, the more broadly conceived view of the analytic situation, not only in Fairbairn but in object-relations theory more generally, admits the analyst-object as a real object. For Lacan, this was anathema: the extension of the so-called objectified imaginary (from the schema of the individual to that of the analysing situation) compounds the essential confusion in Fairbairn and the object-relations approach *per se*.

Lacan's criticism of Fairbairn, which set the agenda for a comprehensive critique of object-relations theory, was aimed at (a) the recourse to the objectified imaginary (the ego-ideal, the ideal object, illusion, misrecognition and so on), and (b) the idea of the analyst as a role model, that is to say, the imaginary action of the analyst as an object of identification. Some two years after these remarks appeared in *Le moi dans la théorie de Freud et dans la technique de la psychonalyse*, Lacan's reservations about the plausibility of object-relations theory were expressed at far greater length in his 1956–57 seminar, although as he (1994: 362) noted, the aim now was to 'revise the notion of the object-relation' from a classical Freudian perspective. Despite the fact that it runs directly counter to 'the new-fangled theory' and the concomitant developments in latter-day analytic practice, *La relation d'objet* is nonetheless a remarkable work, clearly conceived, and still one of only a handful of rigorously compiled analyses of object-relations theory. In fact, it may be the most important examination we have of the object-relation in post-Freudian theory. The critical terms of reference inevitably find fault with object-relations theory, but they also provide us with further discursive resources. I shall demonstrate what I mean by this in my comparative reading of Winnicott and Lacan on the gift-object. Meanwhile, let me summarise some of Lacan's more basic definitions and hypotheses.

a The object is only ever a refound object

What is meant by the object? What do objects mean for the human psyche? Lacan takes Freud's (1905: 222) notion of refinding (*Wiederfindung*) as his point of departure: 'The finding of an object is in fact a re-finding of it' along 'anaclitic' and/or 'narcissistic' lines. Lacan (1994: 363; emphasis in the original) in turn postulated that an object is 'something that is assuredly to be conquered, and indeed, as Freud reminds us, it can never be conquered without first being lost. An object is always a reconquest. Only by taking up once more a place that he initially dis-inhabits can man arrive at something that is improperly called his *wholeness*'. The symbolic dimension is accorded a pivotal role insofar as it 'distances the object', precisely 'so that the subject may re-find it' (1994: 312). Lacan describes how the introduction of the Oedipus complex reframes the form and function of the pregenital relation, and posits that the 'optimal' outcome here consists in refinding the object ('marked by the relationship with the primal mother') as 'the object of desire for the object that succeeds the maternal object' (1994: 75). In effect, the mother-infant relationship is conceived in oedipal terms.

b The central object-relation is one of lack

Lacan (1994: 364) maintained that '[t]he whole object-relation such as it has been established in the analytic literature and in Freudian doctrine revolves around the notion of privation'. He (1994: 59) advanced the view that 'the object is instantiated only in relation to lack'. This is how Lacan (1994: 73) characterised 'the child's fundamental disappointment', which functions as a structural determinant when the child 'recognises not only that he is not his mother's sole object, but also that his mother's point of interest is the phallus … On the basis of this recognition, he is to realise in a second moment precisely that she is deprived of this object, that she lacks it'. Anxiety and its relation to the object are thus articulated from the point of view of lack: 'Anxiety is not the fear of an object. Anxiety is the subject's confrontation with the absence of the object' (1994: 335).[6]

c The object-relation is operative on the imaginary plane

Lacan's critique of object-relations theory becomes more complicated in its successive iterations. And yet by comparing certain formulae from Book I and Book IV of his seminar, we can see that the basic argument remains unchanged and is consistently aimed at the 'dyadic relation in primary love'. In particular, the critique is based on an analysis of the object of satisfaction: (a) 'the object-relation is one which conjoins to a need an object which satisfies it' (Lacan 1975: 209); and (b) the satisfaction of a need to which the object corresponds introduces the real, with the inevitable threat of absence, in response to which the infant finds himself confined to the imaginary register as his only recourse. Lacan singles out in *La relation d'object* the fetish object and the phobic object in order to demonstrate, as he (1975: 226) noted in the first year of his seminar, how 'the intersubjective relation is reduced to an inter-objectal relation grounded on a natural, complementary satisfaction'. This is how the relationship of dependence appears from a Lacanian perspective: 'In our time, object-relations, with everything that is normative and progressive about them in the subject's life, with how they are genetically defined as mental development, belong to the register of the imaginary' (1994: 282). Despite the value accorded to this register in Lacan's schema, the assumption is that 'untenable contradictions' come to the fore 'in how this notion of the object-relation plays out when it starts to be expressed in terms of a pre-genital relation that is becoming genital, with the idea of progress that this entails' (1994: 282). The decisive point for Lacan (1975: 212) is that object-relations theory is construed in such a way that genital relations are set out on the same axis as pregenital relations, at both stages 'there will just have to be an object to satisfy and saturate [desire]'. The 'blind alleys' persist, according to Lacan (1975: 220), insofar as Balint, Fairbairn, Winnicott, and others prove themselves incapable of articulating the 'pass over' from the imaginary function to an apprehension of symbolic relations, relying instead on a 'supposedly harmonious imaginary relation, which saturates natural desire'. This results in what Lacan (1975: 223) saw as 'the impasse of the imaginary situation' at the heart of object-relations theory.

d The object as a function of the signifier

For Lacan (1994: 386) objects in the complete sense function as signifiers, precisely where something lacks. The object as a function of the signifier, however, fails to come into play where identification with maternal desire as an imaginary desire, identification with the maternal phallus or the maternal ideal (a function that belongs to the order of the ego ideal), prevents the articulation of signifier-elements with other signifier-elements. For Lacan the creation of meaning, or what I call the reach for meaning, depends on 'passing over' from the maternal world and the object of maternal love to the ternary character of symbolisation, from the first adumbration of the symbolic system to the combinatory value of the signifiers. Taking linguistics as his main frame of reference, Lacan (1994: 335) attempts 'to grasp the object-relations across the different stages of the signifying formation', what he sees as the signifying process of the unconscious.

e Frustration cannot give rise to the maintenance of desire

Arranging the experience of the earliest relationship around the notion of the lack of an object, Lacan (1994: 46) further divided this lack into three levels, namely, castration, frustration, and privation. Problems arise, according to Lacan (1994: 46), to the extent that 'the analysts of today have been reorganising the analytic experience upon the tier of frustration, while neglecting the notion of castration, which, along with the Oedipus complex, was Freud's original discovery'. This prompts the call for a revision of the notion of frustration. Accordingly, Lacan (1994: 172–73) noted that 'frustration is not the refusing of an object of satisfaction in the pure and simple sense', that 'frustration hinges on something else'. In the child's primal relation with the mother, frustration is conceived as 'the refusing of a gift, insofar as the gift is itself the symbol of something that is called love' (1994: 173). Frustration operates along these lines inasmuch as and because it is already situated in the symbolic order: 'any satisfaction that is in question in frustration arises there against the backdrop of the fundamentally disappointing character of the symbolic order' (1994: 175). As such, 'frustration is only ever the first stage of the return of the object' which, as we have seen, 'in order to be reconstituted, must be re-found' (1994: 312).

A few key examples, at this point, will demonstrate that despite the efforts of Lacan and his followers, French psychoanalysis includes an influential tradition of object-relations theory. Maurice Bouvet (1967), the main French proponent of the object-relations model, reconceptualised the transference of 'genital' and 'pregenital' structures, with notable success, along object-relational lines. Together with Lacan, Nacht, Lagache, and Lebovici, Bouvet was among the group who helped rebuild the Paris Psychoanalytic Society after the war. Needless to say, Lacan (1994: 68 *et passim*) reserved some of his more caustic criticism for Bouvet (Vermorel 2005: 50). André Green (2005), on the other hand, acknowledged the clinical usefulness of the distinction between 'genital' and 'pregenital' transference constructs. Green also drew a parallel between Bouvet and Winnicott, particularly with reference to technical innovation and variations in the analytic setting. Indeed, the parallels between Winnicott and French psychoanalysis will be evident throughout the following chapters, although it is important not to overstate the case.

As well as the long-lasting and far-reaching impact of his introduction of Winnicott's works in France, J.-B. Pontalis (1974) was also instrumental in countering Lacan's criticisms of Fairbairn. The first French translation of Fairbairn's seminal paper 'Schizoid Factors in the Personality' (1940) was published in *Nouvelle Revue de Psychanalyse* in 1974, edited by Pontalis. The positive evaluation of Fairbairn on theoretical and clinical grounds is instructive. Pontalis argued that Fairbairn's model of object-relationships represented a necessary consequence of theoretical rigour, rather than an arbitrary generalisation of an 'accident' or 'failing' of the psyche. At the same time, he pointed out that Fairbairn inaugurated a shift in the direction of the analyst's attention, or a change in the action of the analyst: from 'What does it mean?' to 'How does it work in there?' The shift in clinical focus from the neurotic model to borderline-schizoid states (*les états-limites*) marked a shift in clinical thinking – that is, from the realm of meaning, representation, and symbolisation to the corporeal habitus of dependency needs and the primary function of the skin or the narcissistic envelope. Alongside a number of analysts who broke away from Lacan to join the Association Psychanalytique de France, Pontalis insisted on the value of Fairbairn's inaugural contribution to the shift in clinical thinking onto an object-relations plane.[7]

To take one more example: in a singular contribution to the post-Freudian drive/structure model, André Green addressed the problem of the object primarily in terms of the relationship between the life and death drives. As we discussed in the previous chapter, primary object-relations are conceptualised in terms of Freud's final theory of drives, not only as libidinal and destructive forces, but also as functions of binding and unbinding. Thus, Green (2005 119–20; emphasis in the original) maintained that the aim of the life drive is to preserve an 'objectalising function' by transforming structures into objects – the ego *creates* objects out of instinctual activity, when the later, by transforming itself, becomes an object'. Green did not go so far as to acknowledge the structuration of the object by *relations*. This applies equally to his formulation of the death drive, which, he maintained consists of a 'disobjectalising function' that attacks the object-relation, but also 'all its substitutes and, in the long term, the ego itself'. In his preface to Bernard Brusset's *Psychoanalyse du Lien, la Relation d'Objet* (1988), Green expressed his doubts about the value of object-relations theory. The problematic of binding/unbinding, however, offers a further variation on the basic object-relations model, that is to say, 'from the double angle of the bindings within the ego and internal objects, and of those which unite the ego with external objects' (Green 2005: 119).

The theory of dynamic structure

My appreciation of Fairbairn's contribution to the Independent tradition will be evident from the foregoing discussion. I see Fairbairn as the most important relational theorist in the British school. To show why I think this is the case, I shall focus on his basic structural model. A close reading of 'Endopsychic Structure Considered in Terms of Object-Relationships' (1944) will demonstrate the point I wish to make. It will also provide an opportunity to review Fairbairn's contribution more broadly and, thereby, underscore his role as the founder of Independent object-relations theory. The 1944 paper completes a series of wartime papers, including, 'Schizoid Factors in the Personality' (1940), 'A Revised Psychopathology of the Psychoses and Psychoneuroses' (1941), and 'The Repression and the Return of the Bad Objects (with special reference to "War Neuroses")' (1943). The wartime papers represent Fairbairn's major achievement (Beattie 2003).

Taken together, the papers mark a profound shift in psychoanalysis, judged by Greenberg and Mitchell (1983: 151), alongside Sullivan's (1953) theory of the interpersonal field, as 'the purest and clearest expression of the shift from the drive/structure model to the relational/structure model'.

Fairbairn saw the world in a fundamentally different way to Freud, and the wartime papers announced and inaugurated an entirely new psycho-analytic perspective, distinct not only from the Freudian interpretation but also from its Kleinian development. Greenberg and Mitchell (1983: 167) summarise the main differences between the structural models as follows: 'The essential struggle in the classical Freudian model involves conflicts stemming from the person's instinctual impulses, some of these being mediated through internal representation of his early relations with his parents. The essential struggle in Fairbairn's model involves the person's irreconcilable loyalties in his longings for and identifications with various features of his significant others, in the outside world and as they have been internalized in an effort to control them. The problem for Freud is the in-herent opposition among instinctual aims and between instinctual aims and social reality; the problem for Fairbairn is that the person ... is forced to fragment himself to maintain contact and devotion to the irreconcilable features of [relations with others]'.

The 1944 paper begins with the basic theoretic principles of Fairbairn's model: (a) libido is primarily object-seeking (rather than pleasure-seeking); (b) drives constitute the forms of activity in which the life of ego structures consists; and (c) disturbances in early object-relationships lie at the origins of all psychopathology. In this case, the fundamental motivational push 'is not gratification and tension reduction, using others as a means towards that end, but connections with others as an end in itself' (Mitchell and Black 2016: 115). The model of primary connectedness, conceived as a primal dependence on the mother, is predicated on the finding that impulses are simply 'forms of energy at the disposal of ego structure' (1944: 90). For Fairbairn (1946: 149) 'structure divorced from energy and energy divorced from structure are meaningless concepts'. The structuration of energy is seen as an irreducible phenomenon of psyche: '"impulses" cannot be considered apart from the endopsychic structures which they energize and the object-relationships which they enable these structures to establish; and, equally, "instincts" cannot profitably be considered as anything more than forms of energy which constitute the dynamic of such endopsychic structures' (1944: 85).

The inseparability of energy and structure is the principal claim of Fairbairn's revised conception of psychical structure, and among his most important contributions to psychoanalysis. As such, it frames the basic disagreement with Klein as well as Freud. In the Freudian-Kleinian devel-opment, the source of motivational energy is the instinctual impulse. Essentially, for Freud the original impulse has no 'direction' but becomes 'directed upon' objects inasmuch as, and because, they facilitate the reduction of tension. Psychological activity thus consists of directionless energy that is secondarily 'directed upon' objects. In a modified version of the Freudian interpretation, Klein maintained that objects were integral to impulses from the beginning of life. Nevertheless, the underlying presupposition that objects are facilitative of drive activity remained intact in her model.

Fairbairn (1941: 34), on the other hand, proposed not only that energy and structure are inseparable, but also that libidinal energy is primarily object-seeking: 'it is not the libidinal attitude which determines the object-relationship, but the object-relationship which determines the libidinal attitude'. These propositions concerning the energy of the ego ('libido') and its structural nature represent a conception of human activity that is entirely different to the classical theory of motivation. That the acting person, in its libidinal capacity, consists of energy operating in 'directional ways' is something which is to be expected as a natural or logical consequence of living-there. Thus, for Fairbairn (1944: 126) psychic change *is* 'directional'; it amounts to 'changes in structural relationships and in relationships between structures'. The argument is twofold: (a) each structure exists in dynamic interrelation with every other structure; and (b) relations structure objects. The theory of dynamic structure presupposes 'the relationship of various parts of the ego to internalized objects and to one another as objects' (1944: 84–85).

It was clear to Fairbairn that the hypotheses of dynamic structure and internalised object-relationships called for a thoroughgoing revision of Freud's drive/structure model. Starting with the premise that drives 'cannot be considered apart from objects, whether external or internal', and that 'it is equally impossible to consider them apart from ego structure', Fairbairn (1944: 88) set about revising the basic terms of the Freudian interpretation – including, the structural model of the mind; the classical theory of motivation (drive theory); the fundamental principles of mental functioning; and the theory of repression. The argument is presented on clinical grounds. Despite the fact that 'the clinical referents and implications' (Greenberg and Mitchell 1983: 153) may not always be clearly spelled out, Fairbairn (1944: 107) nonetheless based his revised conception of psychical structure on the analysis of schizoid patients: 'Freud's theory of the mental apparatus was, of course, developed upon a basis of the depressive; and it is on a similar basis that Melanie Klein had developed her views. By contrast, it is the schizoid position that constitutes the basis of the theory of mental structure which I now advance' (1944: 107). The theory is based on a clinical reworking of the phenomenology of inner reality from the perspective of multiple internal ego-object constellations.

Fairbairn formulated two contrasting theories of psychopathology. In his earlier papers (1940; 1941) he noted that 'all forms of psychopathology are defences against oral conflicts and anxieties, either of a schizoid [early oral phase] or a depressive [late oral phase] nature, centring on a fear of one's own love or on a fear of one's own rage respectively' (Greenberg and Mitchell: 1983: 170). The child either withdraws from relatedness because he feels his love is 'bad' or he feels he has driven his mother away on account of his own destructiveness. By contrast, in his second theory of psychopathology Fairbairn (1943; 1944) introduced 'a more unified theory of psychopathology based on ego-splitting and schizoid dynamics' (Greenberg and Mitchell 1983: 172). The explanation of psychopathology shifted from (a) the early separation between 'schizoid' and 'depressive' (the Kleinian schema) to (b) the idea that *all* psychopathology originates in the splitting of the ego and the repression of 'bad' objects. By dropping the reference to defences against specific impulses (early and late oral impulses), the second theory was not only more unified but also more fully relational in nature.

Based on the distinction between the melancholic affect of 'depression' and the 'sense of futility' or 'meaninglessness' characteristic of schizoid affect, Fairbairn (1944: 91) sought to clear up what he saw as an underlying confusion in post-Freudian clinical practice. Drawing on his own experience of treating hysterical symptoms, he came to the conclusion that 'the dissociated phenomena of "hysteria" involve a split of the ego fundamentally identical with that which confers upon the term "schizoid" its etymological significance' (1944: 92). The call for a 'return to hysteria' was predicated on these grounds, with profound implications for the structural approach and the theory of repression. Whilst 'the main phenomenon of melancholic depression may be regarded as receiving a relatively satisfactory explanation at the superego level', this is not the case for paranoid and hypochondriacal trends, which, Fairbairn (1944: 93–94) noted 'frequently manifest themselves in melancholics'. For Fairbairn (1944: 94) these accompanying clinical phenomena are oriented towards 'internal objects which are in no sense "good", but are unconditionally (i.e. libidinally) bad'. At the same time, and more importantly, Fairbairn (1944: 94) proposed that it is 'equally difficult to find a satisfactory explanation of the symptoms of "hysteria" at the superego level – if for no other reason than that in "hysteria" the libidinal inhibitions which occur are out of all proportion to the measure of guilt which is found to be present'.

The 'return to hysteria' ushers in a structural approach that is based on neither the id nor the superego as explanatory concepts. Indeed, for Fairbairn (1944: 99–100) 'all psychopathological developments originate at a stage antecedent to that at which the superego develops and proceeds from a level beneath that at which the superego operates'. It is not simply a matter of timing. Fairbairn's radically revised view is levelled not only at the classical structural model but also at Klein's (1928) attempts to link the formation of the superego with the pregenital phases of development. Fairbairn's (1944: 101) insistence on attributing 'overriding psychopathological importance to a level beneath that at which the superego functions' places the revised structural model at odds with the notion of a pregenital superego, particularly Klein's (1928: 187) idea that 'the sense of guilt' attaches itself to oral- and anal-sadistic impulses. Consistent with the primitive, preoedipal origins of psychopathology and its schizoid nature, Fairbairn (1944: 93) specified that (a) *'repression* originates primarily as a defence against "bad" internalized objects (and not against "impulses")' and (b) 'that *guilt* originates as an *additional* defence against situations involving bad internalized objects'. On the grounds that the internalisation of objects is essentially a means of 'coercion' or defence, Fairbairn (1944: 111) maintained that 'it is not the satisfying object, but the unsatisfying object that the infant seeks to coerce', or bring under his control in the inner world. Mitchell and Black (2016: 117) flesh out Fairbairn's point: 'Because the child, in his object-seeking, cannot reach the unresponsive aspects of the parents in actuality, he internalizes them and fantasizes those features of the parents as now being inside of him, part of him'.

Fairbairn attached no meaning to the primary internalisation of a 'good' object, an object that is satisfying from the infant's point of view; nor did he see any need to qualify this basic proposition: 'I can think of no motive for the introjection of an object which is *perfectly satisfying*' (1954: 15 n 2).[8] Fairbairn viewed internal objects and internalised object-relations as neither immanent nor the primary forms of thought and experience. However, he acknowledged that a 'perfectly satisfying' relationship between the infant and his actual mother does not exist in reality but is only 'theoretically possible'. Living-there itself – indeed, in all its diverse intensity and affective complexity – provides sufficient grounds for introjecting the maternal object. Yet based on the assumption that introjection is essentially a *defensive* technique (the first defence adopted by the original unitary ego to deal with an unsatisfying object-relationship), rather than an expression of the infant's instinctive incorporative need, Fairbairn maintained that it is always the 'bad' or 'unsatisfying' object-relationship that is internalised in the first instance. An observation from an earlier paper suggests a certain degree of ambiguity in Fairbairn's thinking: 'the appeal of a good object is an indispensable factor in promoting a dissolution of the cathexis of internalized bad objects' (1943: 74). The 'good' or 'satisfying' object is viewed as something of a compensation in the wake of the internalisation of 'bad' or 'unsatisfying' objects; 'good' internal objects are conceived, exclusively, as defences against 'bad' internal object-relations. Fairbairn regarded internal objects *per se* as 'compensatory substitutes for crucial missing connections with actual others' (Mitchell 2000: 123).

In the 1951 Addendum to the 1944 paper, Fairbairn (1944: 134–35) proposed that 'the object which is originally internalized is, not an object embodying the exclusively "bad" and unsatisfying aspects of the external object, but the pre-ambivalent object … The internalization of the pre-ambivalent object would then be explained on the grounds that it presented itself as unsatisfying in some measure as well as in some measure satisfying'. More specifically, again with reference to the *actual* human situation, Fairbairn (1954: 16 n 2) went on to revise his original formulation to the effect (a) 'that the differentiation of objects into categories to which the respective terms "good" and "bad" can be applied only arises after the original (pre-ambivalent) object has been introjected', and (b) 'that this differentiation is effected through splitting of an internalized object which is, in the first instance, neither "good" nor "bad", but "in some measure unsatisfying", and which only becomes truly "ambivalent" after its introjection'.

Despite certain inconsistencies and omissions in his account of the internalisation of 'good' object-relations, Fairbairn was perfectly clear about the structuration of the unconscious mind. For Fairbairn, the unconscious is structured during the earliest period of development, the period of infantile dependence, in accordance with the schizoid position. Ogden (2010: 101) elaborates on this finding: 'the formation of the internal object world is always, in part, a response to trauma (actual failure on the part of the mother to convey to her infant a sense that she loves him and accepts his love)'. The concept of the 'dynamic unconscious', therefore, is fundamentally redefined: 'I have treated the internalized objects simply as *objects* of the dynamic ego structures ... it is only through [the activity of the ego] that objects ever come to be internalized. However, in the interests of consistency, I must now draw the logical conclusion of my theory of dynamic structure and acknowledge that, since internal objects are structures, they must necessarily be, in some measure at least, dynamic' (1944: 132; emphasis in the original). The argument comprises two basic propositions: (a) internal object-relations form the central part of the repressed; and (b) structural differentiation is essentially a defensive and psychopathological process that arises in response to trauma, rather than a criterion of human development as such.

There have been various attempts to explicate Fairbairn's notion of the unconscious and its origins. In this respect, Rubens singles out 'internalization' as perhaps the single most confused theme in Fairbairn's writings. The confusion arises, according to Rubens (1994: 164), on account of the fact that Fairbairn 'used the concept of "internalization" in two distinctly different ways, while never acknowledging that the difference existed'. Thus, Rubens differentiates between the internalisation of 'good' and 'bad' objects on the basis of two qualitatively distinct modes of internalisation: 'good' objects are not subject to repression, i.e. they are not split-off from the original central ego; whereas 'bad' objects are organised into relatively closed-off dissociated systems, or unconscious psychic structures. It is only the 'unsatisfying' aspects of the object that are 'repressed and internalized in a way that generates structure-producing splits' in the ego (Rubens 1994: 165). By contrast, Rubens points out that 'satisfying' aspects of the object are never 'structurally internalised'. Thus 'non-structuring internalisation' does not result in 'the establishment of any "entity" within the self, but rather results in an alteration of the integration of the self, or in the production of a thought, memory or fantasy within the self' (Rubens 1984: 437). The process of nonstructuring internalisation does not result in the formation of endopsychic structure; it denotes rather a *maturational* process (with progressively higher levels of synthesis and integration), something that tends to remain implicit in Fairbairn's revised theory of psychic structure due to his preoccupation with psychopathology. Nevertheless, Rubens (1994: 172) notes that 'Fairbairn's insistence that structure implies pathology and that wholeness and integration imply health is unique among psychoanalytic theories'.

Despite offering a coherent account of the formation of psychic structure, the distinction between the nonstructuring effects of the internalisation of 'good' objects and the structuring effects of the internalisation of 'bad' objects leaves the introjection of the maternal object unclear. Skolnick (1998: 144) offers an alternative interpretation by suggesting that for Fairbairn whilst 'good' objects may be internalised, they are never repressed. In which case Fairbairn's basic conception of ego-splitting and the formation of internal objects remains intact: the unconscious is structured by the internalisation of interactions with those aspects of the mother that fail to meet the infant's dependency needs at the beginning. This constitutes what Ogden (2010: 102) sees as the core dilemma for the infant or child, that is to say, 'when he experiences his mother (upon whom he is utterly dependent) as both loving and accepting of his love, and unloving and rejecting of his love'. Ogden (2010: 102–103) draws attention to a fundamental ambiguity in Fairbairn's treatment of this core human dilemma: 'Is every infant traumatized by experiences of deficits in his mother's love for him? Or does the infant misinterpret inevitable (and necessary) frustrations as manifestations of his mother's failure to love him?'

Fairbairn lends weight to both interpretations: on the one hand, there is an assumption that 'the traumatic factor in the situation' arises as a realistic perception, that the infant realistically perceives the 'unsatisfying' aspects of maternal love. On the other hand, Fairbairn (1944: 112–13; emphasis in the original) discerns in the infant's response to privation and the contingencies of life an affect-laden sense of intentional rejection on the mother's part: 'what presents itself to [the infant] from a strictly conative standpoint as *frustration* at the hands of his mother presents itself to him in a very different light from a strictly affective standpoint. From the latter standpoint, what he experiences is a sense of lack of love, and indeed emotional *rejection* on his mother's part'. How far can the matter be resolved? It seems to me that, in listening to our patients, we live with this ambiguity as a matter of course, moving back and forth between the two interpretations in accordance with the nature of the transference. Skolnick, for his part, proposes that a clearer delineation between Fairbairn's early and later stages of primary dependence, between dissociation (the early internal objects of infantile dependence) and the problem of ambivalence, allows for the repression of the 'good' object, without necessarily undermining the logic of Fairbairn's main argument. It does so, however, by placing Fairbairn's thesis within a broadly defined Kleinian framework along the lines of paranoid-schizoid and depressive positions.

The idea that repression is primarily directed against internalised bad objects, understood as psychical structures, is an integral part of Fairbairn's thesis – namely, that repression is essentially structural in nature. This points to what Fairbairn (1944: 94) saw as an 'anomaly' in the Freudian interpretation, where the 'agent' (ego) and the 'instigator' (superego) of repression are regarded as structures whilst the repressed consists essentially in 'libidinal impulses', in particular, 'repression arises as a means of defence against impulses involved in the Oedipus situation and treated by the ego as "guilty" in terms of the pressure of the superego'. For Freud the repressed consists of conflictual, forbidden impulses; whereas Fairbairn treated the repressed as well as the agent/instigator of repression as internal structures. The repressed was seen as part of the self 'tied to inaccessible, often dangerous features of the parents, whereas the repressor was seen as a part of the self 'tied to more accessible, less dangerous features of the parents' (Mitchell and Black 2016: 118).

Fairbairn's theory of dynamic structure was based on clinical findings. For example, the alternative view of repression that he put forward as part of his revised theory of psychic structure, was based on the analysis of a patient's dream. The manifest content of the dream is as follows:

> the dreamer saw the figure of herself being viciously attacked by a well-known actress in a venerable building which had belonged to her family for generations. Her husband was looking on; but he seemed quite helpless and quite incapable of protecting her. After delivering the attack the actress turned away and resumed playing a stage part, which, as seemed to be implied, she had momentarily set aside in order to deliver the attack by way of interlude. The dreamer then found herself gazing at the figure of herself lying bleeding on the floor; but, as she gazed, she noticed that this figure turned for an instant into that of a man. Thereafter the figure alternated between herself and this man until eventually she awoke in a state of acute anxiety.
>
> (Fairbairn 1944: 95)

None of the available interpretations that made use of the standard analytic method seemed to satisfy Fairbairn. As we have seen, he employed neither the superego nor the id as explanatory frames of reference. On the contrary, he maintained that all the figures appearing in dreams represent parts of the ego or internalised objects, a view that was integral to his theory of object-relationships and the idea of internalised objects as structures. In a further elaboration along these lines, which set the model directly at odds with the Freudian interpretation, Fairbairn (1944: 99) proposed that 'dreams are essentially, not wish-fulfilments, but dramatizations ... of situations existing in inner reality'. For Fairbairn the latent content of the dream is set out as a series of *dramatis personae*: the figure of the dreamer subjected to attack; the man into whom this figure turns, and who then alternates with the figure of the dreamer as the object of attack; the attacking actress; the dreamer's husband as a helpless onlooker; the observing ego of the dreamer; and the attacking actress not only as another figure of the dreamer but also the dreamer's mother.

Fairbairn offers two observations on this picture of inner reality: (a) the figures fall into two classes – namely, ego structures and object structures; and (b) the ego structures 'pair off' with the object structures. This suggests the following pairs: the observing ego and the observing object representing the dreamer's husband; the attacking ego and the attacking object representing the dreamer's mother; and the attacked ego and the attacked object representing the dreamer's father (and by transference her husband). On the strength of these clinical observations, Fairbairn formulated the structural significance of the dream, precisely in terms of the object-relationships pertaining to the ego structures. The dreamer's ego is split into three separate egos or sub-selves, according to Fairbairn (1944: 101), 'in conformity with the schizoid position'; hence an original 'central ego and two subsidiary egos ... cut off from the central ego'. The subsidiary, dissociated ego structures, which remain tied to compensatory internal objects and, therefore, unavailable for vital relations with real people, are divided as such into the 'libidinal ego' and an aggressive, persecutory ego termed the 'internal saboteur' (subsequently the 'antilibidinal ego'). The former is related to the dreamer's father and, therefore, is 'highly endowed with libido'; the latter is related to the dreamer's mother as a repressive figure aimed at sabotaging the dreamer's libidinal relationship with her father. Fairbairn accorded this structural configuration 'universal' significance.

To appreciate the radical nature of his contribution, it is important we acknowledge the extent to which his notion of 'ego' differs from the use of the term in classical structural theory. The 'pristine personality of the child', according to Fairbairn (1954: 15), 'consists of a unitary dynamic ego', that is to say, an ego with its own energy, rather than energy drawn off from the id. The ego itself – 'directed upon' objects – effects the reach for life and, under conditions of infantile dependence, realises the potentiality of 'more life'. That Fairbairn referred to this primitive state of potentiality as a 'dynamic ego' follows directly from 'his postulate of the inseparability of energy and structure' (Rubens 1994: 156). Rubens underlines Fairbairn's adherence to the 'innate structural integrity' of the ego *contra* the derivative structure of the ego in the Freudian interpretation. Moreover, he points out that Fairbairn conceived the original ego as 'an actual fragment of the self, and not a representation of it' (1994: 159).[9] Similarly, Guntrip (1961: 279) noted that Fairbairn's 'ego' is not 'the superficial, adaptive ego of Freud ... formed on the surface of a hypothetical impersonal id as its adjustment to outer reality. Fairbairn's "ego" is the primary psychic self in its original wholeness, a whole which differentiates into organized structural patterns under the impact of experience of object-relationships after birth'. Fairbairn described how the original unitary psyche undergoes processes of ego-splitting, or dissociation, which assume 'relatively permanent, internal, structural form' (Guntrip 1961: 280).

To recall the basic principle of the relational/structure model, in the situation described by Fairbairn objects do not count simply as a means for 'managing internal pressures and states'; on the contrary, interactive exchanges with and emotional ties to others (external and internal) become 'the fundamental psychological reality itself' (Mitchell 1988: 25). In addition to the dissociation from the central ego, the ego is subject to a further split in conjunction with the split in internal objects. The term 'libidinal ego' describes the dissociated ego-structure cathecting the 'exciting object'; the term 'antilibidinal ego', the dissociated ego-structure cathecting the 'rejecting object'. The former denotes the enticing aspects of the mother coupled with the semblance of the infant's primordial sense of hope, and the latter refers to the withholding, depriving aspects of the mother coupled with the hate and destructiveness attendant on the infant's reaction to frustration. Fairbairn's structural theory privileges the relations among the internal objects and their corresponding subsidiary egos. And what comes to the fore is the extent to which the hopefulness of the libidinal ego and its exciting object (the subject and object of potential relatedness) are subject to vengeful attacks and relentless mockery from the antilibidinal ego.

For Fairbairn, this arrangement represents a major parameter of internal reality and its psychopathological consequences. It accounts, strictly in terms of the ego and ego defences, for what Freud (1926) saw as a fundamental resistance beyond the resistances of the ego – namely, the repetition compulsion and the negative therapeutic reaction, or the unconscious sense of guilt and the need for punishment. Further to the revised theory of psychopathology, the residual nucleus that remains after the exciting and rejecting parts have been split off from it, represents the sufficiently satisfying aspect of the internalised object, what Fairbairn (1954: 17) eventually termed the 'ideal object'. The latter represents the comforting aspects of the infant's relationship with its mother. In each case, the object is significant only in terms of its attachment to a part of the ego; while at the same time, the ego is shaped by its relations with objects.

The 'basic endopsychic situation' thus consists of three ego/object configurations: central ego/ideal object; libidinal ego/exciting object; and antilibidinal ego/rejecting object. The defensive manoeuvres employed in this situation are aimed at the child's 'experience of frustration' in his relationship with his mother and his 'sense of rejection' owing to her actions. Fairbairn (1944: 110) concludes that it is the experience of frustration which 'calls forth the infant's aggression in relation to his libidinal object and thus gives rise to a state of ambivalence'. To recall the point that I made earlier, aggression is not seen as a primary motivational factor but, rather, as the derivative of environmental deficiency and the failure of satisfying object-relationships.

In a summary statement concerning the general setup of internalisation and dissociation, Fairbairn proposed that the infant attempts to deal with the ambivalent situation as follows:

> (1) by splitting the figure of his mother into two objects, a good and a bad, (2) by internalizing the bad object in an endeavour to control it, (3) by splitting the internalized bad object in turn into two objects, viz. *(a)* the exciting or needed object, and *(b)* the rejecting object, (4) by repressing both these objects and employing a certain volume of his aggression in the process, and (5) by employing a further volume of his aggression in splitting off from his central ego and repressing two subsidiary egos which remain attached to these respective internalized objects by libidinal ties.
>
> (Fairbairn 1944: 114)

The explanation of the origin of the basic endopsychic situation is presented, simultaneously, as an explanation of 'the origin of the schizoid position, the origin of repression and the differentiation of the various fundamental endopsychic structures' (1944: 109). Unlike Freud, for whom the oedipal situation was an 'ultimate cause', Fairbairn (1944: 120) advanced the alternative hypothesis of infantile dependence and its primacy: '[the Oedipus situation] is not a basic situation, but the derivative of a situation which has priority over it not only in the logical, but also in the temporal sense. This prior situation is one which issues directly out of the physical and emotional dependence of the infant upon his mother'. This was the crux of Lacan's (1994: 53) critique of Fairbairn: 'from the very first, Freud yoked castration to the central position he gave to the Oedipus complex as the essential articulation of any development in sexuality'. Alternatively, in a definitive break with Freudianism that renders internal objects and the internal object world in hitherto unprecedented depth, the oedipal situation is seen as a secondary formation in relation to a more 'basic situation', namely, the oral-dependent relationship with the mother. The distinction passes into Independent object-relations theory in general and is established as a basic principle.

Here is where we meet

Our being together with one another in the world is the given of human existence. It is only in living and acting *together with others* that the personal ego itself is realised. But what does it mean to live with others? The principal thesis of the present work is that human life *is* the proximity of persons, the proximity of one to the other. A consideration of the human being reveals the extent to which human life equates with the proximity of contact, rather than individual substances, indivisible unities, or autonomous monads. The thesis rests on two propositions. Firstly, sensibility reveals itself as proximity on the surface of the skin, insofar as the egoism of the skin-ego is exposed immediately, without mediation, to the skin of another; touch instantiates the immediate nearness characteristic of the dependence relationship prior to the dialectic of presence and absence.[10] Secondly, I propose we model proximity on the coming into relation of two primordial phenomena of maternity: (a) 'the mother has a breast and the power to produce milk' and (b) 'she would like to be attacked by a hungry baby' (Winnicott 1945: 152), grasped and bitten into by an infant whose hunger incarnates the reach for life. The very ruthlessness of its spontaneity characterises the infant's reach for life as a primary act of love. The scene of devourment may be seen as an expression of ruthless love rather than innate oral-sadism.

Winnicott's characteristic mode of expression is immediately evident in these basic propositions concerning the object that is gifted to the infant (the mother's breast as gift-object) prior to the play of satisfaction and frustration. Indeed, in turning from Fairbairn to Winnicott, I wish to emphasise above all a stylistic shift in clinical and theoretical thinking. As we have seen, Fairbairn and Winnicott disagreed about *this* and *that*. The disagreements between them were far from insignificant; most notably, Fairbairn followed Freud by using the terms 'need' and 'satisfaction' interchangeably. Winnicott (1956a: 301), on the other hand, consistently privileged 'need', as distinct from 'satisfaction', at the level of absolute dependence: 'a need is either met or not met, and the effect is not the same as that of satisfaction and frustration of id impulse'. The emphasis on needs rather than the pattern of the relationship with the object that comes about by frustration, remained decisive for Winnicott's analysis of maternity: 'the recognition of the mother as a person comes in a positive way, normally, and not out of the experience of the mother as the symbol of frustration' (1956a: 304). Winnicott was more explicit than Fairbairn on these points: the infant experiences the mother neither as a type of satisfying object pertaining to archaic symbolisation nor as a symbolic object of frustration. I take up the substantiative differences between Winnicott and Fairbairn at various points throughout the book; but ultimately, what set the founding figures of Independent object-relations theory apart from one another was their contrastive modes of expression. As a comparative reading of their writings demonstrates, Fairbairn and Winnicott provided psychoanalysis with a new sense of origination, while the idiom in which they did so underscored the distance between them.

Our main focus on the object-relation in conjunction with the acting person is underpinned by the idea that life comes into its own where spontaneity, the infant's spontaneous reach for life, is met by the aliveness of maternal care. It is a meeting that is constitutive.[11] The person-action relation rests on the mother's ability to adapt to her infant's needs. In living-there at the beginning, the infant has yet to become someone, a provision has first to be made. In this respect, meeting articulates the actualisation of potentiality; it constitutes the primordial grounds of dynamic structure, understood as the *potentia-actus* correlation of human dynamism. The integral dynamism of the human being, especially in its inner aspect, is evident in what Winnicott called the infant's 'spontaneous gesture'. The latter consists in the spontaneity of freedom, which expresses the potentiality of the personal being of the infant, although it becomes efficacious only through the 'delicate adaptation to exact needs'. What this means for the infant is that the object-world presents itself in such a way that it matches or joins up with the creative imagination of the inner world (Winnicott 1964: 73–74). Adaptation to need, in the form of 'primary maternal preoccupation', enables the spontaneous gesture to unfold *as an experience.*

This is the position that I maintain throughout the present study: that starting with infantile dependence and the infusion of aliveness through the mother, meeting constitutes the decisive factor in a human life. Living beings thrive only where they come into the company of others, initially, under conditions of absolute dependence. The experience is formative. Meeting constitutes the existential groundwork of going-on-being, the enabling of the human being as the person. Milner (1977) made a similar point in terms of the indispensability of a safe and reliable meeting place, which she described as a type of overlapping, or 'area of overlap'. Winnicott, in his approach to meeting, distinguished between the nondifferentiation of subject and object (me and not-me, ego and non-ego) on the one hand and, on the other, the fusion or defusion between the subjective object and the object objectively perceived. Milner was after something rather different, although along similar lines to Winnicott. She emphasised the prelogical fusion of subject and object, the feeling one has of being joined up, merged with the object, as distinct from defusion, the feeling of being separate from the object. The recourse to the problematic of fusion extends the analysis of meeting along the axes of augmentation and formlessness.

Milner (1977: 282) conceived fusion as an augmentation of reality: far from a 'narcissistic impoverishment of one's relation to the external world', the feeling of being joined up, or merged with the object, instantiates an 'actual enrichment' of external reality.[12] Furthermore, Milner identified the fusion characteristic of the dependence relationship with 'the formless core of being', and proposed that formlessness constitutes the basis of new forms; hence 'the inner silence, the basic formlessness from which all form comes, and which at first can feel like total emptiness, annihilation even, and be defended against at almost any cost. And especially so when this inner silence is liable to get mixed up with the phantasy of the destruction of the inner needed object' (Milner 1977: 283–84).

The acceptance of a phase of some kind of fusion, according to Milner (1969: 249), 'was necessary for all creative work, whether the work is within the psyche or in the outer world'. In this respect, the interpretation of preprimitive states does not take its point of departure from the destructive envy of mother's inside; infantile aggressiveness is not conceived as the frustrated destruction of the love-object. Consequently, creativity is not modelled on reparation as a result of the infantile fantasy of a destroyed inner world; moreover, far from 'just an attempted escape' to the imaginary gratification of having been 'the satisfied infant at the mother's breast', Milner (1969: 249) maintained that fusion represents 'one end of a constantly alternating polarity which is the basis of all psychic creativity, and therefore of symbol formation and psychic growth'. We can describe this 'constantly alternating polarity' in terms of the movement between the *creative act*, conceived as a spontaneous gesture, and the *creation of the symbol*.

The same holds for Milner as for Winnicott: the 'area of overlap' actualises the creative imperative, the want to live creatively, and as such provides for an experience of something irreducibly personal. This is a dynamic process that comes to more than basic unity or imaginary harmony. For Winnicott, it is 'creative apperception' more than anything else that makes the individual feel that life is worth living. Creative activity may be seen as the substratum of the person-action relation. In the Winnicottian tradition, primary creativity is simultaneously a condition and the medium of the *personal* structure of being, even as creative activity issues from the formless core of being. Meeting itself may be seen as the quiddity of creative living – indeed, it is on account of meeting that the personal 'someone' becomes real, becomes what Winnicott (1960a: 148; emphasis added) called the true self: 'At the earliest stage the True Self is the theoretical position from which come the spontaneous gesture and the personal idea. The spontaneous gesture is the True Self *in action*. Only the True Self can be creative and only the True Self can feel real'.

The realisation of the true self in acting, the initial fulfilment of oneself in the action of the spontaneous gesture, precedes any reference to objects external to the ego. The reach for life is efficacious prior to the formation of 'unit status', or of the constituent elements of the true self: 'me' and 'not-me' (Winnicott 1950–55: 217). The human being is someone from the very moment of his coming into existence. Yet this has to be realised as a fact of experience – that is, by mother and child living 'an experience together'

(Winnicott 1945: 152). In this respect, the *intentional* object of acting functions as an (imaginative) elaboration of the spontaneous gesture, an elaboration of the reach for life in the form of the true self in the action; it denotes a mature actualisation of the original living-there. As such, the true self embodies the originality proper to worldmaking. The true self is rooted in the spontaneity of freedom, the freedom of the person performing an action. The spontaneous gesture unfolds (under favourable conditions) as the authentic form of the 'act of the person'. The true self is simultaneously an expression of the person who acts and an actualisation of freedom. It proceeds from living-there, or actual existing, and is originally a manifestation of the psyche-soma continuity of being: 'The true self, a continuity of being, is in health based on psyche-soma growth' (Winnicott 1949: 254).

Winnicott may be considered a personalist to the extent that he subscribed to the view that the real is personal; that the person-action relation constitutes the basic pattern of psychic reality; and that it is 'in action' (primary creativity, the spontaneous gesture, the act of living creatively) that the person is disclosed in the human being. Being a person means being 'someone', a true self in the Winnicottian sense, who is capable of spontaneous gestures; hence beings who are also persons. But while being a person manifests itself in action, Winnicott (1970: 287) insisted that one's personal existence is constituted, in the first instance, by the dependence relationship: 'Any discussion of the "paranoid position" in pure culture is futile unless the environmental provision is first assessed and allowed for'. For Winnicott, the relation pertaining between action and an acting being in action depends *as an actual reality* on the environmental factor; true experience issues from the infant's want-to-live being met by the 'good enough' mother. The person is reliant on the environmental provision, which is ruthlessly appropriated at the beginning of life in accordance with one's capacity to be free and to act freely. Outside of this setup the individual can neither realise nor fulfil himself as a person, that is, as the person performing the spontaneous gesture and fulfilling himself in the process of doing so.

The self-dependence of the person, or what Winnicott (1963a) described as being 'towards independence', is an achievement. But despite the fact that only a person could accomplish what is made reliably available, and that feeling real is considered the basis of a worthwhile life and the source of one's happiness, the 'personal idea' does not assume that only persons are real. Winnicott was less interested in the self than in the conditions of its flourishing. Accordingly, his full account of the true self, the complete setup of the person as a human being, confirms that meeting provides the basis for being, precisely as the freedom and efficacy (the *conatus*) of the person. Meeting augments available reality by allowing for the actualisation of potentiality. It enables the human person's freedom to unfold, which means that in the Winnicottian tradition at least, personalism presupposes interpersonal relations.

The acting person originates in its own potentiality, but does not exist *ex nihilo*. The paradox here is that the dependence relationship demarcates the *independence* appropriate to the human person. In Winnicottian terms, the more authentically mother and child *live an experience together*, the more the child's own personal being matures, precisely along the lines of the 'true self'. Winnicott (1960b: 46) described the trajectory of dependence: from 'absolute dependence' through 'relative dependence' to 'towards independence', in terms of the infant's changing relation to the sense of having its needs met. The experience of freedom itself relies on what meeting provides. As such, the experience is rooted in the care about which, initially, the infant 'has no means of knowing' (Winnicott 1960b: 52). The freedom of the person thus carries within it a trace of something unknown, regarding the conditions of one's own possibility.

Ogden (2001: 314) makes the far-reaching claim that 'Winnicott is suggesting (though I think he was not fully aware of this as he wrote it) that he is in the process of transforming psychoanalysis, both as a theory and as a therapeutic relationship, in a way that involves altering the notion of what is most fundamental to human psychology'. In particular, Ogden (2016a: 8) underlines the historic import of meeting in Winnicott; understood in terms of the 'convergence of passions' rather than (say) the keeping of appointments, meeting may be seen as a 'radically new conception' of human relations, a new way of thinking about the development of human consciousness, as well as the formation of the object-world or the world of persons. The 'convergence of passions' – one might go further and describe a primordiality *bondage* of passion – designates the absolute nature of the dependence relationship prior to object-relationships, prior to the objectivity of objects, and before life takes a foothold in the *continuity* of being. The convergence of maternal care and the infant's own sense of aliveness, that is to say, where the responsibility for another is immediately inclined towards the want to live, defines living-there as the grounds for the consciousness of the acting person, the togetherness of living-with, or the assembling of living into a conjuncture. Being in the object-world is derivative of the actualisation of potential space afforded by these nonerotic passions at the beginning of life. Basically, 'meeting' in the preprimitive sense of the term makes human life what it is and each of us living beings.

Winnicott discovered the primordial determination of meeting as the grounds for going-on-being alongside what he called 'transitional objects' and 'transitional phenomena'. The two sets of discoveries go hand-in-hand. Thus, in his account of the vital element, the meaning of transitional phenomena is evident before any correlation – including, the subject-object correlation (the thematization of 'me' and 'not-me') – as a between (*Zwischen*).[13] The latter denotes the intertwined relation of being and its incarnate nature, the original incarnation of *erleben*, which, incommensurable with the synchrony of the correlative, precedes the objectivity (*Gegenständlichkeit*) of the self and the object-world.[14] In this respect, 'between' may be seen as *home* in the discovery/invention of the world; transitional space describes the point at which, and the process by means of which, living comes about in an inhabitable world. The infant thus creates the life creating him, even as he lives in the world before it *is*, before being-in-the-world. For Winnicott (1988: 107) the continuity of being unfolds in the 'no-man's-land between the subjective and what is objectively perceived ... between fact and fantasy'. And he (1960b: 43) consistently maintained that 'the inherited potential of an infant cannot become an infant unless linked to maternal care'. The couple, rather than the individual, is the smallest indivisible human occurrence; the personal is primordially and irreducibly interpersonal. The 'centre of gravity', as Winnicott (1952: 99) noted, does not start off in the infant but *between* mother and infant.

The gift-object

The continuity of being presupposes a primitive emotional tie underpinned by a type of immemorial gift. The infant reaches for *what is there* as a precondition of the reach for meaning. As such, mother and infant each make a gift of themselves, with their whole being, in the form of preoccupation and spontaneity, respectively; and they do so prior to the oedipal structuration of the gift as something one has or does not have, 'the dialectic of having or not having the phallus'. This brings us back to Lacan's critique of the object-relation. As regards maternity, Lacan (1994: 166) presupposes that the dialectical structure of the gift renders the gift as a sign of love: 'the child is faced with a mother as the support of the first love relation, insofar as love is something that is symbolically structured, insofar as she is the object of an appeal, an object which therefore is as much absent as present'. In proposing that the gift arises from 'a zone that lies beyond the object relation', Lacan (1994: 174) advanced the view (a) that this beyond-zone is a function of the 'order of exchange' which the child enters even in the earliest relationship and (b) that it can arise as such only with 'the character that constitutes it as specifically symbolic'.

What does it mean to give? Is it ever the object that is given? Lacan's (1994: 132) response was unequivocal: 'What intervenes in the love relationship, what is asked for as a sign of love, is only ever something that carries worth merely as a sign ... there is no greater possible gift, no greater sign of love, than the gift of what one hasn't got'. Viewed from the perspective of the so-called 'dialectic' of the gift, the satisfaction of need is construed as a 'compensation' for the frustration of love; moreover 'to the extent that the breast becomes a compensation, it becomes the symbolic breast' (1994: 349). The mother is now in a position to refuse love. The child, in turn, according to Lacan (1994: 175), 'quashes ... the disappointing aspect of [the] symbolic interplay by orally seizing the object of satisfaction, the breast in this instance. What sends him to sleep in this satisfaction is precisely his disappointment, his frustration, the refusal that he has experienced'. The very reach for life, conceived as a grasping of the oral object, is consigned to an experience of 'symbolic unfulfillment'. Clearly, the idea that the child comes to 'imagine himself as nothing' (1994: 238) is quite different from the experience of 'disillusionment' in the Winnicottian sense. We shall come back to this distinction in a moment.

For Lacan orality becomes what it is – namely, an eroticised activity – through the substitution of the satisfaction of need for symbolic satisfaction. This in turn is presented as a theory of primitive fantasy. Lacan (1994: 187) noted, for example, that the gaping hole of the Medusa's head is 'a devouring figure that the child encounters as a possible outcome of his search to satisfy his mother'. The situation is presented as a solution to the problem of phobia, in which the theme of devouring is seen as ubiquitous and, moreover, may be traced back to the fear of being 'devoured by the mother'. The argument is based on the following premises. Firstly, anxiety comes into play at the point where 'the imaginary orgy', the child's identification with the mother (his being ensconced in his 'mother's interior'), gives way to a threatened reification of the real – indeed, anxiety itself, which by its nature has no object, is transformed into a fear that something real will happen ('the fear of …'). Secondly, the solution to this problem relies on 'the intervention of the real father' as a condition for the reorganisation of the symbolic world, or the symbolic transposition of the imaginary. The absence of the mother's penis is seen as the 'essential signification' (1994: 349) on both counts.

What does this schema tell us about worldmaking? The infant in Lacan's schematic is not alternately helpless (primary distress) and spontaneously alive (primary creativity) so much as disenchanted, exposed in the case of phobia to a wide-open maw. The onus in this situation is placed on the child. For Lacan (1994: 179) it is a question of how the child manages to get out of this situation: 'It is at the level of the annulled object *qua* symbolic object that the child holds his dependence in check, and precisely by feeding on *nothing*'. The child, in other words, is required to place himself 'between his mother's desire, which he learns to experience, and the imaginary object that is the phallus' (1994: 242). This sums up Lacan's (1994: 262) understanding of the preoedipal nature of the imaginary and symbolic relationship: 'the phallus as an imaginary object of the mother's desire constitutes an absolutely crucial point in the mother-child relationship'. The object is seen as tantamount to nothing, 'a signification that signifies nothing' (1994: 321), and whatever degree of narcissistic injury the child suffers at this level is counted as a 'prelude', if not a 'presupposition', with regards to the later effects of castration.

For Lacan it is the symbolic order that constitutes grounds for the earliest relationship; hence the 'pre-eminence of the phallus across the entire imaginary dialectic' that articulates genital development. The child's entire relations with his mother are seen as played out, symbolically, within the 'imaginary dialectic', precisely in anticipation of the oedipal situation. Indeed, the initial scheme of the child's relation to his mother does not simply precede the Oedipus complex, but also prepares the ground for this supposedly more momentous event. Preprimitive stages thus serve as a gateway, with a range of outcomes for object-relations. The basic assumption here is that 'all that is pregenital can be integrated at the oedipal level' (1994: 390). The child manages psychic reality, according to Lacan (1994: 248), by passing from the 'image' to the 'symbol' along two axes: (a) through discovering that 'the symbolic organisation of the world ... belongs to no one'; and (b) in coming to terms with the absence of anything beyond the imaginary game (the 'luring game') with his mother, a realisation that the (imaginary) game of seeing what cannot be seen, and cannot be seen because it does not exist, has symbolic value.

By contrast, Winnicott approached the object of need in terms of a *bona fide* gift. On the one hand, Winnicott acknowledged the illusion of narcissistic omnipotence and its ramifications for creative living. On the other hand, the positive evaluation of illusion posits the gift as a figure of the 'future-to-come' (*l'à-venir*), a permanently available potential space. Operative beneath the sign and, retrospectively, in excess of the symbolic phallus that exists *qua* absence, the primordiality of the gift constitutes an interhuman relationship in its own right, precisely insofar as it meets certain basic needs. As we have seen, for Winnicott the meeting of needs precedes the dialectic of satisfaction and frustration, and as such the primordial experience of separation and loss results in an unassuaged feeling of longing, rather than an acknowledgement of a constitutive lack. Longing may under adverse conditions become a type of compulsive brooding (*Grübelzwant*), but the sense of longing itself that bears upon primordial objects is an integral part of the horizon of psychic life.

Generally speaking, Winnicott's application of an existential analytic to clinical experience and to human existence at large, is incommensurable with Lacan's articulation of the relations symbolic, imaginary, and real on the model of structural linguistics and through a series of algebraic formulations. It becomes apparent from the perspective of need that the gift which manifests itself *on appeal* is not confined to a (primary) symbolic determination of oral activity; it is not a substitutive satisfaction for symbolic saturation and disappointment; nor does it make sense here to propose an already 'advanced signifying organisation', let alone the 'fixing down' of the acts of primary creativity as so many signifiers (Lacan 1994: 397–98). The primary act of love may be seen as integral to the vital function of living-there. The anteriority of the latter is not subsumed, in retrospect, by the virile function, by the structuration of the symbolic world in the Oedipus complex, or by the symbolisation of the castration complex. The primordial situation is not simply left behind. The vital function takes the form of a primordial gift. The gift is not yet a *sign* of love for either mother or infant, but rather, an act of gratuitous and ruthless love, respectively. This pre-supposes a theory of the unconscious (a) as a psychosomatic phenomenon, distinct from the impersonal symbolic structures of the unconscious (Anzieu 1975), and (b) as a relational rather than a purely intrapsychic phenomenon. Primary maternal preoccupation – including, handling and holding – and the infant's spontaneous gesture are each given before the gift signifies itself as a gift, and before the father becomes a determining function of gift exchange in the anthropological sense.

I want to insist on the distinction between acts and signs, between gestures and symbols. The mother meets the infant's need at the level of absolute dependence solely as an act of love, even as the infant's ruthlessness in relation to the mother may be seen as an equivalent act. The possibility of intersubjective experience is already available in and through these acts of love, where mother and infant propose themselves in their whole being. This is not to say that mother and child are sufficient unto themselves; the earliest relationship is nonetheless integral. The capacity for spontaneous human relatedness is evident from the beginning of life. This is in contrast to the *signification* of the gift, insofar as it requires the intervention of the father *qua* giver. Lacan's (1994: 211–12) interpretation rests on this point: 'The symbolic father is in some sense a necessity of symbolic construction, but one that we can locate only in a beyond-zone, I would almost say in a transcendence'. As such, the father is in a position to give, symbolically, the phallic object, or the gift of the phallus. The latter inscribes the gift relation in the symbolic order, where the gift signifies itself as gift, as a gift from the father. It is the very nature of the symbolic phallus, according to Lacan (1994: 144), 'to present in exchange as an absence, as an absence that functions as such'. The object thus takes the place of lack in the form of an imaginary construct. In a view that is based explicitly on the anthropological model of the gift (Mauss 1950), the symbolic phallus is conceived in terms of a singular relation to an object that is not one.

We are reliably informed that this is not 'an authoritarian intervention that stipulates ... there is nought to be found' (1994: 272–73). Rather, in accordance with the order of the signifier, the father structures what cannot otherwise be symbolically assimilated, what would reverberate unconsciously on the imaginary plane as the equivalence between phallus and child. Accordingly, Lacan (1994: 147) concludes that the love relation unfolds on 'the perverse paths of desire' (fetishism, transvestism, exhibitionism, homosexuality) as an imaginary relation; whereas the symbolic object reveals that 'what is loved in the love-object is something that lies beyond it. This something is undoubtedly nothing ... Since it is a symbol, not only *can* it be this nothing, but also it *must* be'. The trajectory of the signifier describes the movement from 'a phallic apprehension of the relation with [the] mother to a castrated apprehension of relations with the parental couple as a whole' (1994: 276).

Are we naturally disenchanted? The Freudian interpretation explicitly established disenchantment as a criterion of maturity. Freud reworked the Kantian question of enlightenment in relation to disenchantment as a condition of emergence from our self-imposed 'immaturity' (*Unmündigkeit*). Lacan was not the only analyst to follow suit. Yet the 'nothing' that lies beyond (the love-object) is open to any number of interpretations. The so-called 'beyond-zone' does not necessarily presuppose the constitutive function of the phallus as a symbolic object. Analysis of the dependence relationship suggests that the 'beyond' comes into play from the beginning, not in anticipation of the sanctioning intervention of castration, but rather, as a vital function of illusion-disillusionment. Winnicott's theory illusion-disillusionment indicates (a) that we cannot talk of the *want* to go beyond, transcendence is not found by seeking, and (b) that the driving force rather is one of failure (the mother's failing) rather than a combination of infantile intentionality and maternal lack. Winnicott (1971a: 10–11; emphasis in the original) observed that '[t]he good-enough mother ... starts off with an almost complete adaptation to her infant's needs, and as time proceeds, she adapts less and less completely, gradually, according to the infant's growing ability to deal with her failure ... *If all goes well* the infant can actually come to gain from the experience of frustration, since incomplete adaptation to need makes objects real, that is to say hated as well as loved'. Maternal failure is not a type of shortcoming or deficiency; fallibility is integral to maternity. The fallible mother is not the absent or unreliable mother but the mother who remains available as the good-enough mother.

Moreover, insofar as disillusionment, rather than castration, constitutes the way out of illusion, this calls into question the very idea of a 'pre-oedipal' relationship. Winnicott was no less instrumental than Fairbairn in directing the analytic focus away from the role of the Oedipus complex in psychological development, to such an extent that there no longer appears to be a rationale for the term 'pre-oedipal'. It would be more consistent to dispense with the term altogether, and to credit the dependent relationship as entire or whole. As for the Oedipus complex itself, the figuration or symbolisation of lack, including the so-called lack in the maternal object, is by no means synonymous with what Lacan (1994: 220) called 'the game of the imaginary phallic lure'; nor does a simple opposition between presence and absence, any more than the reference to 'good' and 'bad' objects, account for the inherent complexity of ambivalent affects and affections at the level of infantile dependence. To summarise the object-relations perspective: (a) the area of the Oedipus conflict is not the sole or primary determinant of psychic structure; and (b) the oedipal situation is not prefigured by a series of (perverse) imaginary harmonies modelled, as it were, on an extension of Balint's harmonious interpenetrating mix-up to postnatal life.

What do these observations tell us about the primary love relationship? We have summarised Lacan's view. Alternatively, Winnicott's (1971d) theory of object survival and the transformations of identification proves invaluable here, insofar as it allows us to reformulate the nature of the object in relation to absence and the negative. This remarkable late paper opens an entirely new and original path in psychoanalysis, which may yet prove to be Winnicott's lasting contribution. We can highlight the radical import of Winnicott's intuition, particularly in relation to the gift-object, by noting the overlap with Derrida's (1991: 14) insight that 'the simple phenomenon of the gift annuls it as gift, transforming the apparition into a phantom and the operation into a simulacrum ... There is no more gift as soon as the other *receives* – and even if she refuses the gift that she has perceived or recognized as gift'. Lacan focused on what lies beyond the object; whereas Derrida drew attention to the annulment or destruction of the gift as a precondition of what we might call the pure object.[15] The destruction of the object is viewed in terms of its very phenomenality, its appearance in 'the order of exchange' and 'the order of circulation' (Derrida 1991: 13). Importantly, though, the destructive element, in this case, does not amount to annihilation in the Kleinian sense. On the contrary, Winnicott (1971d: 91) noted that destruction plays its part in worldmaking, in making reality a principle of living – that is, by 'placing the object outside the self. For this to happen, favourable conditions are necessary ... the subject is creating the object in the sense of finding external reality, and it has to be added that this experience depends on the object's capacity to survive'. The theory of object survival re-conceptualises the lived experience of absence in relation to the outside world as distinct from a 'beyond-zone'.

In this respect, what the father gives the mother in accordance with the symbolics of debt, is brought into play, retrospectively, through an imaginative elaboration of the primordial gift-object, the gift as an enactment of primary love in the earliest relationship. This is not a theory of recognition. To the contrary, it is precisely the gift that is *not* recognised as a gift that is at stake, as distinct from (say) the fear of annihilation (fragmentation of the ego) as a primordial 'experience' of the death drive, or the catastrophic consequences of 'an insufficient symbolisation of the ternary relationship' (Lacan 1994: 153). Imaginary and even illusory relationships are not merely oriented to the symbolic but, rather, provide the very grounds for living-there as giving. Derrida (1991: 9; emphasis in the original) noted that '[a] gift could be possible, there could be a gift only at the instant an effraction in the circle will have taken place, at the instant all circulation will have been interrupted and *on the condition* of this instant'. How does this breaking open take place? What is it that drives the gift relation? These questions allow us to approach representation (*Vorstellung*) and the symbolic order as irreducibly fissured, overdetermined, in retrospect, by the preprimitive 'event of donation'. The 'instant of effraction' draws its energy from the immemorial gift manifest at the level of absolute dependence.

The overlap here between philosophy and psychoanalysis draws attention to some fundamental questions. The residual impressions, perceptions, and sensations of primary maternal preoccupation and of the infant's spontaneous reach for life, impressions generated by what was always *à venir* ('to come'), continue to interrupt the symbolic series of economy, exchange, and circulation. We have always been given something more to begin with than the *symbolic* object, something for which we continue to yearn. A feeling of longing, as distinct from the constitutive value of absence and the mother's own so-called lack, is integral to a gift that was always *à venir*. The promise of the latter is more amorphous than the desire for some other thing. Consequently, unformulated, unshaped experience persists as a feeling of longing alongside the survival of the object. To be clear, even as the maternal object eventually proves fallible, it confirms the *promise* of more life. This is what Derrida (1991: 14; emphasis in the original) means by the impossible possibility of the gift: '*At the limit, the gift as gift* ought *not appear as gift* … It cannot be gift as gift except by not being present as gift'.

To restate this paradox in Winnicottian terms, it is the 'area of illusion' (Winnicott 1971a) that allows for the possibility of the impossible. The impossible is not simply a capitulation to a nonsolution any more than disillusionment is a negation of illusion. The conclusion I draw from this discussion is that the *experience* of the impossible constitutes a point of departure and, as such, is traced in the immemorial gift – the inaugural human encounter between ruthless love and gratuitous love – as both a condition and an interruption of the 'circle of debt'. As a promise of more life, the experience of the impossible relies on an act of love before there is any question of the *form* of the possible/impossible in the oedipal situation. The order of priority here is both structural and chronological. A large part of *La relation d'objet* consists in Lacan's painstaking analysis of the phases of the signifying structure of 'Little Hans's' myth, the myth of the child's phobia; whereas illusion precedes both mythical structuration and the child's capacity for mythic play. In fact, Winnicott (1960a: 145; emphasis in the original) noted that despite the emphasis in psychoanalytic theory on the term 'symbolic realisation', this tends to miss the essential point 'since it is the infant's *gesture or hallucination* that is made real, and the capacity of the infant *to use a symbol* is the result'. The symbol is an outcome that presupposes a primordial articulation of the threshold between the realisable and the impossible in the 'area of illusion'.

The gift-object operates in this context, prior to the *use* of an object, as part of the necessity of illusion in creative living, a necessity that Winnicott specified in the link between the goodness of the 'good enough' mother and infantile omnipotence. The truth of the 'true self' is characterised by spontaneity which, as a result of 'the mother's relatively successful adaptation to the infant's gestures and needs', may be 'joined up' with the outside world. The gift-object mediates this impossible possibility, or what Winnicott (1960a: 146; emphasis in the original) called the illusion of omnipotence: 'The infant can now begin to enjoy the *illusion* of omnipotent creating and controlling, and then can gradually come to recognise the illusory element, the fact of playing and imagining. Here is the basis for the symbol which at first is *both* the infant's spontaneity or hallucination, *and also* the external object created and ultimately cathected'. Symbolisation presupposes a primordial gift the enactment of which as *l'à-venir* ('future-to-come') designates the 'beyond' as a figure of potentiality. The continuity of being in the primitive structuration of the psyche runs ahead of discontinuity as the mark of the symbol.

Maternité

Being shows up prior to object-relating, and prior to instinctual experience. It appears as a phenomenon of the givenness (*Gegebenheit*) of life itself as distinct not only from the thematization of objects but also from the symbolic representation of absence. Living-there cannot be conceived starting from any category, be it biological, psychological, anthropological, linguistic, or ontological. The interhuman relation consists in living life as a personal and creative experience is among the principal findings of Independent psychoanalysis. The idea is variously elaborated by its most distinguished practitioners – from Fairbairn, Winnicott and Loewald to Charles Rycroft, Marion Milner, John Klauber, Nina Coltart, Neville Symington, and Christopher Bollas.

Yet living-there cannot remain suspended indefinitely without further elaboration. The preoriginal preoccupation of proximity 'comes into a relation' as living-*with*. This involves the movement at the heart of maternity from the by-the-other of proximity (primary maternal preoccupation) to the for-the-other of responsibility, or substitution for another. Consequently, Winnicott (1945: 152; emphasis in the original) proposed that 'these two phenomena [the gift of the maternal body and the susceptibility to the gift] do not come into relation with each other till the mother and child *live an experience together*'. Experience issues out of the proximity of living-there, where primary maternal preoccupation meets the infant's capacity for spontaneous human relatedness. But how, exactly, does the preprimitive state of living-there become living-with? How does an object-relationship arrive at being an object-relationship? This brings us to Winnicott's main question. What does it mean to be a mother? What is a mother? The value of Winnicott's contribution, its real significance, is predicated on this turn from the presence of the Oedipus complex, and the central key of the castration complex, towards maternity as the paradigm of psychoanalytic thought. He was hardly in a position to ignore the father, the oedipal drama, or castration as the sign of the latter; indeed, he (1956b: 125) noted that 'the child provokes total environmental reactions, as if seeking an ever-widening frame' But the 'circle' as he envisaged it had as its 'first example' and integral formation 'the mother's arms or the mother's body'; maternity and the body are the parameters of the 'ever-widening frame'.

Maternity amounts to more than a role, more than a self that is identified with itself, or more than a coinciding of self with self. Maternity is *pre-occupied* prior to commitment, prior to decision; it is giving prior to the intentionality of volitions or the 'given voluntarily'. The mother responds to the child by saying, *Here I am*, rather than, *I am the mother*. It would be more accurate, therefore, to describe maternity in its full content as a vocation (a calling), or an inspiration, the inspiration by the other for the other. To be more precise, we can summarise the question of maternity on two counts: firstly, the mother responds by telling the child where she is rather than who she is; secondly, the 'good enough' mother, in responding in this way, does not choose the good. And no one who has not been called, anarchically (*anarchiquement*) and primordially, can substitute themselves for the mother, who substitutes herself for the infant. Maternity cannot delegate its responsibility; it represents a unique response that has no right to leave the infant alone in the impotence of being. The mothering of one's own baby is entirely personal and, insofar as infantile dependence calls for attention without deliberation, no one else could take over and do as well as the mother herself. The infant relies on the mother responding in this way and remaining preoccupied prior to making a decision. In more concrete terms, the mother holds the infant, even as it has a grip on her; at its most dependent, in a state of helplessness, and subject to primitive agonies of one kind or another, including the horrifying sense of annihilation, the infant makes a claim on the mother's 'adaptative technique' as the embodiment of goodness. In this respect, 'I am inspired' means 'here I am'.

The proximity pertaining to the primary sensory world of mother and infant is the condition for the possibility of 'a bit of experience' showing up in the object-world. The *experience* of proximity is at once an imaginative elaboration and a representation of more primordial proximity that signifies in giving. Winnicott (1988: 19) observed that the psyche begins 'as an imaginative elaboration of physical functioning' – including, not only the 'superimposition' of the self and the body but also the 'binding' of temporality. Psychism thus amounts to a thematic exposition of being, the being of emergent entities ('me' and 'not-me'): to live an experience together (with) signifies being, coexistence, and the visibility and recognition of faces. By contrast, the 'pre-original' signification of proximity – the signification of the-one-for-the-other – *gives sense*, precisely because *it gives* prior to the intentionality of the particular volitions. The infant reaches for meaning as an original creative activity, while the possibility of giving without recognition or recompense involves an 'exposure of being' rather than an 'openness upon being' or a 'discovery of being'.

I am drawing on the work of Emmanuel Levinas for these distinctions. Philosophical tradition and empirical psychology can do no more than overlap with one another: philosophy does not provide confirmation of clinical thinking any more than psychoanalysis illustrates philosophical ideas. Overlap, however, affords sufficient grounds for fruitful comparison. In this respect, I think a comparative reading of Levinas and Winnicott is warranted, largely, on account of the resonance in their respective renderings of 'maternity'. Anodyne readings of the 'good enough mother' obscure Winnicott's more sharply defined views concerning the good before or beyond being, the original goodness of creation. Levinas (1986: 211), for his part, draws attention to the 'traumatic violence' that maternity suffers, which he identifies as a paradigm of the transcendental ego that 'comes from our awakening by and for another', our going out towards the other without hesitation and without recompense.

The 'severe manner' is explicit in Levinas, where maternity is seen as 'substitution' or bearing *par excellence*.[16] Despite the fact that Winnicott was seemingly less emphatic in his approach to maternity, an unsparing attitude is nonetheless integral to his principal claims. In particular, the mother is 'good enough' only inasmuch as and because she is obligated by the good as the responsibility of care. Maternity designates the nature of care. For Winnicott, as for Levinas, maternity embodies this description. Thus, the overlap between Winnicott and Levinas is evident, above all, where they elaborate on the good that 'chooses me' before 'I can be in a position to choose', or before 'I welcome it'. The readiness to strive towards the good, distinct from the ability to make decisions, applies to maternity, but the readiness of 'going out toward ...' also accounts for the very impulsion of the infant's reach for life. The absoluteness of 'absolute dependence' takes on meaning in this relationship, which, in an ethical version of the facilitation of 'primary creativity', Levinas (1981: 125) describes as 'the very overemphasis of a responsibility for creation'. It is not a case of the mother loving her baby as much as she loves herself. Rather, the mother, holding her baby, has the gravity of the world in her arms. This is expressed in the mother's attitude towards her infant '*You mean the world to me*', an attitude in which the mother finds herself beholden.

Let us consider Levinas's exposition. I shall focus on what is most germane to my own study, rather than attempt a comprehensive overview. Maternity (*maternité*) is mentioned only in passing in *Totalité et infini*, originally published in 1961, where Levinas (1969: 278) introduces the term in the context of 'the protective existence of the parents' – indeed, to account for the recourse of filiality. There is no further mention of *maternité* at this stage nor any explanation of its meaning beyond these few brief comments on its relation to fatherland. More than ten years after Levinas's first major philosophical work, *maternité* is presented, together with the analyses of 'proximity' (*proximité*) and 'substitution' (*substitution*), as a central frame of reference in *Autrement qu'être ou au-delà de l'essence* (1974). In the two central chapters of Levinas's expository discourse in *Otherwise Than Being* – 'Sensibility and Proximity' (chapter 3) and 'Substitution' (chapter 4)[17] – maternity is described as the paradigm of the sensibility of proximity. The concept of *maternité*, therefore, occupies a central position in one of the most important and original contributions to contemporary thought.

The later work elaborates on the basic aim of *Totality and Infinity*, namely, to investigate the possibilities of a philosophy of transcendence as distinct from ontology and theology. How is it possible to think transcendence? For Levinas, the question calls for a reorientation of philosophy from ontology to ethics. In particular, he approached what he saw as the 'infinity of the other' through an analysis of subjectivity and its modes of responsibility: 'proximity', 'patience', 'substitution', 'hostage', 'witness', and 'traumatism'.[18] Responsible subjectivity, or what Levinas (1981: 96) terms responsibility of 'the-one-for-the-other', denotes a subjectivity 'traumatised' by transcendence, the 'transcendence of the approach beyond being'. The aim is not to treat being with 'distain' but to approach it on the basis of 'being's other', to credit that being 'takes on its just meaning' on the basis of 'proximity' (*proximité*) (1981: 16). Ricoeur's (1997) critical assessment of *Otherwise Than Being* focuses on what he sees as the 'greatest gamble' of Levinas's work – namely, the idea of placing 'saying' on the side of ethics and the 'said' on the side of ontology. Ricoeur (1997: 82) believed this presents two problems: (a) 'the difficulty, for ethics, of freeing itself from the ceaseless confrontation with ontology'; and (b) 'the difficulty of finding for the ex-ception that disrupts the system of being, the language appropriate to it, its own language, the *said* of its *Saying*'. In fact, Levinas (1981: 16) admits that the otherwise than being is 'understood in a being'. However, it is important to note that in this case 'ontology' refers to being's other (Levinas 1981: 3–4), an ontology derived from ethics, comprehensible only out of proximity. Levinas (1981: 159) was unequivocal on this point: 'Justice is impossible without the one that renders it finding himself in proximity'. For Levinas it is the forgetting of self that provokes justice and determines the possibility of rationality of peace, even as the other is remembered before the third lest it be assimilated to totality. The State thus issues from 'the infinity of the being-for-the-other of proximity ... the proximity of the neighbour' (1981: 161).

Levinas's two major works take a different approach to the same fundamental problem. *Totality and Infinity* is primarily concerned with the 'epiphany of the face' and the alterity of the Other, 'who dominates me in his transcendence' (1969: 215). *Otherwise Than Being* turns to the meaning of the self who *meets* the other and, thereby, is relentlessly exposed to 'the trauma of transcendence' (1981: xlii). In a formulation that opens an entirely new dimension, with respect to the primary love of the earliest relationship, *infinity persecutes the infinite* from the 'epiphany of the face' to 'the trauma of transcendence'. For Levinas, as for Winnicott, maternity is a primordial phenomenon of meeting. As such, *maternité* is introduced by Levinas (1981: 74) to describe the nature of care: taking care of the other's needs *as a giving*, a giving that gives otherwise than being. And the possibility of giving otherwise presupposes the 'happiness' (*bonheur*) of 'enjoyment' (*jouissance*). By 'enjoyment' Levinas (1981: 73) means 'the singularization of an ego in its coiling back upon itself ... the very movement of egoism'. Maternity is conceivable – indeed, as the paradigm of passivity and patience – only insofar as egoism embodies the enjoying of enjoyment. The formulation is uncompromising:

> giving has meaning only as a tearing from oneself despite oneself, and not only *without* me ... to be torn from oneself despite oneself has meaning only as a being torn from the complacency in oneself characteristic of enjoyment, snatching the bread from one's mouth. Only a subject that eats can be for-the-other ... The immediacy of the sensible is the immediacy of enjoyment and its frustration. It is the gift painfully torn up, and in the tearing up, immediately spoiling this very enjoyment. It is not a gift of the heart, but of the bread from one's mouth ... The immediacy of the sensibility is the for-the-other of one's own materiality; it is the immediacy or the proximity of the other. The proximity of the other is the immediate opening up for the other of the immediacy of enjoyment ... altered by the immediacy of contact.
>
> (Levinas 1981: 74)

The analyses of 'sensibility', 'proximity', 'hostage', 'trauma', and 'substitution' fill in the meaning of *maternité* further to the analysis of *jouissance*. In an attempt to replace the subjectivity of intentional analysis with the traumatised subject of proximity, Levinas (1981: 19) proceeds on the basis of the following itinerary: (a) subjectivity denotes 'a sensibility from the first animated by responsibilities', a sensibility in which the subject is permanently under 'accusation' and in the condition of being 'hostage'; (b) 'proximity' *is* 'the sense of the [subject's] sensibility', the proximity of the other is located in sensibility and, as such, 'traumatises' the subject; (c) 'substitution', understood as 'otherwise than being' (*autrement qu'être*), designates the basis of proximity; and (d) 'infinity comes to pass' in the ethical relationship of substitution, a relationship between subject and infinity, 'at the basis of proximity'. Levinas (1981: 19) points out that these concepts 'echo' one another, that 'the themes in which these concepts present themselves do not lend themselves to linear exposition, and cannot be really isolated from one another without projecting their shadows and their reflections on one another'.

Bearing in mind Levinas's caveat, I wish to single out 'proximity' (by-the-other) and 'substitution' (for-the other) as the main points of overlap between Levinas and Winnicott. Levinas (1981: 184) treats signification 'as proximity, proximity as responsibility for the other, and responsibility for the other as substitution'. Let us consider the meaning of 'proximity' and 'substitution' in turn. Levinas assumes that the absolute and proper meaning of proximity presupposes humanity:

> Humanity, to which proximity properly so called refers, must then not be first understood as consciousness, that is, as the identity of an ego endowed with knowledge or (what amounts to the same thing) with powers. Proximity does not resolve into the consciousness a being would have of another being [the me/not-me relation] that it would judge to be near ... Consciousness, which is consciousness of a possible, power, freedom, would then have already lost proximity properly so called, now surveyed and thematized, as it would have already repressed in itself a subjectivity older than knowing or power.
>
> (Levinas 1981: 83)

We can conjecture a number of propositions based on this understanding of proximity. Firstly, proximity 'appears as the relationship with the other ... Proximity is thus anarchically [*anarchiquement*] a relationship with a singularity without the mediation of any principle ... What concretely corresponds to this description is my relationship with my neighbour' (1981: 100). Importantly, the neighbour is a stranger, which means that the responsibility of the-one-for-the-other applies to people one does not even know. Maternity, on the other hand, circulates the 'assignation of me by another' as a kinship relation, although, in this case, assignation by the other designates 'a way of being affected without the source of the affection' (1981: 101) becoming an anthropological theme. Proximity 'is not any kind of conjunction of themes' (1981: 94), and insofar as the psychoanalysis of maternity attends to a relationship with exteriority prior to the act that would bring it about, it is irreducible to ontological as well as anthropological categories.

Secondly, proximity is not a relationship between two terms, between subject and object, or between entities already present in the object-world (me and not-me): 'It is not enough to speak of proximity as a relationship between two terms, and as a relationship assured of the simultaneity of these terms. It is necessary to emphasize the breakup of this synchrony, of this whole, by the difference between the same and the other in the non-indifference of the obsession exercised by the other over the same' (1981: 85). This obsession, a subjectivity obsessed, shows itself as *preoccupation* in maternity, where attention without deliberation holds one hostage.

Thirdly, proximity is an approach towards and contact with the other; it is a state of primary participatory belonging, rather than a primary total undifferentiated state. As such, proximity is 'contact with the other' rather than 'fusion': *to be* 'in contact is neither to invest the other and annul his alterity, nor to supress myself in the other' (1981: 86). As figures of being's other, preoccupation and participation do not cohere into a basic unity, but remain subject to an asymmetrical relationship, insofar as one is beholden to the other.

Finally, exposure to another in proximity is 'the immediacy of a skin and a face' (1981: 85); a face 'does not function in proximity as a sign of a hidden God who would impose the neighbour on me' (1981: 94). On the contrary, a face is 'a trace of itself', a trace 'expelled in a trace', which, as such, 'obsesses the subject without staying in correlation with him' (1981: 94). The *for* pertaining to proximity is a *for* of 'total gratuity', rather than 'an ontological conjunction of satisfaction' (1981: 97). Levinas (1981: 97) insists that the capacity of a being 'is insufficient to contain the plot which forms in the face of another'.

We can extrapolate a similar series of basic propositions from Levinas's text regarding the term 'substitution'. Firstly, 'under accusation by everyone, the responsibility for everyone goes to the point of substitution' (1981: 112). Responsibility for the other, when taken to the point of substitution, describes the ethical trajectory from 'the for-the-other proper to disclosure' to 'the for-the-other proper to responsibility' (1981: 119). The point is that the 'I' is sought out by the other. In this respect, substitution presupposes a new understanding of the person conceived 'under the weight of the universe, responsible for everything'. This is what Levinas (1981: 116) means by the movement of 'accusation' as an ethical trajectory: 'The unity of the universe is not what my gaze embraces in its unity of apperception, but what is incumbent on me from all sides, regards me in the two senses of the term, accuses me, is my affair'. Substitution for the other amounts to the 'expulsion' outside of oneself, the 'emptying' of oneself (1981: 110–11). Levinas (1981: 120) maintained that the 'gratuity of sacrifice' confirms the person under accusation as the-one-being-hostage-for the other.

Secondly, substitution has meaning only as 'an upsurge in me of a responsibility prior to commitment' (1981: 103), a situation that bears no resemblance whatsoever to self-consciousness. It is attention without deliberation. To be more precise, consciousness is affected 'before forming an image of what is coming to it, affected in spite of itself' (1981: 102). Levinas terms this 'persecution by another', a 'being called into question prior to questioning, responsibility over and beyond the logos of response' (1981: 102). Levinas allows that responsibility prior to any free commitment *is* a relationship, but a relationship 'that is not reducible to an intentional openness upon oneself, does not purely and simply repeat consciousness in which being is gathered up' (1981: 108). The 'accusative that derives from no nominative [*du se-accusatif ne dérivant d'aucun nominatif*]' (1981: 11) determines the sense of the 'oneself', precisely, as 'a responsibility that rests on no free commitment, a responsibility whose entry into being could be effected only without any choice' (1981: 116). It is in this sense that we can talk of the infinite persecuting the finite.

Thirdly, 'maternity' (*maternité*) embodies the proper sense of the 'oneself' as substitution, understood as a preoccupation prior to any commitment and incommensurable with consciousness. The involvement in 'maintaining oneself, losing oneself or finding oneself' is not 'a result, but the very matrix of the relations or events that these pronominal verbs express' (1981: 104). Levinas notes that the 'evocation of maternity in this metaphor' is confirmation of the proper sense of the 'oneself'. Maternity bears the other within the oneself, without recourse to fusion or basic unity: 'In maternity [*maternité*] what signifies is a responsibility for others, to the point of substitution for others and suffering both from the effect of persecution and from the persecuting itself in which the persecutor sinks. Maternity, which is bearing *par excellence*, bears even responsibility for the persecuting by the persecutor' (1981: 75).

Dependence and preoccupation

How far are these views applicable to Winnicott's thought? Winnicott envisaged meeting in terms of the infant's first 'environment', the mother's body and the mother's arms. The primordial presociological sociality of the maternal holding environment (space signifying potential), represents Winnicott's first major and most important finding. Holding also and equiprimordially exercises a *hold on* the mother, resulting in what Levinas (1981: 15) described as a 'trauma suffered by a hostage'. As such, holding demarcates a going beyond the spatial in the conventional sense of the term, an excess inherent in a worlding environment that precedes any sense of reality, society, or representation of the world. One's picture of the world is always a secondary elaboration based on sensations, rhythms, unformulated experiences, and the emergent shapes of the earliest phase of infant life. Looked at from this point of view, meeting is not primarily a mode of access to objects but, rather, an expression of the givenness of phenomena. In concrete terms, experience is given as the goodness of maternal giving. One has to be sufficiently enlivened, that is to say, held and handled in a sufficiently alive way, in order to 'live an experience'. The first semblance, in which illusion precedes the distinction between subjective and objective, presupposes a primordial accommodation and bestowal of goodness. In Winnicottian terms, the latter consists of a responsibility belonging to the 'good enough mother'. Maternity, conceived as holding *par excellence*, provides for the 'objective transcendence' of living-there by way of tolerance and understanding, passivity and patience, and substitution or bearing.

It is the very gratuitousness of maternal care that instantiates the primordial *tie* – the provision of nourishment, the tearing away of the mouthful of bread – as a phenomenon of primal semblance. The mother's patience, the concrete circumstances of maternal care, are founded on an essential indifference towards compensation in reciprocity. To begin with, living-*there* latches on by means of 'holding' and 'handling', and only then proceeds towards living-*with* by way of 'object-presenting' and the increasing objectivity of the object-world. Living-there is now open to the continuity of being. Winnicott attempted to define this process in his paper 'Primary Maternal Preoccupation' (1956a), which focuses on what it means to be a mother at the level of absolute dependence. The basic theoretic distinction is set out in terms of 'the good enough environment' and 'an environment that is not good enough'. Winnicott (1956a: 303; emphasis added) proposed that 'if the mother provides a good enough adaptation to need, the infant's own *line of life* is disturbed very little by reactions to impingement'. The infant's innate potential, including his need to act freely, unfolds most favourably with minimal disruption, or with a minimum of environmental intrusion.

It is 'enough' sometimes *not* to enter into the infant's feel of things – that is, to allow for the innate reach for life to proceed unimpeded towards the continuity of being: 'a good enough environmental provision in the earliest phase enables the infant to begin to exist, to have experience, to build a personal ego, to ride instincts, and to meet with all the difficulties inherent in life. All this feels real to the infant who becomes able to have a self that can eventually even afford to sacrifice spontaneity, even to die' (Winnicott 1956a: 304). Winnicott shares Levinas's (1986: 212) view concerning the anteriority of the good over and against 'evil'. Life is seen as antecedent to the so-called death drive. This is evident in the statement that the 'Good invests freedom – it loves me before I love it. Love is love in this antecedence. The Good could not be the term of a need susceptible of being satisfied, it is not the term of an erotic need, a relationship with the seductive which resembles the Good to the point of being indistinguishable from it, but which is not its other, but its imitator. The Good as the infinite has no other, not because it would be the whole, but because it is Good and nothing escapes its goodness' (Levinas 1981: 187 n 8).

Levinas (1981: 75) emphasises 'the anarchy of the Good', insisting that the good is 'better than being' (1981: 19). Winnicott, on the other hand, discerns the goodness of the good in the facilitation of being as living-with. Applied paradigmatically to environmental provision, the good may be determined first and foremost according to whether it promotes or hinders human flourishing. The good-enough environment enables the infant's life to come into its own; it meets the infant's need to act freely and, as such, provides a 'setting' for the infant's innate sense of aliveness to flourish. Essentially, the 'environment mother', as distinct from the 'object mother', provides for the *continuity* of potentiality insofar as the mother's breast becomes felt by the infant to be what he needs. The inner relation of spontaneity is a dependent relation. It presupposes a meeting-place based on a paradox, that is to say, where the infant imaginatively creates what he finds.

Dependence is integral to the inner personal structure of the 'true self'; it is simultaneously a condition of being alive and a structural trait of the whole person. In this respect, psychoanalysis, which is not a philosophy of the will, has discovered the clinical fact that lived experience is not a given; that primary creativity requires a meeting place at the origin; that the person exists of its own right (*persona est sui iuris*) only under certain conditions. We attain this basic insight from the classical Freudian interpretation: the 'want-to-be' is not equivalent to 'I will'. In more concrete terms, the infant *acquires* an experience of himself, that is to say, a self-experience as well as the possibility of self-realisation, only on account of a facilitative environment. The environmental factor forms the basis of experience: the diverse moments or states pertaining to the being of the emergent ego are situated, in accordance with its own potentiality, within the living structure of the acting person. This means that the good is a condition of being in the object-world; potentiality unfolds as inner continuity, as the persistence of the person or the personal ego, within the framework provided by the 'good enough' environment mother.

On the other hand, '[m]aternal failures produce phases of reaction to impingement and these reactions interrupt the "going on being" of the infant. An excess of this reacting produces not frustration but a *threat of annihilation*. This in my view is a very real primitive anxiety, long antedating any anxiety that includes the word death in its description' (Winnicott 1956a: 303; emphasis in the original). There is *something more* than death in the primitive anxiety of annihilation. The 'something more' in this case presents itself clinically as blank pain, unthinkable anxiety, or inner deadness, a 'primitive agony' that comes about under threat of extinction or oblivion. The threat of annihilation is incommensurate with the anticipation of dying. In fact, 'without the initial good-enough environmental provision, [the] self that can afford to die never develops. The feeling of real is absent and if there is not too much chaos the ultimate feeling is of futility. The inherent difficulties of life cannot be reached, let alone the satisfactions. If there is no chaos, there appears a false self that hides the true self, that complies with demands, that reacts to stimuli, that rids itself of instinctual experiences by having them, but that is only playing for time' (1956a: 304–305). In effect, Winnicott's analysis of reactivity: the reduction of the act of living to a mere *act in return*, draws attention to the two ends of life; it points to the fact that postnatal existence is already taking care of dying.

Somatic reactivity interrupts the continuity of being; whereas the act of living indicates the extent to which one is urged and directed towards more life. In this respect, the reach for life is inherently a reach for meaning, or what amounts to the same thing, for a life worth living. Moreover, Winnicott did not make a categorical distinction between 'reaction' and 'emotion' as qualitatively different types of dynamism. He (1956: 305) focused instead on the emotive dimension and the psychical consequences of somatic reactivity: 'where there has been failure [in the] first phase, the infant is caught up in primitive defence mechanisms (false self, etc.)'. While essentially reactive in nature, the 'false self' is nonetheless part of the personal structure of the human being and, as such, possesses its own dynamism. The 'false self' is a phenomenon of psyche. It structures the somatic ability to react as a psychical function.

The Winnicottian analysis of the ego and the mechanisms of defence focuses not only on the nature of reaction but also on what the infant reacts to. This brings us back to the 'severe manner', so to speak, of Winnicott's idiom and his 1956 paper concerning the mother's 'special psychiatric condition'. Winnicott's reference to 'normal illness' is consistent with his broad definition of what is 'normal'. In maternity, the state of being preoccupied with the infant to the exclusion of all other interests is described as follows: 'It gradually develops and becomes a state of heighten sensitivity during, and especially towards the end of, the pregnancy. It lasts for a few weeks after the birth of the child. It is not easily remembered by mothers once they have recovered from it. I would go further and say that the memory mothers have of this state tends to become repressed' (1956a: 302). Directly equivalent to Levinas's recourse to 'obsession', 'persecution', 'trauma', and so on to designate the one-for-the-other, Winnicott (1956a: 302) compared maternity at the earliest phase of infant life with 'a withdrawn state, or a dissociated state, or a fugue, or even with a disturbance at a deeper level such as a schizoid episode in which some aspect of the personality takes over temporarily'. This disturbed and restless state of 'heightened sensitivity' is clearly not all that the good-enough mother provides in meeting the child's needs. Yet the capacity for this extreme preoccupation may be seen as the indispensable groundwork for any further environmental provision in which the child is able to find meaning.

Based largely on the concept of 'preoccupation', Winnicott's (1960b: 42) theory of maternity epitomised the view that 'the infant exists only because of maternal care'; that living-there becomes living-with as a primitive developmental achievement: 'the infant and the maternal care together form a unit ... at the earliest stages the infant and the maternal care belong to each other and cannot be disentangled' (1960b: 39–40). The view was shared by a generation of postwar British analysts for whom the concept of infantile dependence, and the mother's identification with the infant, was *the* shared example of clinical thinking. Repeated in various ways in the founding works of the Independent tradition, we find a series of interconnected claims: (a) the baby is entirely dependent on the mother at the earliest phase to meet its needs; (b) the infant becomes *an* infant only insofar as the mother provides an environment that facilitates the infant's innate reach for life; and (c) the mother handles things, to begin with at least, in such a way as to spare her baby the shock of dependence.

Winnicott discovered that life becomes living on the condition that the infant feels held together by his mother. Living as *going on being* is inconceivable apart from the love that the infant receives from its mother, the availability of a so-called 'average expectable environment' (Winnicott 1965). Life persists in and through the infant's experience of a 'facilitating environment'. Experience itself is constituted on this basis. This is a clinical finding based on the analyst's 'acceptance of the reality of dependence' (Winnicott 1960b: 42) in the transference. Winnicott (1960b: 54) thus advanced the concept of 'dependence' as a transference-countertransference construct, distinct from both the biological concept of 'adaptation' and the sociological concept of 'socialisation': 'work on infantile dependence derives from the study of the transference and counter-transference phenomena that belong to the psychoanalyst's involvement with the borderline case ... this involvement is a legitimate extension of psycho-analysis, the only real alteration being in the diagnosis of the illness of the patient, the aetiology of whose illness goes back behind the Oedipus complex, and involves a distortion at the time of absolute dependence'. One is not dealing in this case with observational data; nor is observational research a source of psychoanalytical understanding. The same holds for Winnicott as for Freud: 'Freud was able to discover infantile sexuality in a new way because he reconstructed it from the analytic work with psycho-neurotic patients. In extending his work to cover the treatment of the borderline psychotic patient it is possible for us to reconstruct the dynamics of infancy and of infantile dependence, and the maternal care that meets this dependence' (1960b: 55).

Winnicott's reference to Freud is instructive. There is a celebrated footnote in 'Formulations on the Two Principles of Mental Functioning' (1911) that reveals the extent to which Freud (1911b: 219–20 n 4) simultaneously acknowledged and passed over the *fact* of dependence. Winnicott (1960) was among the first to clarify the fundamental limitations of the Freudian interpretation in this paper. On the one hand, Freud credits in passing the provision of maternal care, 'the care [the infant] receives from its mother' at the beginning. Taken at face value the brief reference in Freud's statement to 'care' seems to support the theory of absolute dependence. One could take the footnote to mean that Freud had mentioned an important matter, something that he intended to come back to under the heading of (say) 'helplessness'. The fact that he did not actually return to consider the matter need not be taken as a principled dismissal on Freud's part of its importance. This reading does not rule out the possibility of a throughgoing theory of early psychic life based on dependence, proximity, and maternity.

On the other hand, however, Freud (1911b: 220 n 4) states that the baby 'probably hallucinates the fulfilment of its internal needs; it betrays its unpleasure, when there is an increase of stimulus and an absence of satisfaction, by the motor discharge of screaming and beating about with its arms and legs, and it then experiences the satisfaction it has hallucinated'. For

Freud the infant who fails to find the breast turns to hallucinatory satisfaction, which, inevitably, proves unsatisfactory and therefore prompts
the infant to cathect reality. The infant is under pressure to accept the necessity of reality on the grounds of dissatisfaction. It appears that the more
frustrating it is, the more available reality becomes. On this view, thought
issues from an excess of dissatisfaction, while contact with reality is cast in a
universe of one's own choosing. The stoicism of Freud's position is re-
nowned. The criterion of necessity, however, proves inadequate on at least
two counts. Firstly, the acceptance of the 'reality principle' is modelled on a
solipsistic actor driven by intrapsychic forces. Freud's explanation fails to
credit the infant's emotional sense of living-there in terms of the two-body
formation of dependency and primary maternal care. Secondly, Freud's
statement refers not to the earliest stages of interactional life, the undifferentiated mother-baby matrix; but rather, to a more differentiated
object-relationship in which instinctual satisfaction and internal unconscious fantasies are already in play.

Freud viewed the basic human situation consistently in terms of the
drives. Consequently, Freud takes for granted 'the earliest aspects of maternal care' and concentrates instead on the situation of 'relative dependence' in which 'the infant can become aware of the need for the details of
maternal care, and can to a growing extent relate to personal impulse'
(Winnicott (1960b: 46–48). The Freudian interpretation does not allow for
the aboriginal feeling of being held together (living-there) prior to the drives,
the basic situation that pertains at the beginning of life where the infant 'has
no means of knowing about the maternal care' but receives what it needs
without recognition. The theme recurs throughout my essay that under
primitive conditions, the mother meets the infant's *want to be* without reserve. In this respect, mothers allow their infants to enjoy the illusion of
omnipotence *as an experience*, even as they themselves experience being
found/created. The emergence of mind out of life relies on the fact that
illusion opens the world to a particular *way of life*. Distortions are, to a
greater or lesser extent, inseparable from the infant-mother relationship.
Fairbairn established this as a basic principle of his psychopathology; whereas
Winnicott perceived fallibility as integral to going-on-being. By presenting the
lifeworld to the infant in 'small doses', while at the same time registering her
own fallibility, the mother ensures that the process of disillusionment is neither catastrophic nor comprehensive. A vital impression of the foundational
event – namely, needs being met – remains alive in the absence of the object.
The omnipotent illusion of 'creating' the breast (Freud's hallucinatory satisfaction) *lives on* in the no-breast experience as a trace of infinity.

I have focused in this section on Winnicott's rendering of maternity,
drawing certain parallels with Levinas's account, in *Otherwise Than Being*,
of a Self (*l'ipséité*) who meets the other. At the same time, I have avoided
presenting the acting person as an introject of maternal care, let alone a mere

product of the environment. As I have been at pains to point out, children are not simply the by-product of mothering or parenting. On the infant's side, there is a spontaneous manifestation of self-making, a freely defined movement towards living-with, in the very *activity* of the acting person. Winnicott located the 'transcendence' of the person in maternal care, but also *in the action* of a 'spontaneous gesture'. Accordingly, the infant's state at the earliest phase is seen in terms of 'constitution', 'sensation', 'innate developmental tendencies', 'sensitivity', 'spontaneous motility', and 'return from activity to rest'; 'instincts' may be included at the stage of absolute dependence only on the basis of ego development (the reach for life), otherwise reference to instincts is inappropriate. Winnicott gave us the clearest statement of this view that we have:

> The mother who develops [the] state that I have called 'primary maternal preoccupation' provides a setting for the infant's constitution to begin to make itself evident, for the developmental tendencies to start to unfold, and for the infant to experience spontaneous movement and become the owner of the sensations that are appropriate to this early phase of life. The instinctual life need not be referred to here because what I am discussing begins before the establishment of instinct patterns.
>
> (Winnicott 1956a: 303)

Analytic therapy is based on the assumption of an innate reach for life. There must be a sufficient determination of freedom – a constitutive 'act of freedom' (Symington 1983) – for the possibility of psychic change to mean anything at all. The concept of the 'acting person' presupposes an infant with innate potential. Life can come only from life. The potentiality of living is a given. This applies even under adverse conditions where life has yet to be lived. In this respect, at least, the psychoanalysis of maternity ventures beyond phenomenology, with respect to the caress of love prior to object-relationships, prior to living-with. The relationship between mother and infant accounts for the consummation of the ego as the one-for-the-other beyond egoism. It also constitutes the origins of psychic contents on the infant's part. Winnicott, in sum, extended the fundamental insight that relations structure the object, precisely insofar as preoccupation meets the capacity for spontaneous human relatedness.

Notes

1 See Winnicott's (1949; 1970) notion of the psyche indwelling in the soma, the psyche-soma continuity of being.
2 The combination of background and reach – feeling safe and being fully alive – places the drive in an irreducibly relational context. See Tustin (1985) for 'the rhythm of safety' as an interactive reciprocal relationship. Also, see Sandler (1960) for 'the background of safety'; Grotstein (1980; 1981) for the provision of

safety by the environment-mother, understood as the 'background presence' of
primary identification; and Alvarez (1992) for the capacity of the 'good object' to
back up 'feelings of safety' at the beginning.

3 See Winnicott and Khan (1953) for a critical review of Fairbairn's *Psychoanalytic
Studies in Personality*. The authors took exception to the idea that Fairbairn's
theory supplants Freud's theory.

4 Winnicott (1967: 101) only rarely acknowledged the fact that he was working in
'the territory of Fairbairn'.

5 Compare Symington's (1996: 120) notion of aggression as 'a natural endowment
of human beings' available for either 'destructive' or 'constructive' uses.

6 See Lacan (2004) for a further commentary on anxiety and the status of the
object.

7 The publication of the *Collected Works of Ronald Fairbairn* (1988–2005) in three
volumes in a translation by Pierre Lecointe, marked 'a turning point in the dissemination of Fairbairn's ideas' in France (Vermorel 2005: 53).

8 Mitchell (1981: 392) viewed the 'failure to account for the residues of good object
relations and the structuralization of the self on the basis of healthy identifications' as possibly the weakest aspect of Fairbairn's structural model. The basic
principle of compensatory internal objects is not in question; nevertheless,
Greenberg and Mitchell (1983: 180) clearly believe that Fairbairn did not provide
a sufficiently comprehensive account of internalisation, particularly with respect
to 'the residues of good experiences and gratifying relationships'. In his fully
considered view of Fairbairn's account, Mitchell (2000: 123) concluded that
'good and loving experiences, like bad and hateful experiences, also leave internal
residues', which cannot always be integrated with one another insofar as they
embody 'intensely affective experiences organized into different, multiple versions
of self with others'.

9 See Kernberg (1980) for an alternative view of Fairbairn's 'ego'.

10 Didier Anzieu (1989: 40) introduced the idea of the skin-ego as 'a mental image of
which the Ego of the child makes use during the early phases of its development
to represent itself as an Ego containing psychical contents, on the basis of its
experience of the surface of the body'. See also the ground-breaking papers of
Esther Bick (1968, 1986) on the experience of skin in the primitive holding together of the infantile body-ego. The skin comes into play, here, as a pre-object
relationship consisting of 'mother-and-child-in-the-family'. As such, it forms the
preprimitive groundwork for the operations of projection, introjection, and
splitting.

11 'The *Thou* meets me through grace – it is not found by seeking ... The *Thou* meets
me. But I step into direct relation with it. Hence the relation means being chosen
and choosing, suffering and action in one ... The primary word *I-Thou* can be
spoken only with the whole being. Concentration and fusion into the whole being
can never take place through my agency, nor can it ever take place without me. I
become through my relation to the *Thou*; as I become *I*, I say *Thou* ... All real
living is meeting' (Buber 1959: 11).

12 Compare Alice Balint's (1939) analysis of the pre-oedipal situation, an archaic
object-relation lacking any sense of reality, in which 'the frontiers of ego and
external world merge into each other'.

13 See Merleau-Ponty (1964: 166) for the 'interval' *between* the intentional structure of
the noetic-noematic: 'There is undeniably something between transcendent Nature,
naturalism's being in itself, and the immanence of mind, its acts, and its noema. It
is into this interval that we must try to advance'. The 'advance' is made in the
present study in terms of the object-relation in conjunction with the acting person.

14 'The introduction of the other is not what produces the "objective transcendence": the other is one of its indexes, a moment of it, but it is in the world itself that the possibility of the other will be found' (Merleau-Ponty 1968: 172).

15 We can speak of the primordial gift only as a pure object, an object outside any system of exchange and reciprocity, prior to the correlation of subject-object: 'For the gift to be pure of any movement of exchange, it would have to go unperceived by the donatee, not be received as a gift, not be a gift at all. The gift only "exists" or gives in an exchange in which it already gives no longer ... What is commonly called a gift or present is therefore only the trace of a pre-archaic event of donation ... This gift which does not present itself as such precedes any exchange' (Bennington 1991: 190).

16 See Ricoeur (1997: 93) on the 'verbal terrorism' of Levinas's ethical discourse.

17 Levinas (1981: 193 n 1) identifies chapter 4 as 'the germ of the present work', the principal aspects of which were presented in a public lecture at the Faculte Universitaire Saint-Louis in Brussels, on November 30, 1987. The 'talk was a continuation of the lecture entitled "Proximité" given the prior day', and was 'substantially the same text as the study entitled "Langage et Proximité" which subsequently appeared in the second edition of *En découvrant l'existence avec Husserl and Heidegger* (1974).

18 See Levinas's 'The Ethical Relationship as a Departure from Ontology' (1976), which was delivered during his last year at the Sorbonne (1975–76) as part of a lecture course on 'God and Onto-Theo-Logy'. Levinas (1976: 181) summarised the implications of the ethical relationship beyond (*au-delà*) being: 'The subject – the famous subject resting upon itself – is unseated by the other [*autrui*], by a wordless exigency or accusation, and one to which I cannot respond with words, but for which I cannot deny my responsibility'.

Chapter 3

Prospective identification

Freud has been the central figure for Independent psychoanalysis throughout its 70-odd year history and, in the previous chapters, I focused on the object-relation, the acting person, and dependence as the basic frames of reference in the Independent dialogue with Freud. In the two remaining chapters, I focus on the temporal nature of relational being. How do human beings experience their being in time? The prospective-retrospective structure of lived time is an intrinsic aspect of affective human experience; the 'percept can only acquire existence after affect has endowed it with duration' (Spitz 1972: 733–34).[1] Starting with the rhythms of maternal care and the infant's spontaneous gesture, the feeling for time is manifest as a dynamic, intersubjective phenomenon that admits renewal and renovation as well as frustration, defeat, and decline. The claim holds good for the full range of early mother-baby interaction – including, the innate aliveness of unintegrated, noninstinctual, and intractably silent ways of being. Freud addressed the phenomenon of psychic temporality in relation to the discipline of Ananke, a worldview that admits death as time's response to life. In the meantime, however, there is a possibility of more life – indeed, as we have seen, living *is* the pressure for more life.

In the following chapters, I address the experience of living-there and living-with in terms of hopes and memories. I discuss memory and reclamation in the final chapter; but I begin in this chapter with the limit-idea of hope. The phenomenon of hope reveals the extent to which one finds oneself in time (*zeitlich*); and by 'hope' I mean *living towards a possible future*. What Hans Loewald called the 'inner future', conceived as a projected action of the ego of the person, consists in the future that *I seem to see* but has yet to occur. Loewald's view of the temporal dimension of psychic reality is based on Heidegger's fundamental insight in *Being and Time* – i.e. that time is the horizon, the ground, or 'upon which' (*Woraufhin*) of the projection of beings. The Heideggerian influence is all-pervasive in Loewald. This is evident, for example, in the principal claims set out in 'The Experience of Time' (1971b): (a) we are through and through temporal in our way of being; (b) we 'encounter time in psychic life primarily as a linking

DOI: 10.4324/9781315280899-4

activity in which what we call past, present, and future are woven into a nexus'; and (c) the mode of linking itself is 'not so much one of succession but of interaction' (1971b: 143). Loewald reconceived states of mind as 'action patterns' on these grounds. Moreover, he is among only a handful of psychoanalysts who have acknowledged the value of hope – with respect, that is, to the relations pertaining among the modalities of time. And yet, as far as I know, there exists no critical interpretation of the influence of Heidegger's existential analytic of temporality (the *ecstases* of temporality) on Loewald's post-Freudian analysis of the 'correlative' modes of time.

The aim of this chapter, then, is to consider in detail Loewald's Heideggerian approach to time as an original and profound contribution to psychoanalysis, a contribution which counts among the major achievements of Independent Freudian thought. The idea of hope as a fundamental motivational force, indeed coextensive with the structuration and movement of life itself, highlights a major conflict of interpretations. Freud (1919: 236) consistently emphasised the illusory nature of hope from the psychological point of view of the ego-ideal or superego: 'the unfulfilled but possible futures to which we still like to cling in phantasy, all the strivings of the ego which adverse external circumstances have crushed, and all our suppressed acts of volition which nourish in us the illusion of Free Will'. The analytic emphasis on the disenchantment of hope does not end with Freud but remains pervasive and extends to even the most radical post-Freudian contributions. For example, despite his thoroughgoing revision of the structural model, Fairbairn's relational analysis retained a decisive negative evaluation of hope, with respect to the dissociated structure of the libidinal ego and its relationship with the exciting object. The promise of love in the future situates hope, conceived as a type of frenzied, need-driven longing, in terms of an 'obstinate attachment' to 'bad' objects (Fairbairn 1944: 117). The illusory power of the latter accounts for the negative evaluation. Expressed in terms of a radically new version of the libido theory, hope is nonetheless viewed from the familiar standpoint of ('schizoid') psychopathology, rather than normal emotional development. In a familiar scenario of emendable illusion, the hope for future love is treated in psychopathological terms as a defensive internalisation of 'bad' objects, what amounts to a defensive compensation for environmental failure.

Heidegger, on the other hand, maintained a strictly ontological focus on the meaning of the future. For Heidegger (1962: 395–96 [345]) the mood of hope is 'ontologically possible only if Dasein has an ecstatico-temporal relation to the thrown ground of itself'.[2] Thrown (*geworfen*) into the future that is coming towards us, we remain hopeful as part of a living way of life, a life that involves an understanding of being. Hope is part of how we are in the midst of things. We find ourselves affectively disposed towards hopefulness from the beginning of life. As such, 'what is decisive for the structure of hope as a phenomenon, is not so much the "futural" character of that *to which* it relates itself but rather the existential meaning of *hoping [Hoffen] itself* (BT, 395–96 [345]). The radical import of this view is discernible in the theory of potentiality. The envisioned future denotes 'the future to come' (*l'à-venir*), rather than the life that I will someday live; it presupposes the act of hoping (*Hoffen*) beyond what is identifiably mine in that which is 'hoped for'. Far from a mechanism of defence, hope is seen from this viewpoint as the embodiment of 'being as act and as potentiality' (Ricoeur 1992: 317).

Geworfenheit and dependence

The philosopher and psychoanalyst Jonathan Lear, for whom Loewald's work represents something of a beacon, draws explicitly on psychoanalytic thinking in his attempt to understand the end of hope and its 'radical' return. What should one make of an ego-ideal representative of a world that has collapsed? Lear has worked out part of what I mean by prospective identification – including, not only the action of identifying the future as such but also the identification of the acting person with the envisioned future. In his book *Radical Hope*, Lear conducts an ethical inquiry into the value of the future under conditions of 'cultural devastation'. The value of hope is starkly underlined in these conditions and I am indebted to Lear for his account of 'radical hope' as a peculiar form of hopefulness, an expression of virtue in which one remains committed to the inherent goodness of life. Lear (2006: 95) notes (a) that one remains hopeful beyond any understanding of what the commitment to do so might actually mean, that hopefulness is prior to commitment, and (b) that one is hopeful in terms of one's commitment 'to a good that transcends … finite ethical forms'. A trusting expectancy in the goodness of life, modelled on the infant's reach for a mother who *is there*, provides both a moral and an existential context for the futurity of hope.

The idea of *adventus*, a coming or arrival, may be seen as emblematic of the situation or 'radical hope'. Optimists appear to be buoyant in themselves and, indeed, confident about their *likely* prospects. By contrast, hope sustains us originally and primarily when we do not and cannot know what it is that we are hoping for from life. To underline the main point, quite apart from the 'hoped *for*', hopefulness consists in our feeling moved to invest in more life. Lear's discussion of the radical form of hopefulness expressed by the last great Chief of the Crow Nation, Plenty Coups, is an exemplary account of hope as a type of prospective identification. In this respect, hopefulness involves a reach for meaning *as* a reach for a living way of life, something that involves a spontaneous claim on living-there. The hopefulness of the acting person may be seen as a primordial expression of oneself, what Heidegger (BT, 334 [288]) described as Dasein's 'taking action in itself [*in sich handeln*]'. For Heidegger (BT, 183 [144]), Dasein's being-possible as '*thrown possibility*' is primordial. As such, Dasein's directedness has its basis in its 'thrownness' into its future possibility, or what Heidegger saw as its being towards death (*Sein zum Tode*).[3] The idea that Dasein has death 'ahead of' and 'behind' itself confirms the equiprimordiality of human relatedness and human directedness.

The Heideggerian hypotheses of 'thrownness' (*Geworfenheit*) and projection (*Entwurf*) reset the philosophical parameters of my inquiry. In terms of projection, Heidegger proposed that Dasein projects itself on its 'ownmost' possibility, precisely in terms of the possibilities open to it. Repetition (*Wiederholung*) is attributed positive value along these lines as anticipatory resoluteness: 'Repeating is handing down explicitly – that is to say, going back into the possibilities of the Dasein that has-been-there [*Die Wiederholung ist die ausdrückliche Überlieferung, das heist, der Rückgang in Möglichkeiten des dagewesenen Daseins*]' (BT, 437 [385]). For Heidegger (BT, 372: 325) 'letting-itself-come-towards-itself [*auf sich Zukommenlassen*] ... is the primordial phenomenon of the future as coming towards [*der Zu-kunft*]'. In terms of the past and future reaches of time, Dasein can only be its 'having-been' and, on the other hand, can only take over its primordial situation by anticipating its end: 'Only insofar as Dasein *is* as an "I-*am*-as-having-been", can Dasein come towards itself futurally in such a way that it comes *back* [*Nur sofern Dasein überhaupt ist als ich bin-gewesen, kann es zukünftig auf sich selbst so zu-kommen, dass es zurück-kommt*] ... Anticipation of one's uttermost and ownmost possibility is coming back understandingly to one's having been' (BT, 373 [326]).

Dasein exists by way of the past to which it returns, and for which it assumes responsibility, on the basis of the future; hence Heidegger's (BT, 373 [326]) fundamental claim concerning the future as the primary meaning of existentiality: 'The character of having-been arises, in a certain way, from the future [*Die Gewesenheit entspringt in gewisser Weise der Zukunft*]'. Dasein is always 'futural' (*zukünftig*) – it is always coming, or yet to come. And only 'an entity which, in its Being, is essentially futural ... can let itself be thrown back upon its factical "there" ... only an entity which, as futural, is equiprimordially in the process of having-been, can, by handing down to itself the possibility it has inherited, take over its own thrownness [*Geworfenheit*] and be in the moment of vision, for "its time"' (BT, 437 [385]).

Heidegger fashioned the term *Geworfenheit* from the perfect participle – 'thrown' (*geworfen*) – of *werfen*, 'to throw before, throwing before'. In setting the scene for the Heideggerian influence on Loewald's idea of the 'inner future', we can see the extent to which the *Geworfenheit* of the dependence relationship, manifest in the mood of hope, places human meaning more profoundly in its existential context. In particular, it reveals the extent to which hope instantiates the 'that it is and has to be' (BT, 174 [135]) of living-there. As such, the *Geworfenheit* of dependency is evident on four counts: firstly, dependency means being handed over: 'The expression "thrownness" is meant to suggest the facticity of its being delivered over [*Der Ausdruck Geworfenheit soll die Faktizität der Überantwortung andeuten*]' (BT, 174 [135]). Secondly, one is dependent beyond any say one has in being handed over: 'As existent, [Dasein] never comes back behind its thrownness in such a way that it might first release this "that-it-is-and-has-to-be" from its *Being-its-Self* and lead it into the "there" ... Dasein *is* constantly its "that-it-is"' (BT, 330 [284]). Thirdly, being towards independence is an expression of one's *ongoing* dependence: 'Thrownness is neither a "fact that is finished" nor a Fact that is settled [*Die Geworfenheit ist nicht nur nicht eine "fertige Tatsache", sondern auch nicht ein abgeschlossenes Faktum*]' (BT, 223 [179]). Fourthly, dependence is the doing of a certain kind of action, the taking over of thrownness (without getting behind it) in and through its 'projection'; hence dependence as 'thrown projection' or primary creativity: 'All projection – and consequently, even all of man's "creative" activity – is thrown, i.e. it is determined by the dependency of Dasein on the being already in the totality, a dependency over which Dasein itself does not have control' (Heidegger 1973: 161).

On all four counts, our dependence is revealed by the 'being already in' of hopefulness. We go on hoping for something as an expression of difficult freedom. All one's future possibilities – above all, the possibility of no more possibilities (*Sein zum Tode*) – are at stake in the irrevocable violence of time, its discriminations, divisions, and differences. The inner future of prospective identification is inscribed in the movement towards a future that has not yet taken place, but also in relation to one's own mortality. While the futurity of hope is immanent in the very movement towards no more possibilities, Heidegger's analysis of 'being toward death', or being-mortal, ties future time irrevocably to Dasein's 'for the sake of itself' (*das Umwillen seiner selbst*).[4]

To return to 'radical hope', Lear's central theme of 'cultural devastation' is underpinned by Haugeland's (2007b) reading of Heidegger's 'being toward death' (*Sein zum Tode*) applied to the *dying out* of a way of life. The latter comes about when it no longer makes sense for anyone to live in ways, and in accordance with the meanings and values, that prevailed hitherto. As such, the possibility of collapse is inherent in the reach for meaning itself. The possibility of the unintelligibility of an understanding of being – 'the possibility of the impossibility of any existence at all' (BT, 307 [262]) – is an ineliminable condition of all understanding. Lear (2006: 6) refers to this as a peculiar form of human 'vulnerability', the possibility with which we all live of happenings' breaking down. As we shall see in the next chapter, Winnicott's (1974) 'fear of breakdown' is a version of this primitive form of anxiety, an anxiety which tests hope and hopefulness in the face of despair. The patient's innate capacity for hope is called up under conditions of hopelessness.

Generally speaking, we find ourselves committed in the midst of life to a way of life that may nonetheless turn out not to be intelligibly possible. This results in what we might call a dialectic of hope and despair; by which I mean the enactment of a living way of life that embodies an understanding of being on the one hand and, on the other, the falling away of any meaningful possibility of doing so, the impossibility of all our possibilities. This accounts for the extent to which anxiety threatens to become persecutory under primordial conditions of infantile dependence. Klein has given us a thoroughly detailed account of this situation as an intrapsychic phenomenon. The account is based, specifically, on the innate disposition to destroy the goodness on which one is dependent. For Klein (1957: 183) the infant is anxious that he has inflicted damage on the primal good object due to the sway of primitive 'envy': 'I have often described the sadistic attacks on the mother's breast as determined by destructive impulses. Here I wish to add that envy gives particular impetus to these attacks. This means that when I wrote about the greedy scooping out of the breast and of the mother's body, and the destruction of her babies, as well as putting bad excrements into the mother, this adumbrated what I later came to recognize as the envious spoiling of the [good] object'.

A more comprehensive account of the situation places dependence in its environment. In fact, it is only in an interpersonal, environmental field that hope *takes over* despair and reclaims life. The process of 'taking over' in the service of life occurs by means of 'anticipation' (*Vorgriff*), the vital meaning of which, in the Heideggerian sense, involves the projection of oneself on one's possibilities. Not everything, of course, is provided by the mother; the range of possibilities in human maturation varies depending on whether the growing infant is 'resolute' (Winnicott prefers the term 'ruthless') or not in sustaining the reach for life.[5] Potentiality is not a matter of confidence and certainty; nor is hope an entirely conscious phenomenon. Nevertheless, prospective identification constitutes the implicit ground of any new beginning: 'It is not necessary that in resoluteness one should *explicitly* know the origin of the possibilities upon which that resoluteness projects itself ... The resoluteness which comes back to itself and hands itself down, then becomes the repetition of a possibility of existence that has come down to us' (BT, 437 [385]). Looked at from a Heideggerian perspective, the world handed down by the mother may be seen more clearly as an inheritance, something which she makes available to the infant in conjunction with hopefulness as a vital example in the workings of the imaginative life.

The primacy of hope

The hope that takes over despair *from the beginning* – that is, under the traumatic conditions of absolute dependence and helplessness – is distinct from a 'wish' in the Freudian sense. We imagine more than we lack, even as the approach (*adventum*) of hope is irreducible to the fulfilment of a wish. The distinction between hopefulness and wish-fulfilling optimism is central to my understanding of the 'inner future'. In addition to the basic frames of reference afforded by proximity and action, prospective identification provides a further framework for Independent thought, precisely on the grounds that the gratification of a wish and the espousal of hope represent two contrasting uses of the imagination. The distinction is based on the fact that wishes presuppose the satisfactions that hopes envisage and espouse. Wish is based on a prior experience of satisfaction and, therefore, cannot be a phenomenon of primary internal reality.

Freud viewed the link between wish and temporality as follows:

> The relation of a phantasy to time is in general very important. We may say that it hovers, as it were, between three times – the three moments of time which our ideation involves. Mental work is linked to some current impression, some provoking occasion in the present which has been able to arouse one of the subject's major wishes. From there it harks back to a memory of an earlier experience (usually an infantile one) in which this wish was fulfilled; and it now creates a situation relating to the future which represents a fulfilment of the wish. What it thus creates is a day-dream or phantasy, which carries about it traces of its origin from the occasion which provoked it and from the memory. Thus past, present and future are strung together, as it were, on the thread of the wish that runs through them.
>
> (Freud 1908: 147–48)

The Interpretation of Dreams (1900; 1900–1901) is the canonical reference point here.[6] The Freudian interpretation is modelled on an analysis of the hallucinatory reality of dreams, or the dream mechanism of negative hallucination, where the tension relief afforded by the hallucinated wish is seen as the motivating factor in wishful thinking. Ferenczi (1913: 221) noted that the model posits an intrinsic connection between wishing and hallucination based on the 'hallucinatory re-occupation' of a previously 'satisfying situation'. If, as Ferenczi (1913: 221–22) adds, the 'first wish-impulse' of the infant consists in the reclamation of the situation of satisfaction, then 'hallucination is in fact realised'. The infant imagines the wish has been realised; looked at from a subjective point of view, the infant 'needs only to seize the wish-aims in a hallucinatory way (to imagine them) and to alter nothing else in the outer world, in order (after satisfying this single condition) really to attain the wish-fulfilment' (Ferenczi 1913: 222). Consequently, the infant feels 'himself in the possession of a *magical capacity* that can actually realise all his wishes by simply imagining the satisfaction of them' (Ferenczi 1913: 222; emphasis added).

The account that Ferenczi provides of the magical character of wishful imagining may be set alongside Freud's account in the third chapter of *Totem and Taboo* (1913c) of the 'omnipotence of thoughts'. In the chapter, Freud defined the latter as 'the overvaluation of mental processes as compared with reality' (1913c: 87), a situation which he attributed not only to neurotics – including, the symptomology of obsessional neurosis (he cites the case of the 'Rat Man'); but also, in the analogous psychical situation of the primitive and the child. Children and primitive peoples alike are satisfied with the substitutive pleasures of play and imitative representation, according to Freud (1913c: 84), as a result of 'the paramount virtue they ascribe to their wishes'. The defensive tendency to imagine wishfully is thus linked to the technique of animism in which omnipotence of thoughts prevails. Freud (1913c: 89–90) made a further link between magical thinking and narcissism; he maintained that 'whether the libidinal hypercathexis of thinking is an original one or has been produced by regression', it results in 'intellectual narcissism and the omnipotence of thoughts'. The same argument concerning both the autoerotic projection of wishes upon external reality and the link with narcissism is repeated in 'On Narcissism' (1914b). Once again, Freud (1914b: 75) described the 'megalomania' of primitive thought and the infantile belief in magic in similar terms: 'an over-estimation of the power of ... wishes and mental acts, the "omnipotence of thoughts", a belief in the thaumaturgic force of words, and a technique for dealing with the external world – "magic" – which appears to be a logical application of these grandiose premises'.

The burden of Freud's argument is that wishes provide a narcissistic fantasy in mitigation of reality; hence a wishful replacement for an unbearable or intolerable reality. Yet the argument is not altogether clear. Bass (2000) is helpful here. He draws out the implications of Freud's idea that the wish is the revived memory of the experience of satisfaction; the idea that wish-fulfilling perception is brought about in order to avoid a 'registered reality'. The point is that in affording tension relief (the infant's experience of having hunger relieved), the hallucinated wish allows the infant to avoid an unsatisfying experience that has been registered unconsciously. In what amounts to a wide-ranging elaboration on the Freudian theory of magical-hallucinatory omnipotence, Bass emphasises the splitting of the ego for defensive purposes between 'registration' and 'repudiation'. The critical import of this reading applies not only to Freud's earliest ideas about tension regulation and hallucinatory wish-fulfilment, but also to the late work on disavowal and the generalisation of fetishism as a psychic structure.

Bass (2000: 104–105) relies on Loewald and his conception of time in differentiating the 'temporal immediacy' of wish-fulfilment from the 'intrinsic temporal' process of internalisation: 'Identification and wish fulfilment are atemporal in that they attempt to perpetuate an eternal present. Temporality, Loewald writes, is the possibility of a future reintegration with the environment which does not magically and exclusively attempt to make good a loss in the present, as happens in every dream'. Time is conceived as intrinsic to internalisation and its hopeful substratum. As such, the duration of internalisation 'implies the possibility of change of internal elements, because it is intrinsically open ... the time of an opening to the future' (2000: 105). This anticipates my own reading of Loewald. It is also consistent with my analysis of hopefulness – the idea that the internalisation of interaction denotes 'a time of differentiation and delay, the temporality of "not now"' (Bass 2000: 105). The vitality of hopefulness is not equivalent to wishful omnipotent longing, hallucinatory wish-fulfilment, or dream-like fantasies of wish-fulfilment. Admittedly, longing – including the longed-for revival of primary love – may be expressed in wishes as well as hopes; but unlike the 'de-differentiating identification of subject and object in wish fulfillment' (Bass 2000: 105), hopefulness is structured as an open-ended relation towards the future.

Wishing and hoping are distinct modes of the inner future, they cannot be defined under one head. The hope-impulse is primordial and irreducible to the first wish-impulse, the perceptual experience of hallucinatory recall of memories of previous satisfaction. In contrast to the synthetic activity of wish-fulfilment, absolute hope anticipates a possible future from the beginning – indeed, as the possibility of experience itself. It represents a primordial impulse in the infant, an impulse to reach towards life, rather than an attempt to relieve a painful, tensive reality by means of a wishful replacement. In the revived memory of the experience of satisfaction, the infant imagines the wish has been realised. The synthesis of temporality, according to Freud (1908: 148), rests on the 'thread' of psychic life (phantasy) that the wish affords us. By contrast, hope is essentially 'ahead (of itself)' – (*im sich*) *Vorweg*; it imagines forward (of itself) as an original manifestation of living-there. Wish comes under the heading of unconscious fantasy; it operates as such, in accordance with the pleasure principle, as part of the primary process. Hope, on the other hand, may be seen as a psycho-physical phenomenon (registration and perception); an inarticulate, preverbal urge of life; a primordial existential phenomenon that inheres in the first breath.

Identification and internalisation

Loewald provides a general framework for an object-relations theory of time. He published two key papers on time, 'Internalization, Separation, Mourning, and the Superego' (1962a) and 'Superego and Time' (1962b), which set out his main arguments on the topic.[7] We can add to these a third, shorter paper, comprising Loewald's contribution as Chairman of the Panel on 'The Experience of Time', held at the Fall Meeting of the American Psychoanalytic Association in New York in 1971.[8] Taken together, these papers present a remarkable trilogy on the mutually generative and open-ended meanings of past, present, and future.

Loewald approached the problem of time from what he saw as two complementary standpoints. Building on the 'paradigm-challenging difficulties' (Whitebook 2017: 315) in Freud's 'On narcissism' (1914b) and 'Mourning and melancholia' (1917b), as well as the revision, brought about by the second theory of the psychical apparatus in *The Ego and the Id* (1923b), Loewald's analysis of time was based first and foremost on the Freudian notion of 'internalisation' (*Verinnerlichung*).[9] In addition to the revised concept of primary narcissism and Freud's formulation of the structural theory (id-ego-superego), Loewald also relied on Heidegger for the idea that our being is itself, at bottom, temporal (*zeitlich*); that we understand being in temporal ways.

To begin with Freud and the concept of internalisation, Loewald based his innovative theory of time on a critical rereading of the structural point of view. Although he focused primarily on the futurity of the superego, Loewald (1949: 7) acknowledged that 'Oedipus, castration complex, superego, have all forerunners or developmental stages going back to much earlier ages than those originally postulated by Freud'. The acknowledgement of precursors of the superego has wide-ranging implications for our understanding of psychic structure. Ferenczi (1925: 267) pre-empts this line of thinking with his concept of semi-physiological 'sphincter-morality', the 'anal and urethral identification with the parents [as] a sort of physiological forerunner of the ego-ideal or superego'. Loewald, for his part, subscribed to the idea of very early psychological mechanisms that constitute 'forerunners' of the superego.[10] On this reckoning, the basic habits of learning – including, the internalisation of prohibitions – are acquired very early on prior to the decline of the Oedipus complex and the concomitant internalisation of the conflict of authority with the father.

The idea of preoedipal precursors of the superego invites comparison with the Kleinian development. Broadly speaking, the Kleinian application of 'internalisation' as a synonym for 'introjection' concerns the installation of objects or part-objects as the constitutive elements of the internal world. In this respect, as Loewald (1962b: 48) noted, 'object and ego become differentiated one from the other' through 'interactions' between internal and external reality. To be clear, Loewald was not convinced by the idea of a premature superego (existing at the oral stage) so much as mechanisms operating prior to superego formation that prefigure its existence. But while he did not necessarily find himself in agreement with Klein's metapsychology any more than her theory of clinical technique, Loewald (1977: 377) nonetheless allowed that 'problems of self-object differentiation [from primary narcissism] ... probably are not less but more universal and deep-seated than psychosexual conflicts of the oedipal nucleus of neurosis'. This amounts to a thoroughgoing reassessment of preoedipal object-relations.

In a model of ontogenetic development that allows for a degree of rapprochement between Freud and Klein, as well as certain Independent contributors, Loewald (1962a: 265) maintained that internalisation is 'structure building'. This means that internalisation constitutes the groundwork of differentiations and bounded structures in the maturing psyche. There are two aspects to this. Loewald maintained that the structuration of psychic life proceeds from an original, primal unity, 'a primitive stage of primary narcissism and primary aggression' (an early predifferentiated period) through 'externalisation' to 're-internalisation'. Furthermore, he argued that having become object-cathected in the process of externalisation, neither drive nor object is the same as before, but rather, is reinternalised at a further level of differentiation. It is also assumed that the ego itself becomes further differentiated in the process of structuration. The latter thus involves two types of identification – 'those that precede, and are the basis for, object cathexes and those that are the outcome of object cathexes formed in the oedipal phase' (1962a: 258). The early, less differentiated 'emotional ties', comprising ego identifications, take place prior to the constitution of inside and outside ('me' and 'not-me'). On the other hand, oedipal identifications, constituting the elements of the superego, are brought about by 'new experiences of deprivation and loss'. Oedipal identifications are seen as 'new versions … of identifications which preceded the oedipal situation' (1962a: 264). The 'new versions' inscribe the 'forerunners' of the superego, or ego identifications, at a further or higher level of differentiation.

Loewald (1962a: 258) did not maintain a hard and fast distinction between these two types of identification, but allowed for a continuum between the two with 'much overlapping and intermingling of them'. Nevertheless, based on the crucial distinction between 'a relationship to fantasy objects', on the one hand, and 'an internal relationship that is a constituent of ego structure' (1962a: 262), on the other, it is possible to set out a thoroughgoing theory of primitive emotional development based on the undifferentiated quality of early life. On this view, primary reality comprises the introjections and identifications which precede the oedipal phase. It remains a moot point whether or not they are preparatory in relation to oedipal structuration. Loewald's point was that later forms of organising experience do not transcend but, rather, rework the earliest form of experience, the undifferentiated union of mother and baby. As for the principal tenet of Independent thought, the constitutive role of 'dependence' in this undifferentiated matrix is evident in terms of 'the child's frequent experience of an impotent, helpless ego' (1962a: 268). The future is clearly at stake from the beginning.

That the superego is 'heir' to the Oedipus complex (Freud 1923b: 38–39 *et passim*) is not in question. Loewald did not posit a preoedipal superego.[11] Instead, he followed classical theory on two fundamental points. Firstly, he assumed that by relinquishing his libidinal and aggressive oedipal desires, the child transforms his cathexis of his parents into an identification with them – or, more accurately, into an identification with his parents' superego, understood as the repository of tradition (Freud 1933 [1932]: 67). Secondly, the same holds for Loewald as for Freud: superego morality is seen as the highest form of moral agency, rather than 'a first stratum of morality that has the function both of preparing the way for autonomy and of retarding it' (Ricoeur 1970: 449). For Loewald the agency of the ideal, understood as the heir to primary narcissism, is not in any way a restrictive category but extends throughout the moral life.[12]

Alongside the formation of the ego, Loewald elaborated on the transposition of a relationship, rather than an object, from the external to the internal world – most notably, the internalisation of the relation of authority between father and child in the relation between superego and ego. Modelled on the normal resolution of the Oedipus complex, elements of the relationship with the relinquished object are internalised, which also prefigures 'subsequent separations in which successful mourning takes place' (1962a: 274–75). The superego is defined as 'an enduring structure pattern whose elements may change and move either in the direction of the ego core or in an outer direction toward object representation' (1962a: 275). The definition allows for the continuous movement between internal and external reality as characteristic of psychic life.

The superego is conceived on the basis of the structural theory – that is, as a further 'grade' or 'differentiation within the ego' (Freud 1923b: 28). For Loewald, as for Freud, superego identifications consist of identifications with differentiated objects of libidinal and aggressive cathexis. With respect to the origins of the superego, Loewald (1962a: 257) consistently argued that the constitutive identifications of the superego are 'the outcome of a relinquishment of oedipal objects'. Again, rather than a premature or preoedipal superego, Loewald (1962a: 257) introduced the idea of 'degrees of internalisation' of greater or lesser 'distance from an ego core'. He substantiated this claim on the grounds that 'the introjects constituting the superego are more on the periphery of the ego system but are capable of mobility within this system and may thus merge into the ego proper and lose their superego character'. It is the degree of tension between the ego core and the superego, according to Loewald (1962a: 271), that renders them 'distinguishable'.

The concept of 'degrees of internalisation' underpins Loewald's general theory of structuration as a temporal phenomenon. Firstly, it underlines the significance of dynamic structuration (structure-in-process), with respect to 'shifting distances of internalised "material" from the ego core and shifting distances within the ego-superego system, as well as transformations in the character of the introjects according to the respective degrees of internalization' (1962a: 275). Secondly, the degrees of internalisation are conceived as temporal in nature, 'representing relations between an inner present and an inner future' (1962b: 276). The latter comprises what I call prospective identification.

Temporality

Considered by a growing number of admirers from across the board as 'one of the most seminal and influential thinkers in modern psychoanalysis' (Fogel 1991a: 4), Loewald may be seen as among the most important precursors to contemporary Independent thinking. The integrative reach of his perspective places Loewald at the forefront of the Independent tradition, equal in stature to the likes of Fairbairn and Winnicott in the British school. Chodorow (2003: 898) supports this view, describing Loewald as the 'founding father' of an incipient American Independent tradition, as well as an indispensable resource for British Independents 'who wish to ground Winnicott in a more precise and articulate metapsychology and conceptualization of the analytic process'.[13] I take issue with the second point. It is not possible to 'ground' Winnicott in Loewald's thought. They approached the task of thinking itself from entirely different perspectives, even if they shared certain preoccupations and themes.

What did Loewald bring to the post-Freudian development? Freudianism was the main frame of reference for Loewald, although I am hardly alone in assuming that an appreciation of his contribution, particularly, with regards to the articulation of time and conscience, depends on a full acknowledgement of the Heideggerian influence on his thought. Mitchell (1998: 835) surely overstates the case by suggesting that 'Loewald's life's work might be regarded as a kind of Heideggerian reworking of Freud's basic concepts'. Heidegger's influence is nonetheless all-pervasive in Loewald's account of the past and future reaches of time. Freud was the main source for Loewald's theory of the superego, understood as the intrapsychic representation of the future; but he was no less indebted to Heidegger for the *scope* of the theory. This presents us with a challenge. As well as one of the most strikingly original thinkers of the twentieth century, Heidegger is also a notoriously difficult thinker. This is not the place to address the difficulties one encounters in reading Heidegger.[14] Instead, I will comment on Heidegger's interpretation of 'the meaning of being' before turning to my main theme: Heidegger's ecstatic interpretation of temporality as a framework for Loewald's account of the inner future.

Heidegger affords Loewald access to the fundamental question of how human beings experience their being in time. His primary concern in *Being and Time* was to raise the question of the sense of being – to make sense of our ability to make sense of things – and to 'reawaken an understanding for the meaning of this question' (BT, 19 [1]). Everything in *Being and Time* proceeds from this 'reawakening' against the background of the forgetfulness and abandonment of being. The question about the sense of being, according to Heidegger (BT, 21 [2]), 'provided a stimulus for the researches of Plato and Aristotle, only to subside from then on *as a theme for actual investigation [als thematische Frage Wirklicher Untersuchung]*'. The understanding of being, in ways that Heidegger was at pains to demonstrate, matches the know-how of acting persons going about their ordinary, everyday lives. The understanding of being thus tallies with Dasein's understanding of being as a 'concrete' way of life: 'Dasein has grown up both into and in a traditional way of interpreting itself: in terms of this it understands itself proximally and, within a certain range, constantly' (BT, 41 [20]). The fact that understanding itself is Dasein's characteristic way of being itself provides the starting point in *Being and Time*: 'Dasein understands in its Being, and ... to some degree it does so explicitly. It is peculiar to this entity that with and through its Being, this Being is disclosed to it. Understanding of Being is itself a definite characteristic of Dasein's Being' (BT, 32 [12]).

The question of time is already and necessarily apparent in the fundamental question concerning the sense of being: 'whenever Dasein tacitly understands and interprets something like Being, it does so with *time* as its standpoint' (BT, 39 [17]). For Heidegger (BT, 39 [17]) all ontology operates in the horizon of time; he proposed that 'time needs to be explicated primordially as the horizon for the understanding of Being, and in terms of temporality as the Being of Dasein, which understands Being'. The explication, however, is not available in the extant publication; it would have been the topic of the unpublished third division of *Being and Time*. Nevertheless, in making the case that 'the central problematic of all ontology is rooted in the phenomenon of time' (BT, 40 [18]), Heidegger instituted a radical break with the subjectivist (Husserlian) conception of the subject. The explicit removal of time from the domain of *psychical* entities, where Heidegger believed it had been assigned by the tradition, places philosophical reflection on consciousness and its internal temporality on an entirely new footing. This is the topic under consideration, namely, Loewald's attempt to conceptualise the 'inner future' in the wake of Heidegger's irrevocable break with the concept of 'subjective time'. The further point I wish to make is that the 'inner future' reveals itself in lived experience as a type of prospective identification.

Heidegger uses two distinct terms for time, *Temporalität* and *zeitlich(keit)* – the canonical English translation renders these terms as 'Temporality' and 'temporality', respectively. For Heidegger, only Dasein is *zeitlich*, in time; whereas *Temporal(ität)* applies to being, not to Dasein or to any other entity. Being cannot be understood except 'by taking time into consideration'; while being and its 'modes and characteristics have their meaning determined primordially in terms of time'. Heidegger (BT, 40 [19]) refers here to 'being's "*Temporal*" determinateness [*seine* temporale *Bestimtheit*]'. In Division Two of *Being and Time*, he (BT, 38 [17]) elaborates on the fundamental claim concerning the inextricability of being, Dasein, and time: 'We shall point to temporality [*Zeitlichkeit*] as the meaning of the Being of that entity which we call "Dasein"'. Again, we have only the first two of the projected six planned divisions of *Being and Time*, and the extant publication concentrates almost exclusively on Dasein's temporality (*Zeitlichkeit*). The temporal structure of Dasein takes precedence in the order of argumentation, insofar as the temporal character of being itself may be approached only via the ontological analysis of Dasein as the entity that understands being. There is nonetheless a clear indication in the Introduction of the trajectory of Heidegger's thinking – 'the fundamental ontological task of Interpreting Being as such includes working out the Temporality [*Temporalität*] of Being' (BT, 40 [19]).

Assuming that the features we use to structure experience will necessarily be found in everything we experience, placed Heidegger in general agreement with Kant's critical project.[15] Loewald, in turn, challenged psychoanalytic orthodoxy with respect to the interpretation of the ego and its relation to reality, and in so doing relied on Heidegger's extension of Kant's argument. In particular, Loewald elaborated on the idea that time alone can account for all the ways we experience and understand the world and ourselves. Heidegger, however, went further than Kant in his attempt to 'temporalize' Kant's account of the transcendental subject. In this respect, 'Heidegger may be said to argue (*contra* Kant) that there is a more fundamental condition for the possibility of experience than Kant's categorical principles or synthetic *a priori* judgement(s) – the projective unity of the subject's transcendental, imaginative synthesis, and the unity of time itself' (Zucket 2007: 216). Loewald, for his part, adopted the general idea that time is not an entity but a dynamic process, or what Heidegger in his later writings and lectures increasingly referred to as an 'event' (*Ereignis*). The idea is already set out in *Being and Time*: 'Temporality "is" not an entity at all. It is not, but it *temporalizes* itself ... Temporality temporalizes, and indeed it temporalizes possible ways of itself. These make possible the multiplicity of Dasein's modes of Being' (BT, 377 [328]).

I have allowed that Heidegger is a difficult thinker and, as I think this last quote demonstrates, his analysis of time accounts for some of the more impenetrable passages of *Being and Time*. Loewald, on the other hand, believed firmly in the value of plain speaking, and he certainly did not ape the style of his philosophical mentor; nor did he concern himself unduly with the multifaceted complexities of Heidegger's philosophy. Despite the obvious benefits of Loewald's approach, the straightforwardness comes at a price. Loewald seems to have glossed over the fact that fundamental ontology, according to Heidegger, cannot be rendered as a psychological 'explanation'. This is a matter of some importance, as it concerns the basic distinction in the Heideggerian interpretation between the factual analysis of things (the ontic) and their mode of being (the ontological), between entities themselves and the being of those entities, or between Dasein's own being and being as understood by Dasein.

At the most basic level, Heidegger distinguished between entities, understood as anything and everything there is or could be, and the being of entities, which 'is' not anything at all – 'the Being of entities "is" not itself an entity' (BT, 26 [6]). The Heideggerian interpretation rests on this basic phenomenological contrast between (a) grasping what is and what is not true of entities, understood as *discovering* entities, and (b) grasping them in terms of a distinction between what is possible and impossible for them, understood as *disclosing* the being of entities.[16] Generally speaking, Heidegger and Loewald approached an entity of the character of Dasein (the entity that we ourselves in each case are) from different vantage points, but in terms of a common preoccupation with the past and future reaches of time.

An appreciation of these distinctions is necessary if we are going to consider Heidegger's influence on Loewald – indeed, even a rudimentary understanding of Heidegger's claims will allow us to consider his influence on Loewald with a certain degree of clarity. Loewald himself leaves these more general philosophical matters implicit in his writings. He was after all writing for psychoanalysts, not for philosophers. Moreover, it seems to me that Heidegger exerts no influence whatsoever over a large part of Loewald's contribution to psychoanalysis. From a Heideggerian perspective, Loewald was engaged in developing a regional ontology of psyche, or of the objects understood by modern psychology. Mitchell (1988: 835) proposed a comprehensive view, arguing that Loewald's life's work was tantamount to a Heideggerian reworking of Freudian metapsychology. It is hard to see how this view stands up to scrutiny. Loewald was nonetheless explicit in his intention to approach the 'conscience' of the ego-superego system from a Heideggerian interpretation of the future, '*(im sich) Vorweg*' – the ahead (of itself), or forward (of itself).

Further clarification of basic terms is in order. The fact that Heidegger tended not to use the standard philosophical vocabulary adds to the difficulty of his work. In his aim to 'reawaken' a feeling for the importance of the forgotten and abandoned question of the sense of being, he relied on a new set of vocabulary. The terms that he used for the interpretation of time divide roughly into 'two main groups – in effect, one for "temporality" [*Zeitlichkeit*] and one for "Temporality" [*Temporalität*] – each of which has a threefold articulation' (Haugeland 2002: 232). A summary account of the latter will allow us to see what Heidegger meant by Dasein's 'ekstatic-horizonal unity'. Heidegger takes up temporality as the ontological meaning of 'care' (*Sorge*) and 'concern' (*Besorgen*) in §65 of *Being and Time*, where he treats the sense of Dasein's being as the sense of care. The care of existence itself is understood in terms of temporality. As such, the temporal nature of care is revealed in its specific structural aspects – namely, forward-of, amidst, and already-in. These aspects correspond to the structural determinants of Dasein's temporality (*Zeitlichkeit*) – namely, the coming-toward (itself), the making-present (of entities), and the coming-back-to (itself). Dasein's temporality is set out, in these terms, as a process of temporalizing in the unity of the 'ekstases of temporality' (*Ekstasen der Zeitlichkeit*).

The analysis of what Heidegger called the temporal 'ecstasies' introduces yet more unfamiliar terms and concepts, although we have already touched on some of what Heidegger intended by the use of these terms. Dasein is seen as temporally 'ecstatic', which means that Dasein is 'thrown' beyond the here-and-now, beyond the immediacy of beings in their actuality, and projected into the futurity of the 'has-been'. The Greek word *'ekstasis'* means 'displacing' – from the verb meaning 'to put something out of its place'. Dasein thus stands outside itself; more precisely, it runs ahead of itself in the 'ecstatic' reach of tensed utterance and, according to Heidegger (BT, 437 [385]), is 'resolute' (*entschlossen*) in its anticipation of a future-oriented 'retrieval' (*wieder-holen*) of the past: 'The resoluteness [*Entschlossenheit*] which comes back to itself and hands itself down, then becomes the repetition [*Wiederholung*] of a possibility of existence that has come down to us'. I discuss the radical implications of §74 of *Being and Time* – the idea that 'history has its roots [essentially] in the future' (BT, 438 [386]) – in the final chapter on memory.

Suffice it to note here that Heidegger set out the meaning of the 'ekstases of temporality', specifically, with respect to the horizonal schemata of the ekstases: 'The existential-temporal condition for the possibility of the world lies in the fact that temporality, as an ecstatical unity, has something like a horizon' (BT, 416 [365]). Heidegger (BT, 416 [365]) was not concerned with the psychological meaning of ekstases as 'raptures' or 'ecstasies', nor yet with the sense of one's being 'carried away', so much as the movement of the ekstases towards the horizonal schemata – the '"wither" of the ecstasis'.[17] In his attempt to get at the gist of Heidegger's ecstatic interpretation of primordial temporality, Haugeland (2002: 235) proposes that 'the schemata are ... where the ekstases are "going"'. This is essentially what the ekstatic-horizonal unity has to tell us about the phenomenon of time conceived from a schematic point of view.

The horizonal schemata are divided as follows. Firstly, Dasein's 'for the sake of itself' is understood in terms of its 'ability-to-be'; hence a committed 'ability to be' towards entities *as entities*: 'The schema in which Dasein comes towards itself futurally, whether authentically or inauthentically, is the "for-the-sake-of-itself"' (BT, 416 [365]). Secondly, the horizonal schema of making present is defined by 'the "in-order-to"' (BT, 416 [365]). Again, what is defined by the latter is 'equipment' (*Zeug*), although as Haugeland (2002: 234) notes 'this must be just a special case – the horizonal schema of enpresenting entities has to be *entities* in general ... Although, one might *suggest* that there is a single horizon of enpresenting with several schemata – different ones for different sorts of entities'. Unfortunately, the extant text does not help us much in deciding the matter. Thirdly, the schema of the past ('what has been') is defined in terms of 'that *in the face of which* [Dasein] has been thrown and that *to which* it has been abandoned' (BT, 416 [365]). This characterises the horizonal schema of the past: reference back. The world 'in the face of which' Dasein is thrown and 'to which' it is abandoned defines the ekstasis of the coming-back-to (itself), while *at the same time*, Dasein is making itself present in the 'in order to'. Dasein *takes over*, becomes responsible, in a fundamentally 'resolute' way, for its being towards the ends of the limit, its mortality. The horizon thus demarcates the constrained finitude of human longing taken over as one's own. We experience the horizon as something like a facilitative bind, or enabling tie – indeed, a primitive type of identification with *both* the dead *and* our own mortality.

How one goes about understanding *the binding of the inner future* is a problem that Loewald inherited from Freud but also from Heidegger's ecstatic interpretation of temporality. The conflict of interpretations vis-à-vis Freud and Heidegger come sharply into focus here. If Dasein is not a person but a living way of life that embodies an understanding of being, then death cannot be understood simply in terms of the end of a person's life. Death and dying do not designate *this* or *that* moment of human perishing. Freud (1915c: 300) defined the acceptance of death as a task: '*Si vis vitam, para mortem.* If you want to endure life, prepare yourself for death'; whereas Heidegger understood Dasein's 'being toward death' as the horizon of the ekstasis of the future. Together, the horizonal schemata of the has-been, enpresenting, and the future designate the 'ecstatical unity' of temporality. Essentially, this is what Heidegger's interpretation of time amounts to: the ekstases of past, present, and future are each seen as a horizon – not things or events as such but a transformable field in which things and events take place. As such, the ecstatic-horizonal unity makes possible a world and the entry of entities into it: 'on the basis of the horizonal constitution of the ecstatical unity of temporality, there belongs to that entity which is in each case its own "there", something like a world that has been disclosed' (BT, 416–17 [365]). Elaborated in §69 (c) under the heading of 'the transcendence of the world', Heidegger concludes that horizonal time constitutes the world of beings, that it functions as the horizon for our understanding of being.

Conscience

Being and Time moves from an analysis of care to an analysis of temporality. Thus, before turning to temporality as the ontological meaning of care in §65, in the preceding chapter Heidegger sets out an account of conscience as the call of care. Loewald is indebted to Heidegger for an understanding of the care of existence from the standpoint of temporality. In particular, Heidegger's interpretation of the 'voice of conscience' (*Stimme des Gewissens*) underpins, arguably, the single most innovative aspect of Loewald's theory of time and the superego.[18] Loewald combined the key findings of Freud's structural point of view with Heidegger's observations concerning the existential-ontological analysis of conscience. In working out his own theory of the superego, Loewald took something from each of his two main sources: Freud was the model; Heidegger, the indispensable precedent. In effect, Loewald set about the task of integrating two sets of radically new ideas about time and moral life, with respect to the *temporalisation of conscience.*

My more immediate aim in this section is to summarise Heidegger's account of conscience, which differs in fundamental ways not only from the scepticism of the Freudian interpretation, but also from the prevailing traditions of moral philosophy. Broadly speaking, Heidegger challenged the 'ordinary interpretation' of conscience on two counts. Firstly, he privileged the ontological interpretation of conscience and guilt over any consideration of ethical content: 'The primordial "Being-guilty" [*Schuldigsein*] cannot be defined by morality, since morality already presupposes it for itself' (BT, 332 [286]). The interpretation concerns the structure that must be in place before the phenomena of having a 'good' or 'bad' conscience (a sense of 'good' or 'bad' objects) can occur. For Heidegger, the capacity for being 'answerable' (*verantwortlich*) is immanent, a claim that is upheld in terms of Dasein's 'authentic' (*eigentlich*) being itself, its receptiveness to a call to be itself. Being ready to receive the call is what Heidegger described as 'resoluteness' (*Entschlossenheit*), Dasein's undertaking of its own potentiality; understanding the call means 'wanting to have a conscience' (*Gewissen haben woollen*).

'Resoluteness' is Heidegger's best answer to the question of how the horizon of Dasein's coming-towards, the ahead of itself, can demarcate finitude. One is ready to receive the call, a readiness that is constitutive of the fundamental human situation: 'Wanting to have a conscience is ... the most primordial existentiell presupposition for the possibility of factically coming to owe something. In understanding the call, Dasein lets its ownmost Self take action in itself [*in sich handeln*] in terms of that potentiality-for-Being which it has chosen. Only so can it be answerable [*verantwortlich*]' (BT, 334 [288]). Taking-action, the doing of a certain kind of action, takes over the want to have a conscience. For Heidegger (BT, 338 [291]) conscience is not the 'certainty' (Gewissheit), or the 'making-certain' (*Sichvergewissern*), that one has not done something and, therefore, is not guilty: 'Becoming certain [*Gewisswerden*] that one has not done something, has *by no means* the character of a conscience-phenomenon'. The Heideggerian interpretation, which rests on the distinction between 'conscience' (*Gewissen*) and the adjective 'certain' (*gewiss*) and its derivatives, is clearly not a moral philosophy in the traditional sense.

Secondly, Heidegger did not treat conscience and the legitimacy of its voice – what we might call the authoritative voice of the ideal – as empirical matters of 'fact'. There is no attempt in *Being and Time* to trace conscience back to a psychical faculty in accordance with the ordinary ontical way of understanding conscience. Viewed from a Heideggerian perspective, conscience and guilt are not psychological problems, for instance, in the sense of our 'being burdened with inhibitions' (BT, 345 [299]). Properly speaking, Heidegger provides us with neither a psychology nor a moral philosophy; nor yet, a moral psychology. Instead, he approached the phenomenon of conscience in terms of a constitutive division of Dasein into a caller and a called. There is no suggestion that Dasein is *at the same time* both the caller and the called. The 'call' (*Ruf*) to take over responsibility for one's life and one's way of life is nonetheless seen as immanent in the human situation, although Heidegger believed that it is something we tend to evade or ignore. Here, as elsewhere, Heidegger reclaimed the language of Christianity; the fact that theology is seen as complicit in the forgetting of the question of being does not mean that Heidegger simply ignored the legacy of Christianity. On the contrary, his understanding of care, including 'caringness' (*Fürsorge*) for others, is profoundly indebted to the Christian tradition. This is evident in the key terms of his analysis: 'Being-guilty' (*Schuldigsein*); 'wanting to have a conscience' (*Gewissen haben woollen*); 'hearing the call' (*Ruf hinhören*); and 'fallenness' (*Verfallen*).[19]

Partly, then, through a reworking of Christian tradition, Heidegger provides us with the conceptual basis for a phenomenology of the well-formed conscience. Concentrating in the second chapter of Division Two of *Being and Time* on the ontological roots of the phenomenon itself, he treats the bifurcation of Dasein in terms of the following aspects of conscience: the existential-ontological foundations of conscience (§ 55); the character of conscience as a 'call' (*Ruf*) (§ 56); conscience as the call of 'care' (*Sorge*) (§57); understanding the 'appeal' (*Anruf*) and guilt (§ 58); ontological-existential analysis and the everyday ways in which conscience is experienced and ordinarily interpreted (§ 59); and the authentic potentiality for being oneself which is attested in the 'summoning' (*Aufruft*) of conscience (§ 60). I shall focus on three questions arising from these discussions that bear directly on Loewald's articulation of time and the superego. Taken together, the questions presuppose the radically new way of addressing ourselves that closes the Marburg lecture: not '*Was ist die Zeit?*' ('What is time?') but '*bin ich meine Zeit?*' ('am I my time?').

Approaching the question of time *as mine*, raises a first question concerning the call: to what is one called when one is 'appealed to' (*angerufen*) by the voice of conscience? For Heidegger one is called to the possibility for being oneself; the call appeals to our potentiality for being a self. Potentiality is accorded primacy over the postulate of a separate innate self. Heidegger was consistent in proposing that the 'call of conscience has the character of an appeal [*Anruf*] to Dasein by calling it to its ownmost potentiality-for-Being-its-Self' (BT, 314 [269]). We are 'summoned' (*aufgerufen*) as such *in potentia*. The hearing which 'genuinely corresponds to the calling' (BT, 324 [279]) simultaneously enacts the possibility of an inner future that incorporates an understanding of being. Hearing corresponds to a call that 'points forward', a call that is basically a 'calling-forth': 'when the call is rightly understood, it gives us ... the ownmost possibility which Dasein can present to itself, as a calling-back which calls it forth' (BT, 341 [294]). In the call – in 'wanting to have a conscience' (BT, 334 [288]) – we are invariably ahead of ourselves, reaching towards some future which beckons. In short, 'The appeal calls back by calling forth [*Der Anruf ist vorrufender Rückruf*]' (BT, 333 [287]).

Secondly, what does the call put before the person to whom it appeals? What does the 'appeal' (*Anruf*) say? Contrary to the ordinary, everyday interpretation of conscience as a sense of moral correctness, Heidegger is adamant that the call does not precipitate 'a conversation with itself' in the self that has been summoned. The so-called 'argument' of the self with itself is seen as a 'vulgar' recourse compared to our keeping silent in conscience. Conscience alerts us to the silence. Heidegger (BT, 318 [273]) refers to the 'reticence' (*Verschwiegenheit*) proper to the self as opposed to our everyday recourse to 'idle talk' (*Gerede*). Reticence thus denotes our 'wanting to have a conscience' (BT, 342 [296]). At the same time, the call extends beyond the jurisdiction of conscience; it does not place the self on trial through the familiar *agon* of self-consciousness: '"Nothing" gets called *to* [*zu-gerufen*] this Self, but it has been *summoned* [*anfgerufen*] to itself' (BT, 318 [273]). Strictly speaking, the call has *nothing* to tell us; it 'says' nothing which might be 'spoken of'; nor does it give us any information regarding events in the world. The call is not a type of reproving or approving conscience, accusing or excusing; 'in the content of the call, one can indeed point to nothing which the voice "positively" recommends and imposes' (BT, 340 [294]). The reticent, empty word of the call prompts Heidegger's (BT, 318 [273]) astonishing claim that conscience 'speaks' solely and constantly in the (uncanny) mode of silence.

Thirdly, who is the caller in conscience? The short answer is that we call ourselves in a well-formed conscience. The transcendent reach of the call is reckoned in ontological terms. Heidegger is not suggesting that Dasein is *at the same time* both the caller and the called. The emphasis on our being called *in potentia* mitigates against the conflation of caller and called. Loewald relies particularly on Heidegger's insistence that the self is called from its potentiality *as a potential self*. The formulation is concise but profoundly wide-ranging: 'The call comes *from* me and yet *from beyond me* [*Der Ruf kommt* aus mir *und doch* über *mich*]' (BT, 320 [275]). The impersonal nature of the call – '"It" calls [*"Es" ruft*]' – indicates the extent to which we ourselves have neither planned nor prepared for the call, nor yet purposefully brought it about. In Freudian terms, the ego is called – put under pressure, pressed in upon – by the combined forces of the id and the superego. As such, one cannot will the call any more than one can assume the spontaneity and force of nature (Loewald 1988: 79). But Heidegger (BT,

320 [275]) is equally clear that 'the call undoubtedly does not come from someone else who is with me in the world'.

This suggests a further paradox in which conscience not only 'speaks' in the mode of silence, but also reaches towards itself by way of 'an *alien* voice' (BT, 320 [275]). Dasein itself calls as conscience, and yet it does so only to the extent that 'it calls me [*es ruft mich*]' (BT, 322 [277]). Again, Heidegger makes no appeal to a being unlike Dasein when attempting to account for the caller. Rather, he emphasised the 'uncanny' situation of conscience in which the call issues from the potential self on the one hand and, on the other, is not something which is 'explicitly performed by me' (BT, 320 [276]). The call is seen to reach us in conscience 'from afar unto afar' (BT, 316 [272]) – precisely, to the extent that we have readily allowed for the constitutive gap in ourselves, that we are ready to overhear ourselves. What is called in the call of conscience is apparent 'in our understanding of the appeal [*Anruf*] when we *hear it authentically*' (BT, 341 [294]; emphasis in the original).

Inner discrimination

I have summarised the relevant Heideggerian hypotheses in sufficient detail to assess the use that Loewald makes of them. Loewald's writings seldom draw attention to philosophy; nor are there any direct references to Heidegger in his papers on time. While the 'trained eye' may discern the influence of Heidegger throughout Loewald's work, as Bass (2000: 288n17) notes 'there is never any direct citation'. The Heideggerian influence is discernible only through a critical reconstruction of Loewald's philosophical antecedents.[20] As regards temporal-ecstatic existence, Loewald was centrally concerned with the horizon of the ekstasis of the 'ahead (of itself)', *(im sich) Vorweg*, which Heidegger used as 'a formally undifferentiated term for the future'. While the future temporalizes itself 'authentically as anticipation' (BT, 387 [337]); the 'ahead (of itself)' indicates the neutral sense of the future that has yet to be realised either 'authentically' or 'inauthentically'. Loewald's (1962a: 273) theory of the superego is predicated on the inner future as *(im sich) Vorweg*; the idiom, as well as the claims themselves, are consistently and unmistakably Heideggerian: 'Only insofar as we are ahead of ourselves, insofar as we recognize potentialities in ourselves, which represent more than we are at present and from which we look back at ourselves as we are at present, can we be said to have a conscience'.

We are now in a position to appreciate Heidegger's influence on Loewald's account of internalisation and the formation of ideals. The central issue concerns the extent to which we are beholden, primordially, to a demand that comes to us from the future. Loewald (1962a: 270) describes this demand in terms of 'beckonings from a future'. In so doing he relies on Heidegger's notion of 'wanting-to-have-a-conscience' (*Gewissenhabenwollen*), which involves a fundamental choice between taking over responsibility for a shared way of life pertaining to the world of acting persons, or falling in with the way of the world by not taking one's responsibility responsibly. As an account of the moral life, the hypothesis of futurity represents a critical distance not only from the conjunction of the future and obligation (a 'should') in the tradition of Platonic and Kantian idealism; but also, from the Freudian interpretation of the ideal and the 'unconscious sense of guilt' (1924b: 166).

The problem of futurity enters the Freudian interpretation as part of the economics of ideals and demands. Together with an account of its origins, Freud (1933 [1932]: 66) assigns the superego the functions of watchfulness, conscience (*Gewissen*), and the maintenance of the (ego) ideal. We are left in no doubt about Freud's understanding of the relationship between the superego and the law. The relationship is defined unequivocally in terms of the internalisation of prohibited oedipal wishes. This interpretation seems to have proved itself in clinical terms. The question is whether it allows for a sufficiently comprehensive theory of anticipation and aspiration. Does the classical interpretation allow for the expectant nature of the well-formed conscience? Is there, in other words, an understanding of the nonderivative nature of hope in the Freudian theory of the superego?

Loewald provides new ways of thinking about these questions. In the third and final section of the first of his two main papers on time, and in the whole of the second paper, he elaborates a theory of inner ideals, demands, expectations, and hopes, on the one hand, and of inner doubts, fears, guilt, and despair, on the other. The aim is to cover our 'reaching toward or feeling defeated by a future' (1962a: 273). How should we understand this 'reaching toward'? What does the term 'reaching' mean in this context? Essentially, the postulated gradations of the ego – ideal ego, ego-ideal, and the superego – provide the conceptual basis for Loewald's theory of futurity. Combined with Heidegger's existential interpretation of conscience and the idea of 'anticipatory intervention' (*Vorausgriff*), Freud's alternate conceptualisations of the differentiating grade in the ego provide a comprehensive frame of reference for 'the future in us' (1962a: 274). The latter comprises an ideal that we have failed or have yet to realise. Once again, compare the decisive passage in Heidegger (BT, 314 [269]: 'The call of conscience has the character of an *appeal* to Dasein by calling it to its ownmost potentiality-for-Being-its-Self; and this is done by way of summoning it to its ownmost Being-guilty [*Der Gewissensruf hat den Charakter des* Anrufs *des Daseins auf sein eigenstes Selbstseinkönnen und das in der Weise des* Aufrufs *zum eigensten Schuldigsein*]'. The call thus embodies a fully extended reach for meaning. Heidegger (1962: 243) defined this in terms of a reach beyond the thing and, simultaneously, back behind us; hence a reaching-before and a thrown-back, or prospective identification and reference back.

Loewald integrates the ecstases of time with an account of the ideal agencies. The far-reaching implications of this conceptual move may be seen against the background of wider developments in contemporary psycho-analysis. Loewald remained faithful to Freud's structural point of view; he addressed the intrapsychic representation of the future in terms of Freud's alternate conceptualisations of the differentiating grade in the ego, which he conceived as 'successive stages in the development towards su-perego structure' (1962b: 46). For Loewald, as for Freud, the ideal ego (*Idealich*) represents 'a recapturing of the original primary-narcissistic, omnipotent perfection of the child by a primitive identification with the omnipotent parental figures' (1962b: 46). This summarises the gist of Loewald's argument on the matter – the idea that the agency of the ideal, in its increasingly differentiated form, is the heir to primary narcissism. Loewald posits something like a hallucinated or fantasied state of 'perfec-tion', which recalls Freud's (1895: 326–27) initial definition of 'primary process' – namely, 'wishful cathexis to the point of hallucination [and] complete generation of unpleasure which involves a complete expenditure of defence'. In line with the classical emphasis on the wishful, hallucinatory revival of the memory of a previous satisfaction, Loewald argued con-sistently that infantile narcissism provides the psycho-somatic grounds for narcissistic omnipotence not only as a fact of experience, but also as the impetus for the ideal.

But unlike Freud, Loewald made a distinction between the ideal ego and the ego-ideal; he may be counted among those analysts who do not treat the ideal agencies as interchangeable. There is a coherent precedent for this view in post-Freudian thought in Hermann Nunberg's 1932 lectures (1955) and Daniel Lagache's important 1958 paper '*La psychanalyse et al structure de la personnalité*' (1961). For Lagache (1961: 39) 'the superego corresponds to authority and the ego-ideal to the way in which the subject must behave in order to respond to the expectations of authority'. This allows for 'aspira-tion' and 'interdiction' as two distinct but continuous psychical structures. The distinction addresses Greenberg's (1991: 10–12) critical point that '[a]lthough most analysts follow Freud and stress the forbidden when they discuss oedipal resolution, the consolidation of what is permitted is at least equally important'; that the developing child 'feels pride in her new capa-cities, ambition to use them in a variety of ways, and excitement about her prospects for the future'. Furthermore, despite their conceptual disagree-ments, Nunberg and Lagache identify the ideal ego as a primary-narcissistic formation. Loewald, in turn, adopts the idea of the ideal ego as a discrete psychical structure characterised by a narcissistic ideal of omnipotence. Loewald is also indebted to Lagache for the emphasis on omnipotent pri-mary identification (with the mother), primal differentiation, and the structuration of the ego in general.

Freud was silent on the contrasting incentives of fear and love in relation to the superego and ego-ideal, respectively, although in a late formulation he (1939: 117) concedes that prior to the internalisation of parental authority as a superego, 'the threat of loss or love and the claims of instinct' are coupled with 'an instinctual renunciation out of love for one's parents'. Freudian metapsychology restricts elaboration on these distinctions; whereas Loewald invites discussion of the different motives of inner discrimination. In elaborating on the theory of ideal agencies from a combined Heideggerian and Freudian perspective, Loewald privileged the not-yet-conceived significance of the past in relation to the future as 'coming towards'. The not-yet-conceived is not a reference to the Freudian notion of repression; nor does it call for the lifting of the repressed on the model of the neurotic transference. In discussing the function of repression, Loewald emphasised the 'loosening' of the connections between primary and secondary process thinking, rather than the denial of access to consciousness for an impulse, thought, image, or memory. This, in turn, delimits the form and function of the futurity of the ego-superego system. The 'not yet' denotes more than a future that will one day be present. The additional emphasis on incompleteness, understood as an inherent aspect of temporal structuration, refers to the potentiality of life itself manifest as psychical and existential movements into a future. The 'not yet' consists of 'beckonings from a future' (Loewald 1962a: 270) that will never exist in the present. Even as our needs are met and our wishes are fulfilled, the coming-towards (itself) 'futurally', in such a way that it comes-back, exerts a pressure for yet more life. Beckonings from the future denote the existence of 'non-climatic' phenomena in psychic life – indeed, phenomena that 'have a status of their own, as opposed to being derived from discharge processes' (Loewald 1988: 27).

In order to account for the pressure towards more life as integral to psychic temporality, we need a primordial definition of hope and the mechanism of prospective identification. I propose we reserve the notion of 'hope' – in the primordial sense – for that which opens us to time, namely, hope as the reaching-forward with respect to the possibility of being ourselves. Hope thus announces and inaugurates an inner future that is always heterogeneous to the present. Hope will always press for more. But can we speak coherently of an ethics of hope? In response to this question, my proposal is that imaginative elaboration furnishes the agency of the ideal, the inner moral workings of the acting person, with an extended existential and psychological reach. Loewald (1949: 6) advanced a coherent argument along these lines, in which the ideal, understood as an unconscious identification, seeks to reclaim an 'original identity' with the environment: 'As the mother becomes outside, and hand in hand with this, the child an inside, there arises a tension system between the two. Expressed in different terms, libidinal forces arise between infant and mother. As infant (mouth) and mother (breast) are not identical, or better, not one whole, any longer, a libidinal flow between infant and mother originates, in an urge towards re-establishing the original unity'. Looked at from the perspective of temporal-ecstatic existence, the longed-for restoration of original, primal unity, the reclamation of primary narcissism, is open-ended in nature. In conjunction with the constitution of a libidinal object, the ideal that proceeds from the constitutive imagination of early life inscribes in the psyche an immemorial beckoning from a future that we envisage but never reach. Prospective identification sustains the reach for meaning along these lines, that is to say, as a type of primary identity in which the mother reflects back to the infant a sense of its own living-there.

The infant's imaginative elaboration of psychosomatic life proceeds from prospective identification to the coherence of the object-world. Fantasy and the ideal work in tandem: far from distorting reality, the infant's imaginative experience, in due course, facilitates a more realistic comprehension of the object-relationship and its potentiality. At the same time, the ideal reveals the extent to which imagination and hope are indissociably linked. A revival of this primordial situation is observable in the analytic encounter: 'We know from analytic as well as from life experience that new spurts of self-development may be intimately connected with such "regressive" rediscoveries of oneself as may occur through the establishment of new object-relationships, and this means: new discovery of "objects." I say new discovery of objects, and not discovery of new objects, because the essence of such new object-relationships is the opportunity they offer for rediscovery of the early paths of the development of object-relations, leading to a new way of relating to objects as well as of being and relating to oneself' (Loewald 1960: 225).

An increasingly realistic comprehension of the potentiality of object-relationships presupposes the continuity of enchantment-disenchantment, as well as primary and secondary processes. The 'perfectibility' (Loewald 1962a: 269) of the idealised object maintains its roots in the primitive imaginative activity that defines living-there, and as such provides the vital means of linking the ego and reality. The object-world is structured in a mutual relation with an increasingly organised and organising ego capacity rooted in the agency of the ideal. For Loewald (1962b: 47) the state of 'perfection' of the ego denotes 'the ideal undifferentiated phase where neither id nor ego nor environment are differentiated from one another'. At the most primitive level of primary nondifferentiation, one cannot speak of 'projection' or 'introjection' as defences against intrapsychic conflict or environmental deficiency. Unlike Klein or Fairbairn, Loewald does not allow for the processes of defensive projection and introjection from the beginning of life. In a more broadly conceived critique of the contemporary psychoanalytic literature, Loewald (1988: 77) focused on internalisation, structuration, and identification, rather than unconscious internal objects and the idea of 'a separate innate, individual core or a core self in the infant'.

I shall come back to Loewald's theory of projection/introjection in a moment, but first I want to draw attention to his emphasis on the problem of boundary formation, rather than defence mechanisms: 'primary externalization signifies that *externality is being established*; primary internalization signifies that *internality is being constituted* (1962a: 266; emphasis in the original). The point is that projection and introjection operate as comprehensive mechanisms only after the formation of externality and internality, after boundaries and structures have been established by means of primitive links. The same applies to libidinal and aggressive drives, which cannot be directed towards an object or towards the ego (subject) prior to the formation of inside and outside. For Loewald (1960: 235) 'the world is not organized by the primitive psychic apparatus in such a way that objects are differentiated'. This rules against the possibility of primitive 'part-objects' or 'object-fragments', a conceptualisation of early psychic life which Loewald (1960: 236) discounted in favour of the existence of 'shapes' or 'configurations of an indeterminate degree and a fluidity of organization'. Primary identity operates in this context, that is to say, where the maternal environment provides the infant with an 'indeterminate' configuration as part of the groundwork of self-experience.

Loewald described an inner reality in which things take shape for an increasingly differentiated ego. The latter, in turn, shapes itself, its drives, and its experience of the outside world in the form of ever-increasing differentiated unities. A combined ego-psychology and object-relations approach is clearly evident in this account of how minds develop and identities form. The principal claim is that whatever drives the infant is shaped by interaction with the mother; that emergent object-relationship depends on the libidinal cathexis of the mother. Loewald takes his lead from the later Freud of *Civilization and Its Discontents*, while at the same time allowing for the full complexity of the Freudian interpretation: 'While the picture of the ego as a pathetic "frontier creature" trying to fend off intrusions of the external world, is a dominant image in Freud's writing, Loewald reminds us that it is not the only image to be found there' (Lear 1996: 129). Accordingly, Loewald (1978a: 194) cites a passage from *Civilization and Its Discontents* in which Freud, turning his mind to the emerging ego of the new-born child, assumes that the ego and external reality 'differentiate from and organize each other instead of being seen as accomplished facts *ab initio*'.

Further to the reclamation of infantile fantasy (the lost unity of the mother-baby matrix) in the ideal ego, the narcissistic perfection of the latter is cast before the ego in the ego-ideal (*Ichideal*). The reach for life becomes a reach for something; Eros expresses itself as a definite developmental force on the grounds that something that matters is put before the ego. Freud introduced a terminological distinction but did not differentiate conceptually between the 'ideal ego' (*Idealich*) and the 'ego-ideal' (*Ichideal*). Nevertheless, he treated the latter as a specific agency based on the idealisation of the ego, understood as a reformation of primary narcissism, combined with an identification with the parents. The classical theory also accounts for the way in which the ideal is cast before the ego – that is, in terms of the narcissistic perfection of early infancy: 'What [the child] projects before him as his ideal is the substitute for the lost narcissism of his child-hood in which he was his own ideal' (Freud 1914b: 94).

Loewald defined this more differentiated psychical arrangement from the perspective of projection-introjection. He argued that further to primary externalisation-internalisation (and I would add primary identity), the ideal is formed by means of the mutual interaction between parents and child – including, the projective unconscious fantasies of the parents, as well as the, fantasises of the child. For Loewald (1962a: 269) the deeply interactive nature of this process comprises the 'infantile projective fantasies of the parent's omnipotent perfection', on the one hand, and the 'parental projective fanta-sies of the child's narcissistic perfection and wholeness', on the other. Following the reciprocal co-creation of the mouth-breast event, the ideal itself is seen as an irreducibly intersubjective phenomenon, where the child's ex-perience of omnipotence is coupled with parental idealisations of the child at a more differentiated level of internalisation and externalisation.

In a radically revised version of the structural model, the agency of the ideal is situated in an interactive context. The ideal thus operates through the processes of mutual cathexis and mutual projection, understood in terms of the child's and the parents' projective and prospective fantasises. In this context, the ideal becomes an ideal *for* the ego. This forms part of what Freud (1921: 105) described as 'the irresistible advance towards a unification of mental life'. Loewald developed this idea far beyond anything we find in Freud. In a thoroughly positive reevaluation of the ideal and its imaginative substrate, Loewald (1962b: 47) reiterates the connection between perfection and the future in terms of the unifying *conatus* of psychic life (Eros): 'Perfection now is to be attained by participation in [the parents'] perfection and omnipotence on the basis of an as yet incomplete distinction between inside and outside, between ego and parental object'. Evidently, Loewald was not preoccupied with structuration to the exclusion of the 'magical' dimension of human experience: the ego-ideal involves a type of 'magical participation' that is no less indebted to imaginative elaboration than the ideal ego. It would be a mistake to set Loewald's emphasis on mutual ca-thexis and the child's and parents' projective/prospective fantasies apart from his abiding concern with 'magical' communication and participation. Indeed, in a further elaboration of 'the future in us', the ideal is cast before the ego by means of an identificatory merger with the 'magical object'. The process is conceived as a beckoning of the future, a future that is envisaged *for* the ego, although it is not yet a future *of* the ego (Loewald 1962b: 47).

Imagination and reality

Loewald's theory of inner discrimination is based on the classical structural model. A further advance along these lines is discernible in his critical en-gagement with Winnicott. The question of illusion brings Loewald's disagreements with Winnicott into focus. Why did Loewald object to Winnicott's theory of illusion? Essentially, he believed, not unreasonably, that '*being deceived about the reality of something* is central to illusion' (1988: 70; emphasis in the original). The idea that illusions are beliefs motivated by wishes is authorised by Freud and promulgated by the culture at large. Loewald appears to be at odds with Winnicott on these grounds. We can summarise his objections on three counts.

Firstly, Loewald (1988: 72–73) argued that it is 'misleading to speak of the infant's primary creativity as purely subjective' on the grounds that psychic development originates from an undifferentiated state 'prior to the differentiation of subjectivity and objectivity'. Winnicott (1988: 104) proposed that at the 'early stage' of its life the infant enjoys 'the illusion that what is created out of need and by impulse has real existence'. Loewald countered that, to begin with, there is no 'subjective' or 'objective' world about which to have illusions. Secondly, Winnicott (1971a: 3) proposed that the 'intermediate state between a baby's inability and growing ability to recognize and accept reality' pertains to 'the substance of illusion'. Far from deceiving the infant about reality, Winnicott maintained that illusion actually affords the infant access to external reality. Loewald (1988: 71) rejected the idea of 'transitional space' as the province of illusion: 'Prior to sorting out inner and outer reality there is no "room" for an intermediate third area, no space in which to distinguish or oppose illusion and reality'. The transitional or intermediate area depends on the prior distinction of inner and external reality. Thirdly, Loewald (1988: 77) disagreed with those analyst – including, not only Winnicott but also Freud, Klein, Hartmann, Kohut, and others – who postulate 'a separate innate, individual instinctual core or a core self in the infant'. Everything in the developing infant, according to Loewald, is the outcome of interaction, identification, and internalisation. This includes the formation of the id, which Loewald treated as an interactional construct rather than a biological constant. For Loewald (1988: 78), mental life begins with interactions, not with instincts; it made no sense to him to think of the early stages of life in terms of 'a subjective instinctual or ego (self) core as opposed to objects'.

I think these objections are valid, although it seems to me, they reveal a shared approach to the imaginative basis of lived experience. At the same time, the objections reveal genuine weaknesses in Winnicott's account – including, his reliance on a conventional view of so-called objective reality. Winnicott went along with the commonsense view that objective reality constitutes the epistemological vantage point from which the mature adult refuses to challenge the infant's spontaneous, subjective gesture. The good-enough mother does not challenge the 'illusory' nature of the infant's 'transitional object'; she makes the 'moment of illusion' possible, precisely by meeting the infant's subjective gesture. But as Mitchell (1998: 843) points out, 'Winnicott characterizes experiences in these moments as illusions, unreal in reference to an objective, conventional reality in which he himself is anchored'. Winnicott (1971a:12) insisted that one does not present the infant with the question 'Did you conceive of this or was it presented to you from without?' Loewald's critique casts this insistence in a more dubious light.

The view of reality implied by Winnicott's theory of illusion, a view that is expressed repeatedly not only throughout his own writings but also in the secondary literature, is pulled up short by Loewald's (1949: 11) more trenchant insistence on the irreducible integrative mix-up of fantasy and reality: 'The relatedness between ego and reality, or objects, does not develop from an originally unrelated coexistence of two separate entities that come into contact with each other, but on the contrary from a unitary whole that differentiates into distinct parts. Mother and baby do not get together and develop a relationship, but the baby is born, becomes detached from the mother, and thus a relatedness between two parts that originally were one becomes possible'. The original affective 'density' of human experience is seen as no less real than 'secondary process' experiences; the former is not seen as a fantasied distortion of the latter. The mutuality of primary and secondary processes results in a generative tension *within* an increasingly comprehensive sense of reality.

Loewald alerts us to the tendency in psychoanalysis (starting with Freud) to treat the ego as external to reality. By contrast, for Loewald the ego does not develop by making contact with reality, or establishing a relationship with the object-world. On the contrary, he posited a primitive experiential process in which 'the ego detaches from itself an outer world. Originally the ego contains everything. Our adult ego feeling, Freud says is only a shrunken vestige of an all-embracing feeling of intimate connection, or, we might say, unity with the environment' (1949: 5). Loewald postulated something like a primary ego-feeling of merger, distinct from the ego-feeling of maturity under conditions of separation and differentiation. Winnicott, of course, came to similar conclusions – and yet he lacked the conceptual means with which to explicate his notion of an environment-individual set-up.

Loewald draws our attention to a confusion that persists in psychoanalysis insofar as one relies on a subjectivist epistemology to account for the infant's undifferentiated state. Winnicott may be seen as the source of this confusion in the contemporary English school. Lear (1996: 316–17 n. 8) provides a useful clarification, here, regarding the Kantian and post-Kantian implications of Loewald's theory of psychic reality, the idea that 'a person's "reality" is, in fact, *reality*', that 'objective reality must ultimately be understood as reality for a subject'. This does not entail an idealist reduction of the object-world. Rather, the Kantian distinction between the empirical and the transcendental allows for a distinction between the realm of space and time, on the one hand, and the conditions for the possibility of empirical experience, on the other. Lear notes that for Kant 'the only way to succeed at being an *empirical* realist – namely, that there really is an objective world, not of my own making – is to be a *transcendental* idealist – to accept that the mind has organizing conditions which underlie the possibility of there being experience of a genuinely objective world'. In short, the object-world is realised only in self-experience.

In the course of disagreeing with Winnicott, particularly over the use of the notion of illusion, Loewald clarified some general misunderstandings in Freudian and post-Freudian thought. In the event, he held more rigorously than Winnicott to the idea that 'the psychological constitution of ego and outer world go hand in hand'. For Loewald the ego's relation to reality does not, and cannot, emergence from an experience of illusion in the Winnicottian sense. Rather, the primal, dense unity of the mother-baby matrix is understood in terms of an interactive, imaginative process, where 'the maternal breast is the medium of the infant's creative tension even as the infant in its creative tension is the medium of the mother's creative breast' (1988: 75). Looked at from this perspective, the extent to which the baby has created or invented the available breast is *not* an illusion; nor does it appear as such when looked at *from any vantage point*. To say that the baby has actually created the breast – that is, as part of an interactive process – is an accurate description of psychic reality. We routinely meet a resistance in our patients' insistence that their feelings do not correspond to the way things are in reality. Loewald reminds us that primitive infantile experience (primary reality) is a form of life in its own right and, as such, is no less real than the more mature experience of adults. Babies are not simply waiting to become adults in order to be more fully human; they are alive to themselves from the beginning, alive to others, and alive to a sense of reality.

The fact that fantasy and reality are not experienced as antithetical to, or separable from, one another was a matter of central importance to Loewald. He continually returned to this problem, insisting that as adults we do not occupy a position in reality that is substantially different from that of the infant: 'Reality testing is far more than an intellectual or cognitive function. It may be understood more comprehensively as the experiential testing of fantasy – its potential and suitability for actualization – and the testing of actuality – its potential for encompassing it in, and penetrating it with, one's fantasy life. We deal with the task of a reciprocal transposition' (1974: 368). The point is that we do not acquire forms of secondary-process experience over and against the sensory and sensual primary-process experience operative at the beginning of life. In fact, too strict a separation of fantasy and reality, of the primary and secondary processes, is understood as a result of repression and pathological splitting. Human experience is innately resonant – unless that is, it becomes somehow distorted, inhibited, compromised, or otherwise rendered timid. Loewald (1960: 251) defined the therapeutic action of psychoanalysis along these lines: 'Our present, current experiences have intensity and depth to the extent to which they are in communication (interplay) with the unconscious, infantile, experiences representing the indestructible matrix of all subsequent experiences'. It was a matter of vital importance to Loewald that the dissociation of the primary and secondary processes owing to the 'wrong connections' in neurotic functioning, should not be replicated more widely, especially, under the auspices of scientific materialism. He (1951: 30) cautioned that psychoanalytic thought itself 'has unwittingly taken over much of the obsessive neurotic's experience and conception of reality and has taken it for granted as "the objective reality"'.

Loewald emphatically rejected the idea that the mother allows the baby an 'illusion' of having created the breast *ex nihilo*. Instead, he proposed the more expansive notion of 'invention', conceived as an interactive phenomenon of early human life. For Loewald mother and baby 'invent each other in the mouth-breast encounter' (1988: 76). The basic assumption is that the 'nursing experience is one in which self and other are not clearly differentiated' (Mitchell 1998: 844) but merged in a generative form of proximity: 'The infant is not allowed the illusion of having created the breast, nor does he discover the breast as something pre-existing but hitherto unknown to him; rather, infant/mother invents the mouth/breast "combination", which comes into existence in the manner of a newly invented instrumentality' (Loewald 1988: 76). It is the use the couple make of what they invent, according to Loewald (1988: 76), that confirms 'the reciprocal complementary tension and readiness of agent and "material"'.

There are clearly real philosophical differences between Winnicott and Loewald, some important aspects of which I have mentioned in the foregoing discussion. Nevertheless, Loewald's account of the reciprocal co-creation of the 'mouth/breast' complements the vital imaginative thread in Winnicott's thinking – namely, from the spontaneous gesture through destruction/survival of the object to object-use. Theoretically, Winnicott continued to rely on the idea of reality as an independent phenomenon; but his epistemological bias was evidently at odds with his phenomenological account of undifferentiated infantile states. Winnicott's way of understanding 'creative living' seems to me consistent with Loewald's views on the perpetual reconciliation and interpenetration between imagination and reality. In fact, I suspect that Winnicott's account of a world woven into the texture of the imaginative life of the infant afforded Loewald an opportunity to clarify his own views on the relationship between imagination and reality.

It was Winnicott (1952: 99), after all, who proposed that 'there is no such thing as a baby'; that the 'centre of gravity of the being does not start off in the individual'; that 'the unit is not the individual, the unit is an environment-individual set-up'. Despite the philosophical inconsistencies in his ontology, Winnicott did not reduce the psychic apparatus to a self-enclosed unit; nor did he mean to imply that the illusory nature of creative living was, therefore, less real. This is how I understand the central Winnicottian insight that the sense of reality admits illusion. Winnicott seems to have been looking for ways in which to express the sort of activity that is instantiated in psychosomatic life. This is a problem that has continued to exercise post-Freudian thought. Winnicott tended to confuse matters by treating the transition from relating to 'subjective objects' to relating to 'objects objectively perceived' as a movement towards outer reality. The confusion persists insofar as one assumes that the infant is engaged in making contact with an already constituted world. The idea of illusion, however, is accorded deeper meaning through Winnicott's principal preoccupation with living-there 'in the area of the adapting environment'. The infant's reality is real enough. In fact, the essential problem for Winnicott and Loewald alike concerns the gradual separation of the individual from its human environment: 'What the ego defends itself, or the psychic apparatus, against is not reality but the loss of reality, that is, the loss of an integration with the world such as it exists in the libidinal relationship with the mother' (Loewald 1949: 12). Primary identification provides the framework for creative living, subsequent to which the contact that separation allows between the self and the object-world augments available reality.

Something that makes for living

There is further common ground between Loewald and Winnicott in their respective views on the drives. For Winnicott, as for Loewald, drives are regarded as phenomena of differentiation and maturation, rather than primary forces that seek out objects by means of which to discharge themselves. Independent object-relations theory is predicated on this distinction. Loewald (1971a: 127–28), for his part, consistently maintained that 'instincts, understood as psychic, motivational forces, become organized as such through interactions within a psychic field consisting originally of the mother-child (psychic) unit'. In the beginning is the 'field', the original affective density of living-there; instincts are conceived in this situation as 'forces within the psychic organization and not stimuli which operate on that system from without' (1971a: 123). Loewald (1978: 208b-9) clearly retained the notion of 'instinct', but as a simultaneously structural and relational phenomenon: 'Understood as psychic phenomena or representatives [of organismic stimuli or needs], instincts come into being in the early organizing mother-infant interactions ... Thus I conceive instincts (considered in the framework of psychoanalytic psychology), and the id as a psychic structure, as originating in interactions of the infantile organism and its human environment (mother)'.

Although Loewald was more systematic than Winnicott, they agreed on the basic idea that instincts are created through interactive processes. Loewald (1972b: 321–22) was adamant that drives cannot be taken as given: 'instinctual drives in their original form are not forces immanent in an autonomous, separate primitive psyche, but are resultants of tensions within the mother-child psychic matrix and later between the immature infantile psyche and the mother. Instincts ... are to be seen as relational phenomena from the beginning and not as autochthonous forces seeking discharge ... understood as some kind of emptying of energy potential'. For Loewald internalisation predates the drives; it organises or shapes drive potential (primary narcissism and primary aggression) into drives.

Similarly, Winnicott (1952: 98) proposed that the relationship between the baby and the mother is of 'vital importance, but yet it is not a derivation of instinctual experience, nor of object relationship arising out of instinct experience. It antedates instinct experience'. This accords with Loewald's principal claim concerning the primacy of interaction, the view that the emergent ego shapes drive potential out of the 'enchantment' of early experience. Again, leaving aside epistemological differences, Loewald's notion of 'enchantment' may be seen as comparable to Winnicott's 'moment of illusion'. Despite the use of different vocabularies, they held similar views on the question of structuration-maturation and the role of narcissistic cathexis. Loewald (1978a: 195–96) formulated the principal claim *contra* the given or a priori: 'there is not a given structure ... that is invested with a charge of psychic energy ... these very structures come into being, are maintained and restructured by virtue of objectifying cathexis ... ego and superego come into being, are maintained and modified by virtue of narcissistic cathexis'.

Loewald himself admitted the common ground between his and Winnicott's thinking, with regards to the psychological birth of the human infant. In a suggestive series of reflections on the meaning of 'subjectivity' as a spontaneous activity of nature, he differentiates the baby's mouth-breast experience from the inner experience of the individual confronted with an already constituted object-world. Prior to the differentiation of subject and object, 'subjectivity' is discernible for Loewald (1988: 79) in 'the creative-destructive spontaneity and power of nature' itself. The argument rests on the distinction between *natura naturans* ('nature naturing') and *natura naturata* ('nature natured'), its philosophical *locus classicus* being Spinoza's *Ethics*.[21]

The Latin *naturans* indicates the present active participle of *naturo* (the suffix '*ans*' is similar in nature to the English suffix '*ing*'); hence nature in the active sense, the doing of certain kinds of action. *Naturata* is the perfect passive participle, which denotes the passive mode of createdness ('thingness') in contrast to active spontaneity. Typically, Loewald did not mention Spinoza by name in this passage, although he alluded to the Cartesian distinction between reality or nature taken as activity (*res cogitans*) and nature taken as objective reality (*res extensa*). The distinction supports Loewald's basic psychological hypothesis that imaginative activity, as it develops from the seamless unity of the mother-baby matrix, is a manifestation of *natura naturans*, of nature's 'subjectivity'. Subjectivity, understood as nature's activity, is seen as the enabling 'environment', so to speak, for human individual mentation and for consciousness. The same holds for Loewald as for Winnicott: the reach for meaning, understood as a reach for life, does not reside in an individual instinctual core. This is clearly at odds with the view most commonly expressed by Freud (1940a: 197): 'The core of our being ... is formed by the obscure *id*, which has no direct communication with the external world and is accessible even to our own knowledge only through the medium of another agency'.

Loewald, however, claimed support for his view of the original situation, in which there is no organisation as such, from a remarkable passage in *Civilization and Its Discontents*, where Freud (1930: 68) admits the 'limit-lessness' pertaining to 'primary ego-feeling' or the 'oceanic' feeling: 'originally the ego includes everything, later it separates off an external world from itself. Our present ego-feeling is, therefore, only a shrunken residue of a much more inclusive – indeed, an all-embracing – feeling which corresponded to a more intimate bond between the ego and the world about it'. The idea that initially the ego includes the external world, rather than mediating between the id (understood as its surface of emergence) and the external world, supports Loewald's views on the origins of living-there. Thus, the reach for life ('reaching for ...') presupposes a thoroughly inter-subjective situation that includes 'the creative-destructive powers of the parental couple' (Loewald 1988: 80) in conjunction with the infant's 'primary ego-feeling'.

Winnicott was no less committed than Loewald to the primacy of life. If one were to accept the prevailing view, then the 'self' and the 'sense of self' would count as the overarching themes of Winnicott's work (Abram 2008: 104). This seems potentially misleading to me. Winnicott (1968b: 239) was concerned, first and foremost, with the 'life force' – including, the destructive aliveness of the infant as a manifestation of being alive. Similarly, Loewald turned the psychological claim, regarding nature as active power, into a comprehensive 'psychoanalytic vision' (Chodorow 2003). The claim and the vision are based on the inextricability of imagination and reality; being alive and feeling real presuppose an imaginative sense of reality. The fundamental view – stated explicitly by Winnicott (1957: 42) but maintained no less emphatically by Loewald – is that 'the baby contains something that makes for living – that is to say, living apart from being kept alive'. An un-compromising humanistic vision is set out along these lines in direct op-position to 'the hegemony of the modern scientific *natura naturata* interpretation of reality' (Loewald 1988: 79).

Loewald attempted to identify this vision with Freud. Freud's final in-stinct theory, according to Loewald (1988: 80), is consistent with an inter-pretation of nature as *natura naturans*: '[Freud] extends the concept of *Trieb* in such a way that it stands for the spontaneous activity of the universe, of which man's psychosomatic life, and particularly his unconscious, is but one manifestation'. This is a moot point. The rapprochement between Winnicott and Loewald seems to me less debatable. Again, Loewald (1988: 80) confirmed the essential complementarity between their respective views: 'I suspect that Winnicott would not have disagreed with an interpretation of subjectivity in a wider and different sense ... and that he spoke of illusion in this context for want of a less traditional conceptualization'. I think Loewald was right. Winnicott did not equate 'illusion' and 'unreality'. Nevertheless, he struggled to find a coherent theoretical framework for the idea of 'imaginative elaboration' in the context of the baby's aliveness.

Loewald, however, gets only so far in his attempt to ground the psychological meaning of the life force in the Freudian interpretation. At which point, he turned to Heidegger for the deeper meaning of 'subjectivity' in terms of 'the future in us'. The theory of psychic life as an instantiation of nature's 'subjectivity' is augmented in fundamental ways by Heidegger's phenomenology of conscience. As the call of 'care' (*Sorge*), conscience animates 'the future in us' from the standpoint of 'the ego's future that is to be reached, is being reached, is being failed or abandoned by the ego' (Loewald 1962b: 45). The immediate and substantive ideals and demands of the superego, understood as the internalised authority of the parents, presuppose a more fundamental readiness, with respect to 'the viewpoint of a future ego' (1962b: 45). More than a simple temporal advance, the superego envisages a future held in distant prospect, even as the parents hold the child's future in mind. Loewald (1960: 225) put forward this view of futurity on clinical grounds, arguing that 'the analyst holds himself available to the patient'. In the reach for meaning *as a new beginning*, the patient enacts a longed-for refinding of primary love. The child accedes to the envisaged future by means of prospective identification, which includes a fundamental readiness of its own. An alive baby manifests 'something that makes for living'. We encounter significant variations on this theme in our clinical work. Transference-countertransference constructs reveal internal situations where the infant has had to rely on its mother to keep its future in mind, a situation that pertains to a greater or lesser extent in standard analysis. Alternatively, our patients make use of us in ways that suggest an internal setup where the pressure to evoke the mother's own inner future rests on the infant.

We have discussed Heidegger's interpretation of this state of readiness in terms of the anxiety of conscience, a 'wanting-to-have-a-conscience'. Importantly, the Heideggerian interpretation emphasises the activity of listening, insofar as we are trying to listen to, and to answer to, the voice of conscience. The ethical basis of this arrangement is unmistakable: the hearing which corresponds to the call allows for an ethical demand, a sense of morality that governs our actions or thoughts. We judge that we ought (not) to do *this* or *that*, as Loewald (1962b: 46) points out, only insofar as we are first of all 'ahead of ourselves, looking back at ourselves from a point of reference that is provided by the potentialities we envisage for ourselves or of which we despair'. The call places the life force in an existential context of care. The discrimination of 'good' and 'bad' objects presupposes a more fundamental relation to time, with respect to the ontological meaning of care, a time *between* hope and despair that is manifest as vulnerability in the situation of dependence.

The agency of the ideal informs us when we have lived up to our expectations, or when we have expected more from ourselves than we could manage. We feel 'guilty', in the ordinary sense of the word, when we find ourselves wanting on moral grounds. Nevertheless, we approve or disapprove of ourselves only on condition that 'conscience speaks to us from the viewpoint of the inner future' (Loewald 1962b: 46), the future which comes towards us (*Zukunft*). The ideal is rooted in a more primordial situation comprising the call and the response (Chrétien 2004). Loewald (1988: 76) spoke of a mother and infant who 'invent' one another in the mouth-breast event. Accordingly, we find 'ourselves' from the beginning waiting-towards that which is coming (the *Zukünftige*), taking responsibility for being forward (of ourselves) – essentially, taking responsibility for our finitude as taking-over being towards death. Heidegger described this situation as a phenomenon of authentic temporality. As such, the sense of something coming, something that makes for living, is prior to the 'conscience' that one encounters in everyday experience as judge and admonisher, and with whom the self 'reckons and pleads its cause' (BT, 339 [293]). Blame and forgiveness are secondary elaborations; they presuppose a more primitive sense of futurity as 'reaching for ...'

Freud furnished Loewald with an example; whereas Loewald turned to Heidegger for the form and function of the 'ideal' beyond 'good' and 'bad' objects. The Heideggerian influence is evident in Loewald's main conclusions concerning the meaning of psychic temporality: (a) the primordial meaning of the call attests to the fact that 'we are in advance of ourselves' (1962b: 46); (b) conscience speaks to us – primarily, 'in the name of the inner future' (1962b: 46) – as a condition of 'good' or 'bad' conscience; and (c) the internalisation of the call-response structure (the mouth-breast event) presupposes a readiness coextensive with being in the world (*in-der-Welt-sein*), rather than merely belonging to the world (*weltzugehörig*) or even being within the world (*innerweltlich*).

The future in us

Where do these hard-won conclusions leave us? Loewald saw the structural point of view as a new departure, as well as a gathering together of the Freudian interpretation. In Freud's structural theory, the superego is indistinguishable from the ego-ideal; Freud postulated a single agency based on identification with the parents following the decline of the Oedipus complex. Loewald upheld the classical view of the superego as 'heir' of the

Oedipus complex. At the same time, he emphasised the ego's futurity, an 'inner future' of the ego that comes about 'once a share of the oedipal objects is relinquished ... the ego envisages an inner future of itself, the superego being the representative of the ego's futurity' (1962b: 47). Alongside the partial relinquishment of the oedipal objects, the internalised demands made by the ideal agencies lose some of their archaic insistence on narcissistic perfection. The routine fluctuations of our patients' self-evaluations, however, indicate the extent to which this is anything but an all or nothing situation.

Loewald admitted that as a late structure (the latest differentiating grade in psychical organisation), the superego is subject to regressive tendencies (de-differentiation) on the one hand and, on the other, to a type of rigid intransigence, an ossification of primary narcissism. But assuming an early internalisation process in which parental expectations are sufficiently empathic, or in tune with the maturational stage of the infant (1962a: 271), the conditions are therefore in place for later emotional development. Again, Loewald (1962b: 47) suggested that 'once the libidinal-aggressional relationship with the oedipal figures ... has been partially given up as an external relationship and has been set up in the ego as an internal relationship ... then the ego envisages an inner future of itself'. The idea is that the superego is installed as the 'representative' of the ego's futurity; in 'the structure of the superego the ego confronts itself in the light of its own future' (1962b: 52).

Loewald's account of the ego's futurity consolidates the basic existential presupposition of prospective identification: the envisioned future instantiates the projection of life itself into the future. The distinction between *Natura naturans* ('nature naturing'), the creative power of 'naturing', and *Natura naturata* ('nature natured') proved indispensable for Loewald's late work on sublimation and symbolisation. It is no less important when it comes to the conceptualisation of active time. In my view, life comes equipped with a general power of action in the manner of Spinoza's *conatus essendi*. The ideal of the *conatus*, conceived in terms of the unifying function of Eros, crystallises Loewald's account of time and the superego. The reach for life (*appetitus*) *is* living-there. As such the *conatus* underpins movements into a future. The 'tendency towards' is not simply a type of self-preservation or a derivative of the sexual instinct. The reach for life exists prior to the instinctual dualism that accounts for the Freudian *Lebenstriebe*. From the point of view of the ego-superego system, 'reaching towards' appears as an irreducible combination of primordial imaginative activity, vital illusion, and inner discrimination. The ego-ideal casts the possibility of the future before the ego; the superego, in turn, envisages a future life of the ego, a life that is yet to come. Movements into a future presuppose the trajectory of the ideal agencies – namely, from infantile fantasy (illusion) through imaginative elaboration and the workings of the ideal ego to 'the point of view of the inner future which we envision' (1962a: 273). Faced with a possible or likely future, the ego also assumes responsibility *for* the future, responding to a demand, a 'beckoning' or a 'call', that comes from the not-yet-conceived.

In the course of living our lives, we experience time, and make use of our temporal experience, in terms of what Loewald (1962b: 48) called 'systems of action-patterns'. These patterns provide the conditions, the horizon of a living way of life that involves an understanding of being, in which states of mind become possible. In his analysis of the breakdown of subjectivity, Lear (2006: 49) notes that 'intending and hoping and wondering and desiring are not just up to me: they are not just a matter of exercising my will. And my inability to do so is not just a psychological issue: it is a question of the field in which psychological states are possible'. The point is that states of mind presuppose ontological 'fields' or 'systems of action-patterns'. Haugeland's (2013: 34 *et passim*) reading of Heidegger is particularly helpful in drawing our attention to the meaning of *Befindlichkeit* not as a 'state of mind' but as 'findingness' – the fact that Dasein 'finds itself [*sich befindet*] in its thrown-ness' (BT, 174 [135]). This confirms the essential link between moods and dependence. The acting person always finds himself already in some definite situation, even as living always finds itself already situated. Heidegger's point is that things matter for Dasein, precisely in the way that it finds itself affected in living-there *as* living-amidst: 'Only an entity ... which in existing, is as already having been, and which exists in a constant mode of what has been – can become affected' (BT, 396 [346]). Haugeland's (2007b: 182) concise formulation is worth repeating: Dasein comprises 'a distinctly human way of living that embodies an understanding of being and for which individual people ("cases of Dasein") can take responsibility'.

The inner discriminations of the acting person presuppose this threefold arrangement: (a) things mattering; (b) affectivity's self-experiencing of self; and (c) situatedness. The continuity in the variously differentiated identifications of the ideal presupposes a general standing commitment. Primary prospective identification reveals a commitment to life itself. The commitment pertains whatever human life turns out to be. As such, primary prospective identification constitutes a horizon that operates beyond the investment of the ideal in *this* or *that* object. Accordingly, Heidegger (BT 382 [333]) described the ontological visibility of Dasein's being in terms of 'the horizon in which the Being of entities other than Dasein ... has been clarified'. The distinction between action-patterns and states of mind is set out on ontological grounds: we remain committed to the ideal within the horizon of intelligibility afforded by our existence in an interactional field, which in turn makes states of mind possible. The distinction is manifest in the act of living up to our ideals, or failing to do so. States of mind are thus expressive rather than constitutive of the deeper existential dilemma of living dependent lives. In living-there, dependent on others, one's life is necessarily exposed to failure or collapse; but it is also driven, primordially, by the impulse to make meaningful contact and to live well, to 'reach for ...' in the realisation of one's potentiality.

Taking up the theme of human interaction, Loewald formulated the idea of 'degrees' of internalisation and externalisation. There is no suggestion here of 'peripatetic particles' adrift between ego, superego, and the object-world. To the contrary, the point Loewald wished to make was that the superego, understood as an enduring structure-pattern of introjections, comprises elements that may nonetheless move in the direction of the ego or in the direction of the object-world. The field in which mental states are possible is itself an open-ended phenomenon; the horizon of meaning is subject to change as a flexible parameter of the co-presence of intelligibility. Indeed, mental states remain viable (or not) depending on the degree of flexibility in these patterns; it is precisely the flexibility of the ideal that accords its horizonal status. In the situation of dependence, the criterion of flexibility applies to the possibility of no more possibilities; it remains receptive to the movement between despair and hope. For example, Lear (2006: 127) describes how the 'voice' of the ego-ideal needs to be 'sufficiently flexible' in order to sustain a hopeful future under conditions of extreme difficulty, which includes a 'flexible-yet-courageous response' to catastrophic disillusionment and cultural collapse.

Loewald provided a psychoanalytic theory that accounts for our orientation towards the future. On the one hand, he maintained that elements of the superego may merge into the ego; the superego 'becomes an ego element, becomes realized as an ego trait rather than being an inner ideal or command' (1962b: 51). On the other hand, superego elements may 'take on the character of object representations (externalization)' (1962a: 275). They may, in other words, be 'given up' or 'expelled' and 'persons in the external world representative of such abandoned elements may be repulsive to the superego' (1962b: 51). There is a prevailing tendency, in the culture at large, to foreground interpretation as demystification. Psychoanalysis perpetuates the influence of a misplaced irony, where patients are found wanting in their recourse to illusion, ill-founded belief and self-belief. The too easy recourse to irony results in an impoverishment of the Freudian interpretation. As analysts we are centrally engaged in the process of psychic change, a process that relies on living towards a possible future. The hermeneutic field in which we operate admits a 'double possibility', comprising not only a 'vow of rigour' but also a reclamation of the reach for meaning, a willingness to listen, and a concomitant 'vow of obedience' in the face of *pathos*. Ricoeur (1970: 27) addressed this conflict of interpretations as a positive challenge, issuing as a *kērygma*, a summons to reconcile 'extreme iconoclasm' and 'the restoration of meaning'. I believe Loewald was after something similar, although in less exalted terms. His theory of time and the reformation of the ego-ideal demonstrates the extent to which a transformation of psychological structure is possible only on condition that the horizon of the inner future remains sufficiently flexible to all one's future possibilities.

Notes

1 See Hartocollis (1972; 1976) for the link between the sense of time and affective life.
2 Hereafter cited parenthetically as BT – including two sets of page numbers, the first (in parentheses) refers to a page of the standard English translation, the second (in brackets) to a page of the standard German.
3 See Demske (1970) for a comprehensive and authoritative treatment of the theme of death through the whole of Heidegger's published works, from *Sein und Zeit* through the turn (*die Kehre*) to the later works. In addition, Haugeland (2007b) provides a succinct but incisive gloss on the phenomena of death and dying in the existential analytic of Dasein – in particular, elaborating on Heidegger's (BT, 291 [247]) claim that Dasein 'can end without authentically dying, though on the other hand, *qua* Dasein, it does not simply perish ... Let the term "*dying*" stand for that *way of Being* in which Dasein *is towards* its death [*Seinsweise*, in der das Dasein *zu* seinem Tode *ist*]'. On the grounds that Dasein is the one and only sort of entity that dies, Haugeland advances two propositions, first, that death is the possibility of no more possibilities, and second, that 'being toward death' (*Sein zum Tode*) involves assuming the conditional 'unbounded risk' of a resolute commitment to this possibility. Dying may be seen therefore as an inner act of freedom; death becomes integral to life and, as such, remains more than our physical 'demise' (*Ableben*). For Heidegger, what matters above all is the attitude of 'running ahead' (*Vorlaufen*) toward one's death. As we shall see, the 'ahead (of itself)' frees one not only for death, but also for all one's possibilities; hence the potentiality of prospective identification: The futurity of anticipation and the freedom to choose one's fate may be seen as two sides of the same process, which Heidegger identified in terms of *Sein zum Tode*.
4 See Levinas (1964: 50) for an alternative approach based on a time 'after my time', a time not only 'beyond the horizon of my time' but also beyond the freedom to die one's own death (*Frieheit zum Tode*). Levinas (1988: 216) *contra* Heidegger throws light on the primordial nature of 'reaching for ...' in terms of the 'humanness of dying for the other'; 'dying for ...' is seen as prior to the 'humanity' that defines itself as *conatus essendi*. The humanness of 'dying for ...' is conceived in terms of 'the primordial inflection of the affective as such'. Importantly, the 'being *for* beyond my death' (*l'être pour-au-delà-de-ma-mort*) does not refer to 'the absence of a future' (Colarusso 2006). It is neither a denial of death nor a turning away from prospective identification and the inner future. Rather, the ethical determination of a 'time without me' presupposes that there will never be a present time of the envisioned future; that the acting person renounces being the contemporary of its outcome. Levinas thus introduced a radically new meaning of the futurity of hope, namely, a future the possibility of which presupposes a primordial being-for.
5 We cannot necessarily rely on Heidegger for the primordial reach for life *in the infant*, insofar as the existential analytic rules that infants and small children, indeed like nonhuman animals, have no understanding of being at all (Haugeland 2007b: 181).
6 Freud held different views about the meaning of dreams at different times in his life, beginning with the idea that dreams are 'psychical phenomena of complete validity – fulfilments of wishes' (1900: 122). In this respect, Parsons (2009b: 24) notes that further to the formulation of dreams as 'the concealed expression of a childhood sexual wish', Freud 'had difficulty ... with the idea that dreams could be creative'. Later, however, Freud (1917a; 1920; 1925b) allowed that dreams are not only disguised gratifications of unconscious wishes, but may also be

representations of anxiety. The revised interpretation lends itself more readily to my argument that wishing and hoping are distinct acts of imagining. Lear (2006: 115–117) cites Freud's change of mind in support of his own more comprehensive perspective on the imaginative reach of dreams, particularly the idea of dreams as imaginative responses to reality, rather than a turning away from reality. My understanding of the 'inner future' is based on a similar distinction between wishful omnipotent longings and vital acts of imaging, in which illusions as well as dreams may function as imaginative expressions of hope. I believe that an illusion may act as a creative response to reality, in which case a dream may express a hope for an envisaged future. Illusion and hope thus coalesce in the operation of *avant-coup* as the 'future' counterpart of creative apperception (Parsons 2009b: 20).

7 While the two papers were published in the same year, the former was written two years earlier, versions of which were presented to the Topeka Psychoanalytic Society (1959), to the Western New England Psychoanalytic Society (1960), and at the December meeting of the American Psychoanalytic Association in New York (1960). The original version of 'Superego and Time' was presented as part of the Panel on 'The Superego and the Ego-Ideal' held at the 22nd International Psychoanalytic Congress in Edinburgh in 1961. It effectively extends the argument in the previous paper.

8 The first of Loewald's three papers on time seems to me no less 'radical' than his earlier paper on the nature of 'therapeutic action'. I do not share Chodorow's view of the paper as more 'cautious' and less 'innovative' than his classic paper on the analyst's therapeutic role. The papers address different themes and rework different aspects of Freud's metapsychology, but I do not see the first of the papers on time as any less innovative than 'On the Therapeutic Action of Psychoanalysis' (1960).

9 Loewald maintained the conceptual distinction between (a) 'identification' with objects and (b) 'internalisation' of intersubjective relations; a distinction that does not apply *strictō sēnsū* to the concept of prospective identification.

10 See also Fraiberg (1952), Reich (1954), Weissmann (1954), Glover (1956), Beres (1958), and Spitz (1958) for comparable views.

11 Compare Rosenfeld's (1962) Kleinian view on the continuity between the early and later superego.

12 Ricoeur (1970) credits the contribution of classical theory to an understanding of morality, which extends from St. Paul through Luther and Kierkegaard to Nietzsche's *Genealogy*. However, he notes that Freud's contribution to this tradition of moral critique does not amount to a comprehensive account of the ethical life so much as a theory of premorality and its archaic aspects. The Freudian *ethos* is essentially one of disenchantment, rather than restoration. Yet as Ricoeur's own contribution confirms, the two need not be seen as incompatible.

13 In her introduction to a panel on the Loewaldian legacy in the *Journal of the American Psychoanalytic Association*, Chodorow (2008: 1092) mentions an anecdote from one of Loewald's supervisees, Rosemary Balsam, as confirmation that Loewald saw himself in the 'middle', if not exactly as a latter-day 'middle group' analyst.

14 A reader looking for further clarity in approaching *Being and Time*, might profitably consult Dreyfus (1991), who is probably the most prominent advocate for the view that attributes a degree of autonomy and priority to Division One as an account of Dasein's disclosedness (intentionality). On the question of temporality, see Dastur (1999), Blattner (1999), Haugeland (2002), and Zuckert

(2007). Haugeland (2013) also provides an indispensable interpretation of Dasein as a living-understanding-of-being rather than an individual person.

15 In *Being and Time* but also in *Kant and the Problem of Metaphysics*, Heidegger identified the positive contribution of Kant's *Critique of Pure Reason* not as a theory of knowledge; but more importantly, as a regional ontology of the objects understood by Newtonian physics, or 'what belongs to any Nature whatsoever'. Heidegger understood Kant's transcendental logic as 'an *a priori* logic for the subject-matter of that area of Being called "Nature"'. The characterisation of Kant's project as an 'ontology' is obviously controversial, insofar as Kant's transcendental philosophy is explicitly aimed at the epistemic conditions of human experience, rather than any ontological truths as such. In fact, Heidegger was interested not in the empirical sciences, but in any understanding of and relation towards entities as entities.

16 See Haugeland (2007a) for a commentary on the expression 'to let be' (*sein lassen*), the idea that Dasein lets entities be.

17 See Krell (2015) for a useful commentary on the notion of ecstasy and the *Ekstasen* of time – including, Heidegger's use of the words 'rapture' (*Entrückung*) and the 'suddenness' (*Rapidität*) of the ecstases.

18 For the concept of 'wanting to have a conscience', see Heidegger (BT, 314 [270] *et passim*). Heidegger's interpretation of conscience, as indicative of Dasein's potentiality for being itself, was set out, alongside a number of other key ontological-existential 'theses', on the occasion of a public lecture delivered to the Marburg Theological Society in 1924. The lecture was published as *Der Begriff der Zeit* (1989) and subsequently in English translation as *The Concept of Time* (1992). The theses of the Marburg lecture clearly anticipate those of *Being and Time*.

19 *Schuldigsein*, which has been translated variously as 'being guilty' and 'being a lack', indicates something lacking ontologically. Heidegger uses the terms 'guilt' and 'guilty' in this sense, where the basic meaning of *Schuld* is ontological, rather than ethical or theological.

20 Mitchell (1998) proposed a comparable reconstructive interpretation of Loewald's Heideggerian approach to language. This resulted in some interesting observations rather than a detailed exegesis – including, some preliminary remarks on the idea of language as an intrinsic dimension of human experience from birth onwards.

21 'By *Natura naturans* we must understand what is in itself and is conceived through itself, *or* such attributes of substance as expressed an eternal and infinite essence, i.e. God, insofar as he is considered as a free cause ... by *Natura naturata* I understand whatever follows from the necessity of God's nature, *or* from any of God's attributes, i.e. all the modes of God's attributes insofar as they are considered as things which are in God, and can neither be nor be conceived without God' (*Ethics*, Part I, Prop. 29, Schol.). Loewald's emphasis on the dynamic principle of *Natura naturans* recalls the early German Romantic interpretation of Spinoza's *Deus sive Natura*, the identification of God with Nature, in contrast to the reaction of Spinoza's Christian contemporaries, most of whom rejected his doctrine of God as no more than atheism.

Chapter 4

Memory and reclamation

My account of hope in the previous chapter was framed in terms of a radically new approach to the question of time: 'Am I my time?' (*Bin ich meine Zeit?*) rather than 'What is time?' (*Was ist die Zeit?*).[1] Heidegger (BT, 437 [385]) viewed the future of *meine Zeit* as the primary meaning of existentiality. Dasein, as we have seen, is always 'futural' (*zukünftig*); it is always coming towards its potentiality. Epoch-making as these hypotheses no doubt have proved to be, the analysis of the primordial structure of time is yet more extensive.[2] Looked at from the point of view of the dependence relationship, the experience of time is not confined solely to something like Dasein's coming towards itself; nor does the projection of oneself towards the possibilities of one's existence cover the phenomenon of original and authentic temporality in its entirety. The phenomenological sense of living-there presupposes an extended meaning of *meine Zeit*, insofar as the reach for meaning, understood as the spontaneous expression of the acting person's potentiality, is realised only in a relational field. An emphasis on the relational nature of meaning and its creation does not necessarily require us to come up with an alternative to Heidegger's temporal ecstasies. But it *does* mean giving further thought to the question of the nature of time, including, not only the coming-towards-us of futurity but also the sense of the past, particularly the referential force of the mnemic image.

Repetition

My main thesis in this chapter is that reference back augments available reality, that memory redescribes reality. Heidegger (1992: 15) in fact provides a point of departure with his claim that in 'being futural' Dasein *is* its past; in which case, 'the past – experienced as authentic historicity – is anything but what is past [*Vergangenheit – als eigentliche Geschichtlichkeit erfahren – ist alles andere den das Vorbei*]'. As long as 'the character of "having been" arises, in a certain way, from the future [*die Gewesenheit entspringt in gewisser Weise der Zukunft*]' (BT, 373 [326]) – to this extent, redescriptive memory is grounded existentially in an attitude turned

DOI: 10.4324/9781315280899-5

equiprimordially towards the future and the past.³ The remembered life is not past (*vergangen*) but, rather, the source of more life.

Let us return to the passage from § 74 of *Being and Time*, where Heidegger himself places reference back – the 'I *am*-as-having-been [*ich* bin-*gewesen*]' (BT, 376 [328]) – in the ontological movement of prospection-retrospection. Based on the assumption that the past involves 'Being-already in (a world) [*schon-sein-in (einer Welt)*' (BT, 364 [317]), Heidegger (BT, 437 [385]; emphasis in the original) notes: '*Repeating is handing down explicitly – that is to say, going back into the possibilities of the Dasein that has-been-there* [*Die* Wiederholung ist die ausdrückliche Überlieferung, *das heist, der Rückgang in Möglichkeiten des dagewesenen Daseins*]'. The radical meaning of 'repetition' (in this passage, at least) consists in its *permanent* reach for life; hence going back to the past and retrieving latent possibilities. The active transmission of those possibilities forms an integral part of the inner future. Reference back involves a reprojection of the futurity of anticipation based on the latent potentiality of the 'has-been' (*das Gewesene*). We can infer from this that the possibility of more life depends on the prevalence of unlived life; living necessarily comprises the lived and the unlived, in which case we reclaim the past as a future possibility. The passage continues: 'The authentic repetition of a possibility of existence that has been – the possibility that Dasein may choose its hero – is grounded existentially in anticipatory resoluteness' (BT, 437 [385]).

We can see once again how Heidegger opens up a line of inquiry that the Freudian interpretation tends to obscure with an emphasis on the compulsion to repeat and the conservatism of the instincts. The Freudian 'repetition compulsion' (*Wiederholungszang*) exemplifies the repetition of the same, the tendency of repetition to return to itself *ad nauseam*; whereas in the Heideggerian interpretation repetition differs from itself on at least two counts. Firstly, as 'a mode of resoluteness which hands itself down – the mode by which Dasein exists explicitly as fate' (BT, 438 [386]). Secondly, as a way of living in which history has its essential importance in that 'authentic historizing of existence which arises from Dasein's future', its resolute 'being towards death' (BT, 438 [386]). The Heideggerian notion of active repetition rests on this irreducible combination of retrieval and mortality, of the living past and finite being: '*Authentic Being-towards-death – that is to say, the finitude of temporality – is the hidden basis of Dasein's historically*. Dasein does not first become historical in repetition; but because it is historical as temporal, it can take itself over in its history by repeating' (BT, 438 [386]; emphasis in the original)'. The possibility of historical experience rests on the enactment of 'back to' (*Zurück auf*) as the phenomenal character of 'having-beenness' (*Gewesenheit*).

Robert Harrison provides a particularly insightful gloss on this passage.⁴ While allowing for the complex meaning of authentic repetition as mortality *and* retrieval, Harrison (2003: 96–97) notes that Heidegger was not sufficiently clear about the distinction between 'my dying' and 'my becoming an heir', between 'reaching out to the nullity of death' and 'retrieving legacies in my heritage'. Harrison fully admits the radical import of Heidegger's attempt to link historicity and futurity under the heading of Dasein's 'authentic historicality'. There is no question (in Harrison's mind, at least) about the far-reaching implications of this attempt to root both handed-down possibilities and the act of repetition in the future. Harrison's (2003: 97) point is that the full measure of Heidegger's interpretation comes into view only when we recognise that the future is 'thoroughly populated by the dead as well as the unborn': 'if in my confrontation with my death I am in fact confronted by my dead, and if it is from *them* ... that I receive the sum of those repeatable possibilities that I am thrown back upon in anticipatory resoluteness ... it makes my mortality a coffer of legacies consigned to me from my forebears, awaiting retrieval and renewal'. On these grounds, the acting person assumes the legacy of freely chosen ancestors as well as the posterity of the unborn, those who came before and those who belong in the time to come.

Harrison interprets the meaning of our being-toward-death as a being-toward-the-dead. The need to 'perform our mortality (Wood 2002: 75) is revealed as a need not only to resolutely project a future but also to go back to the past, including the ancestral past as an integral part of one's own lived experience, and to retrieve or fetch back (*die Wiederholung*) possibilities. Freudianism relies here on the figure of archaic mind. In conjunction with the Heideggerian interpretation, psychoanalysis allows for active repetition as an imaginative responsiveness, which renders the sense of the past representable. Time simultaneously (a) recuperates detours and divergencies through memory, history, and retention, and (b) disrupts recuperating temporalisation through the active repetition of imaginative elaboration. I discuss the enactment of memory in this chapter along these lines, that is to say, from the standpoint of the thoroughly historical, nonbiological modes of being of the dead. The attempt to situate the mnemic experience in relation to the inner presence of the dead, understood in Heideggerian terms as our freely chosen ancestors, calls on the Freudian interpretation at its most radical. One could argue further that the problem of memory reveals the Independent dialogue with Freud at its highest point; for Freud, memory was *the* exemplary problem in psychoanalysis and the same is true for a number of key Independent thinkers.[5]

Freud (1909a: 122) formulated the basic psychoanalytic principle of the remembered life – i.e. our going back into the possibilities of the 'has been' – on clinical grounds: 'In an analysis ... a thing which has not been understood inevitably reappears; like an unlaid ghost, it cannot rest until the mystery has been solved and the spell broken'.[6] Leaving aside an insistence on the dissolvability of mystery as well as the familiar construal of interpretation as demystification (Ricoeur 1970), the point I take from Freud is that it requires a job of work for the dead to die in us, rather than to re-peatedly intrude upon us in want of a dwelling-place. It is the work of mourning, broadly defined, that is required here. The figure of the 'unlaid ghost' thus extends our inquiry beyond the link between time and the ego-ideal (the unknown future) to the *transfer* of meaning between the dead and the living, and between the past and the future.[7]

The chapter follows the general pattern of the book. Cognisant of the Independent dialogue with Freud, the dialogue itself is situated in a broadly defined discussion of contemporary thought. I begin with a detailed statement on the idea of memory as transference, which I treat essentially as a transfer *in the imagination*. This involves a discussion of Ricoeur's *La métaphor vive*, particularly the concept of 'semantic innovation', as a theoretical resource for the idea of redescriptive memory. I then go on to identify what I see as a basic tension in the Freudian interpretation between 'recollection' and 'construc-tion', a tension that focuses our attention on the 'considerations of re-presentability' (*Rücksicht auf Darstellbarkeit*) pertaining to the mnemic image.[8] I elaborate on these alternative ways of making sense of the past, what we might call the 'reference-effects' of recollection and construction, in Freudian and post-Freudian thought. And I draw on Derrida's reading of Freud to underscore the shift towards a post-Freudian approach to the problem of memory, in the context of which I discuss the revitalisation of our sense of the past in terms of the not-yet-experienced past.

Metaphor

I aim to demonstrate in this chapter (a) that the act of remembering reshapes the past; (b) that memory manifests its objects; and (c) that the remembered life is something created by the dynamic reality of the acting person. Freud made a singular contribution to our understanding of how we live with the past, and my argument in this chapter is based on Freudian premises. Consider the following statements: firstly, a 'psychological theory deserving any consideration must furnish an explanation of "memory"' (Freud 1895: 299); and secondly, 'Hysterics suffer mainly from reminiscences' (Breuer and Freud 1893–95: 7). Taken from among Freud's earliest works, these statements point to a new and different experience of time based on the temporalisation of the unconscious. Freud outlined this approach, initially, in the *Project for a Scientific Psychology*, relying on the model of hysteria to articulate the theory of repressed memories: 'We invariably find that a memory is repressed which has only become a trauma by deferred action [*nur nachträglich*]' (1895: 356). From the *Project* onwards, Freud (1895: 300) approached memory as the essence of 'psychical processes in general', rather than a psychical property among others.

We are, in many respects, still taking the measure of these inaugural statements, estimating the scope of Freud's contribution in the wider context of what we know about human memory. At the same time, there is an

underlying tension in the Freudian interpretation between the archaeological analogy and the lifting of the repressed on the one hand and, on the
other, the discontinuous conception of time modelled on the dream. The
tension was evident in Freud's work from the beginning. The Freudian interpretation is consistently directed towards an active delay (*Verspätung*)
inherent in memory; hence the work of remembering as deferred action. As
Freud (1893–95: 162) pointed out in the case of Elisabeth von R., following
the death of the patients that she had nursed, 'there would begin in her a
work of reproduction which once more brought up before her eyes the
scenes of the illness and death. Every day she would go through each impression once more, would weep over it and console herself'. Crucially,
Freud adds 'I cannot say whether the work of recollection corresponded day
by day with the past'. An admission of inconclusiveness is hardly anomalous
when it comes to the nature of the remembered life. The complex temporality of the psychic past accounts for why matters have remained open to
new and revised meanings.

   I take my theoretical bearings in this chapter from the Kantian view of the
imagination as the schematisation of our intuition of time.[9] This allows me
to approach the mnemic act from the point of view of the productive imagination. Indeed, the tension in the Freudian interpretation between 'recollection' and 'construction' recalls Kant's distinction between (a) the
empirical or 'recollective' imagination and (b) the poetic or 'productive'
imagination. The Kantian (1781/1998: 257) distinction highlights the tension
in Freud's approach to memory: 'insofar as the imagination is spontaneity, I
also occasionally call it the *productive* imagination, and thereby distinguish
it from the *reproductive* imagination, whose synthesis is subject solely to
empirical laws, namely those of association, and that therefore contributes
nothing to the explanation of the possibility of cognition *a priori*, and on
that account belongs not in transcendental philosophy but in psychology'.
The distinction thus underlines the complex nature of imaginative elaboration: (a) as 'a faculty of the original representation of the object (*exhibitio originaria*), which consequently precedes experience'; and (b) as 'a
faculty of the derived representation (*exhibitio derivativa*), which recalls to
mind a previous representation' (Kant 1798/1978: §28).

   The same holds in both the first and third critiques: (a) the empirical
imagination (understood as a discrete moment of synthesis) is situated between sensibility and the understanding; (b) the productive imagination
encompasses them all, informing all the modes of the synthesis of the
manifold of intuition – namely, apprehension, reproduction, and recognition. In this respect, the constructive role of the imagination, the idea that
the imagination produces an 'original representation of the object (*exhibitio
originaria*)' prior to experience, is consistent with the basic tenets of transcendental or critical idealism. This includes Kant's (1781/1998: 512) central

claim that 'the objects of experience are *never* given *in themselves*, but only in experience, and they do not exist at all outside it'.

In addition to the Kantian schema, Ricoeur's (1978: 194) interaction theory of language suggests a further move in which imaginative elaboration becomes itself 'a properly semantic moment of the metaphorical statement'. For Ricoeur (1991: 173), as for Kant, 'the work of imagination is to schematize metaphorical attribution'. As Ricoeur (1991b: 173) notes, 'before being a fading perception, the image is an emerging meaning'; the imagination furnishes emergent meaning with an image, as distinct from the passage from perception to images. Despite the fact that 'so many prejudices [have] been tied to the idea that the image is an appendix of perception, a shadow of perception', Ricoeur (1991b: 171) posits that the image derives from language rather than from perception. I draw on Ricoeur, then, for the application of the creative imagination and schematism to the phenomenon of redescriptive memory. The Kantian schema supports the idea of the remembered life as an imaginative elaboration. Ricoeur (1978: 208) made the further point that 'a schematism of attribution constitutes the point on the frontier of semantics and psychology where the imaginary is anchored in a semantic theory of metaphor'.

Taking 'metaphoric schematisation' as a pivotal reference point, and concentrating on the link between imaginative elaboration and semantic innovation, I argue that the movement of imagination in its intuitive moment defines the mnemic act. Before pursing this line of inquiry, let me say a bit more about the philosophical parameters of my analysis. Ricoeur (1978: 170) emphasised the extent to which the making of meaning involves 'an event in the realm of discourse'. In this respect, Ricoeur (1991b: 174) postulated on Kantian grounds that imagination is indeed just what we all mean by the term: 'the free play of possibilities in a state of non-involvement with respect to the world of perception or of action'. The (mnemic) image suspends meaning in 'the element of fiction', even as the attitude of 'non-involvement' allows for imaginative experimentation with meanings and values, and, more generally, with ways of living creatively. Ricoeur's postulate is based on the tie between imagination and semantic innovation. The recourse to the theory of metaphor, in this case, presupposes a new way of formulating the problem of the imaginary and its relation to reality. Ricoeur (1991b: 171; emphasis in the original) notes that '[i]nstead of approaching the problem through perception and asking if and how one passes from perception to images, the theory of metaphor invites us to relate imagination to a certain use of language, more precisely to see in it an aspect of *sematic innovation*, characteristic of the metaphorical use of language'.

In his discussion of the semantic theory of imagination outside the sphere of discourse, Ricoeur goes on to stress the 'referential power' of semantic innovation. My view of 'reference back' as the active element of the remembered life is indebted to Heidegger's analysis of the phenomenal character of *Gewesenheit*. At the same time, my view owes at least as much to Ricoeur's (1991b: 174) examination of the power of affirmation in the metaphorical use of language: 'The neutralizing function of imagination [non-involvement] with regard to the "thesis of the world" is but the negative condition for the release of a second-order referential power'. The 'second-order reference' is conceived as the pivotal reference capable of redescribing reality, including, human action itself. This is what Ricoeur (1991b: 176) means when he states that 'the first way human beings attempt to understand and to master the "manifold" of the practical field is to give themselves a fictive representation of it'. The tie between imagination and semantic innovation is operative in the tie between fiction and redescription.

Ricoeur (1991b: 177) notes that we require more from a 'poetics of action' than the mimetic function of fiction or 'narrative play'; in addition, imagination is seen as replete with a projective function, or a capacity for 'pragmatic play', which forms 'part of the very dynamism of acting'. The 'practical imaginary' thus enables acting persons to appropriate the 'immediate certainty' of their power (the power of action) only through 'the imaginative variations that mediate this certainty' (1991b: 178). Once again, the imagination is conceived in Kantian terms as the general function of practical possibilities at the level of the acting person. Moreover, Ricoeur (1991b: 179) extends the power of action to relations between 'diverse temporal fields, those of our contemporaries, those of our predecessors, and those of our successors'. On the grounds that '*like* me, my contemporaries, my predecessors, and my successors, *can* say "I"', Ricoeur (1991b: 180) maintained that 'the principle of analogy between the multiple temporal fields is to the handing down of traditions what the Kantian "I think" is to the causal order of experience'. The act of freely choosing one's ancestors, the freedom to retrieve legacies, is integral to the full meaning of the remembered life. Accordingly, the imagination is at work through 'the analogy of the ego' and its tie to others; the very productiveness of the imagination consists in the schematism of the analogical tie between myself and others like me.

An emphasis on the metaphorical use of language allows us to approach the remembered life in terms of 'recollection' and 'construction' as two contrasting points of mediation. The aim of the chapter is to draw out these different meanings, literal and metaphorical, from Freud's discourse; to identify memory not only as a passive recall but also as the doing of a certain kind of action. It is the *act* of remembering that permits us to speak of the past with conviction; and by 'conviction' I mean a subjective sense of the past, which I treat as a twofold work of discovery *and* creation. My analysis of the mnemic act, therefore, is based on a particular reading of what Strachey in the standard English translation termed 'deferred action'. Winnicott conceived the 'transitional object' in comparable terms, that is to say, as an invention that takes place *between* inner reality and the outside world. As such, the transitional realm constitutes a type of metaphoric schematisation. My argument is that this mode of functioning applies explicitly to our sense of the past. Thus, 'imaginative elaboration', in the Winnicottian sense, articulates the sensorial impressions evoked in memory as an elaboration in imaginative form of primordial relations and transitional phenomena. The primacy of the image is discernible here in the form of 'illusion' as a discovery/invention of primary creativity. Similarly, deferred action reveals itself as a type of metaphorical ('poetical') discourse; the imaginative groundwork of the mnemic act, conceived as a metaphoric schema, exceeds the *cogito* of *meine Zeit*. Remembering *someone* (or remembering oneself *as* another), understood as the work of remembering *par excellence*, presupposes a conviction tied and tasked, from the start, by a time without me, the time of the predecessors and of the successors. One is committed in existential proximity to others, precisely, by the *bound* image of time past.[10]

The imaginative work of remembering, then, is based on certain assumptions about the role of the past in the realm of meaning. Essentially, the metaphoric relationship between past and present may be seen as part of the transfer of meaning in general. An exploration of the metaphoric potential of mnemic experience opens up two specific lines of inquiry, namely: (a) the use of metaphor in ordinary language to *refer* to the past; and (b) the recourse to metaphors (as models) – for example, the central metaphor of the 'unlaid ghost' – in Freudian and post-Freudian theories of memory. Freud leaves us in no doubt that memory and interpretation are inextricably linked as forms of representation; that the answer to the problem of memory lies in the realm of meaning. Freud (1919: 221), however, added an important proviso that leads to the heart of his interpretative system: 'we ourselves speak a language that is foreign'. We simultaneously conceal and reveal ourselves in language, creating radically new meaning through our redescriptive capacity as language users. The pivotal role that Freud assigned to the creation of meaning in language is evident in his early paper on 'screen memories'. In a conversation with one of his patients (a thinly disguised autobiographical portrayal), Freud (1899: 319) identified 'verbal expression' as 'the intermediate step between a screen memory and what it conceals'. We can draw two conclusions from this: (a) that the creation of meaning in language (metaphor) comes alive in its uses; and (b) that act and meaning are coextensive in the 'sense of the past', that something happens in carrying it out.

Hayman (2013: 64–66) notes that the language of psychoanalysis consists in 'the use of metaphor'; hence a type of 'evocative' language that is 'very near to the art of poetry'. At the same time, she upholds the distinction between psychoanalytic and poetic discourse. The distinction itself is well made; the evaluative corollary is less convincing. Hayman (2013: 67) contends that 'however much psychoanalysis is like art, it is certainly something different, and much more'. Despite her clear-mindedness, Hayman surely overstates the case. Are we supposed to abjure the resources of art in our psychoanalytic inquiry into the mnemic act? The censure goes back a long way in the Freudian tradition and, indeed, is rooted in Plato's relatively unfavourable judgement of poetic thinking. While Hayman, for her part, welcomes the rule of metaphor; at the same time, she insists that psychoanalysis must not speak poetically. This is hardly a minority view. Yet the severance of poetising (*poiēsis*) seems ill-advised to me; in fact, I doubt that such a clear-cut renunciation is even possible. One never really knows what is doing the work of thinking in psychoanalysis, insofar as the unconscious is in play.

The reach for meaning through the use of metaphor involves the 'transformation' of the affective *a priori* of primary process and its relational aspect into 'metaphoric expressions of what ... unconscious experience is *like*' (Ogden 1997: 45). For Ogden (1997: 26) this amounts to the very work of analysis: 'At almost every turn, I believe that we as analysts, in our own use of language, are unconsciously teaching and learning the value of the use of metaphorical language'. Freud set discourse to work, under the heading of *transference*, in terms of the discontinuity of semantic modalities; the Freudian interpretation operates at 'the intersection of two domains, metaphorical and speculative' (Ricoeur 1978: 303). Poetry comes into play in telling us 'how things are' by making us 'think more'. Ricoeur (1978: 306) noted that 'poetic discourse brings to language a pre-objective world in which we find ourselves already rooted, but in which we also project our innermost possibilities. We must thus dismantle the reign of objects in order to let be, and to allow to be uttered, our primordial belonging to a world which we inhabit, that is to say, which at once precedes us and receives the imprint of our works. In short, we must restore to the fine word *invent* its twofold sense of both discovery and creation'.

Ricoeur takes up the notion of 'living metaphor' along these lines, linking the twofold movement from reference to ontology, and from metaphor to the concept, under the heading of 'semantic dynamism'. The dynamism of discourse is conceived in terms of a relationship of forces motivated by 'the ontological vehemence of a semantic aim'. We arrive at ontology and the metaphysics of 'metaphorically affirmed being' on the grounds of 'ordered manifolds', which Ricoeur contrasts to 'radically heterogenous' language games in the Wittgensteinian sense. Leaving aside the hurried contrast between Wittgenstein and the hermeneutic of action, suffice to note that the exigency of ontology 'cuts meaning from its initial anchor, frees it as the form of a movement and transposes it to a new field to which the meaning can give form by means of its own figurative property' (1978: 300). Metaphorically affirmed being is discernible in the use it makes of the 'hints of meaning, which are in no way determinations of meaning' (1978: 300).

I shall come back to Ricoeur and the interaction of domains of discourse in a moment; but first, two questions. How does experience express itself with sufficient vitality in language? Meaning sustains its momentum, as well as its reach, by way of 'live metaphor', understood as such by 'virtue of the fact that it introduces the spark of imagination into a "thinking more" at the conceptual level' (Ricoeur 1978: 303). To restate the hermeneutic task in ontological terms: the underlying conflict between demystification and restoration comes to the fore through the effort to 'think more' under the pressure of 'living metaphor'. Living-there is animated by ontological vehemence; to 'think more' is tantamount to 'more life'. Second, how does this affect our sense of the past? The degree to which remembering itself is constitutive of *new* meaning is the theme of this chapter, and the question of memory-as-transference brings us back to the origins of the English school. Ella Sharpe (1940: 155) addressed the problem of meaning from a clinical point of view by focusing on the metaphorical utterances of analytic patients, working her way through words towards 'the sense experience and the associated thoughts'. In tracing the movement from sensorial experience to articulation she relied, implicitly, on a prominent manoeuvre of classical (Aristotelean) rhetoric, regarding the transposition from the empirical ('psycho-physical') to the intelligible.

What does Ella Sharpe mean by 'live metaphor'? How does she conceive of the relationship between *la métaphore vive* and the original psycho-physical situation? Essentially, she (1940: 156) proposed that 'a live metaphor reveals a past forgotten experience', and that the latter was originally a 'psycho-physical' experience. For Sharpe (1940: 168) a patient's spontaneous use of metaphor 'proves upon examination to be an epitome of a forgotten experience'. Concentrated expression in this case comprises an innovation of meaning based upon an amalgam of repressed desire, the early incorporated environment, and early experiences of dependency. Sharpe thus sets the parameters for the present inquiry: the mnemic figures under discussion in this chapter fall under the heading of the concentrated expression of 'epitome'. But while metaphor derives its impetus from primary affectivity – that is, from the preverbal language of affect which 'originally accompanied bodily discharge' – it is not itself a psycho-physical phenomenon. Epitome expresses, in condensed form, a semantic aim in line with the 'unthought known' – a patient 'who speaks vitally in metaphor *knows*, but does not know in consciousness what he knows unconsciously' (Sharpe 1940: 168).

Elaborating on this line of thought, I aim to place metaphor as the doing of a certain kind of action, and to demonstrate that the dynamic aspect of metaphorical expression consists in the disclosure of new meaning. I am indebted on both counts to Ricoeur's study of metaphor, published originally in 1975 as *La Méaphore vive*.[11] Focusing on the figurative inventiveness of metaphor, Ricoeur sets out a tensional theory of meaning in contrast to Lacan's use of linguistics as the theoretical substrate of the Freudian interpretation.[12] Ricoeur's analysis of the 'vital aspects' of language is more germane to my inquiry than Lacan's 'structuralist' perspective, although it would be misleading to insist on a hard-and-fast distinction. Lacan approached the reach for meaning in terms of the repression of the signified and its symbolisation, a process which, he assumed, accounts for the 'splitting' (*Spaltung*) of the subject as a speaking being. The constitution of the unconscious as a hidden structure interior to subjectivity is predicated on these grounds, and remains indebted to the defining Saussurean dichotomies of signifier and signified, synchronic and diachronic, form and substance. But the assimilation of the metaphoric and metonymic processes of language to condensation and displacement, respectively, is not limited to the Lacanian terminology of signifier-signified. Ricoeur, for his part, addressed the reach for meaning in terms of a tensional theory of metaphorical truth, a theory in which the vital aspect of meaning is privileged over the impersonal operations of the signifier and the false pretensions of the *cogito*.

The contrasting approaches of Lacan and Ricoeur may be summarised on three counts: (a) the 'synthetic character of predication' (Ricoeur 1978: 216) is opposed to the differential play of signifiers; (b) the proximity of persons is privileged over the demystification of illusion, idealisation, and the self-satisfactions of *méconnaissance*; and (c) the hermeneutic conception of metaphor presupposes the *reference* of discourse. These distinctions are directly relevant to the present study. In contrast to the monism of semiotic linguistics, Ricoeur (1978: 216) approached metaphor in terms of discourse and its referent: 'the sign points back only to other signs immanent within a system, discourse is about things. Sign differs from sign; discourse refers to the world'. Discourse, 'through its referential function, sets signs fully into relation with things' (1978: 123); the 'question of existence' (1978: 218), therefore, is posed as an integral part of the reach for meaning – that is, over and above the semiotic monism of structural linguistics.[13]

In addressing a misinterpretation of Aristotelian *mimesis* as mere 'imitation', Ricoeur (1978: 39) clarifies a general point: that the 'creative dimension' is inseparable from any 'reference to reality'. Accordingly, he acknowledged with Benveniste that the semantics of discourse (the 'instance of discourse'), as distinct from the semiotics of signification, 'relates to things, to a world'. The spontaneous movement from sense to reference (Frege's two planes of meaning) demonstrates the power of metaphor, or the power of the productive imagination in the Kantian sense, 'to project and to reveal a world' (1978: 92–93). The principle that portrayal is innovative has guided much of my inquiry into the 'acting person' of Independent thought, a principle which allows us to argue from the heuristic fiction *here is where we meet* to 'the revelation of the Real as Act' (1978: 43).

The theory of referential meaning is presented alongside a critique of the sign, following a study of the failure of rhetoric in decline, wherein metaphor remains a substitution of meaning at the level of the word. The substitution theory of metaphor applies to the semantics of the word in post-Saussurean

linguistics – including, the elaboration of structural linguistics in the psychoanalytic theories of Lacan.[14] The correlation of the metaphorical and the
metonymic with a theory of tropes proceeds on the grounds that metonymy
rests on contiguity and metaphor on resemblance. In this methodological
arrangement 'the tropological distinction provides the vocabulary', while the
distinction itself is 'profoundly semiological'. This is the crux of Ricoeur's
(1978: 175–76) critique of the sign: 'Jakobson's analysis completely bypasses
the distinction introduced by Benveniste between semiotics and semantics ...
This monism of the sign is characteristic of a purely semiotic linguistics ...
the model to which a substitution theory of metaphor belongs is one that
ignores the difference between semiotics and semantics and takes the word
and not the sentence as the basic unit of tropology'. Metaphor is characterised, accordingly, as 'a general semiotic process' rather than 'a form of
attribution'.

Put simply, Ricoeur addresses the central problem of 're-description' in
terms of the semantics of discourse, as distinct from the semantics of the
word, and he does so on the grounds that the latter is restricted to the science of signs, whereas the former situates the reach for meaning in the
object-world. For Ricoeur (1978: 125) 'semantic innovation is a way of responding in a creative fashion to a question presented by things' (1978: 125).
My account of redescriptive memory presupposes a context theory of
meaning in which the past, conceived as a metaphorical construct, is
nonetheless considered to be of importance in its own right. As for the
constitution of the subject by accession to the symbolic, Ricoeur (1970: 400)
once again gets to the crux of the matter: 'We are in the presence of phenomena structured like a language [the dream mechanisms of displacement
and condensation]; but the problem is to assign an appropriate meaning to
the word "like"'. His response to this problem, which left him as unconvinced by Lacan as he was by post-Saussurean semantics in general, is
entirely consistent with the more incisive intuitions of the English Freudians.

The idea of seeing things as *actions* places the theory of metaphor on an
entirely different footing to the monism of the sign. The latter, in sum,
presupposes a substitution theory of metaphor in which (a) the difference
between semiotics and semantics is ignored and (b) the word rather than the
sentence is considered as the basic unit of tropology. For Ricoeur (1978:
176) '[t]his is a model that recognizes in the word only its character as a
lexical sign, and in the sentence only the double characteristic of combination and selection'. How does this model compare to the Freudian interpretation? Ricoeur's response is unequivocal:

It is not without reason that Freud does not take language [*le langage*]
into consideration when he treats of the unconscious but rather restricts
its role to the preconscious and the conscious. The signifying factor [*le
significant*] which he finds in the unconscious and which he calls the

"instinctual representative" (ideational or affective) is of the order of images ... The form by which an instinct reaches the psychism is called a "representative" [*Repräsentant*]; this is a signifying factor, but it is not yet linguistic. As for the "presentation" properly so-called (*Vorstellung*), this is not, in its specific texture, of the order of language; it is a "presentation of things", not a "presentation of words".

(Ricoeur 1970: 398)

The mnemic act falls within a general semantic field, where desire comes to the fore through the metaphoric dimension of language. We can support this view with a series of postulates drawn from *La métaphore vive*:

a   Life is sustained in language by metaphor. By which I mean not only that 'language is vitally metaphorical' (Shelley quoted in Richards 1936: 90); but also, more importantly, that the life of words in language is a manifestation of life itself, rather than a mere representation. The criterion of vitality applies to the pure immanence of life, to living-there and living-with, to the existential function of the verb *to be*. Ricoeur (1978: 248) brings home the radical import of this insight: 'In order to elucidate [the] tension deep within the logical force of the verb *to be*, we must expose an "is not," itself implied in the impossibility of the literal interpretation, yet present as a filigree in the metaphorical "is" ... the "like/as" is not just [a] comparative term among all the terms, but is included in the verb *to be*, whose force it alters'. By identifying the 'is' of equivalence, as distinct from the 'is' of determination, Ricoeur revitalises the Aristotelean tradition along hermeneutical lines.

b   There is no 'natural' language, no 'rhetoric degree zero'. An initial 'metaphorical impulse' constitutive of the reach for meaning cuts across the opposition between 'proper' and 'figurative' meaning. This suggests a 'fundamental metaphoric', a bedrock situation in language whereby 'order itself proceeds from the metaphorical constitution of semantic fields' (1978: 23). Ricoeur (1978: 24) identifies the classical source of this claim, which he applies to the reach for meaning at its most extreme – 'the "metaphoric" that transgresses the categorical order also begets it'. In this respect, metaphor may be seen as 'the rhetorical process by which discourse unleashes the power that certain fictions have to re-describe reality' (1978: 7). The link between fiction and redescription proceeds (once again) from Aristotle's finding in *De Poetica* – namely, 'that the *poiesis* of language arises out of the connection between *muthos* and *mimesis*'. I maintain on these grounds that memory manifests its objects.

c   The redescriptive power of metaphor does not operate with full force at the level of the word. Ricoeur's critique, with respect to the rhetorical tradition as well as the semiotic monism underlying what he calls the 'new rhetoric', is levelled at the ill-conceived idea that metaphor is a figure of one word only, a one-word trope. In the rhetorical tradition, metaphor is treated as 'a change or deviation affecting the meaning of the word' (1978: 44). The idea of a 'fundamental metaphoric' realigns the hypothesis of deviation with the initiation of a new pertinence, or 'the properly predicative moment of metaphor'. For Ricoeur (1978: 156) a theory of deviation (or of substitution) becomes meaningful only when aligned with a predicative theory of metaphor: 'the inception of a new pertinence within the metaphorical statement clears the way for linking a lexical deviation with a predicative deviation'. As a phenomenon of predication, metaphor constitutes 'an unusual attribution ... at the sentence-level of discourse' (1978: 44). Taking his lead from the English-language philosophical semanticists (I. A. Richards, Max Black, and Monroe Beardsley), Ricoeur advanced a discursive conception of metaphor based on three distinct levels of discourse: the word, the sentence, and the text. And the 'synthetic character of predication', understood as the central function of discourse is set over and against the mere play of signifiers.

d   What is 'intended' (*l'intenté*) by discourse points to an extra-linguistic reality which is its 'referent' (1978: 216). The theory of intentionality is redefined from the point of view of the referential relationship of the metaphorical statement to reality. Ricoeur effectively extends the phenomenological concept of 'intention' to a general theory of interaction based on the discontinuity of semantic modalities. The referential function of metaphorical discourse (the realism of redescription) is coupled with the discontinuity between speculative discourse and poetic discourse. This presupposes different uses of the imagination. Metaphorical truth is identified with 'the "realistic" intention that belongs to the re-descriptive power of poetic language' (1978: 247). The theory of tension extends the referential relationship of language to reality: 'as the conjunction of fiction and re-description suggests, poetic feeling itself also develops an experience of reality in which invention and discovery cease being opposed and where creating and revelation coincide' (1978: 246). At the same time, the redescriptive 'experience of reality' is subject to an arrangement of 'ordered manifolds' based on the phenomenology of the semantic aims pertaining to modalities of discourse. Ricoeur (1978: 296) concludes that speculative discourse has its 'conditions of *possibility* in the semantic dynamism of metaphorical utterance' and has 'its *necessity* in itself, in putting the resources of conceptual articulation to work'.

The reality of the past

Freud subscribed to the presumption of sense on the grounds that available meaning adheres in various types of hidden meaning (*verborgene Sinn*). The intending of the former, in and through the occurrence of the latter, constitutes the structure of double meaning that delimits the symbolic reach of the hermeneutic field. How does memory fit into this semantic arrangement? Freud remained preoccupied with this question from the 1895 *Project* onwards. In *Moses and Monotheism*, for instance, he (1939: 129) points out that the permanent memory-traces of past perceptions, the living remains of past experience, may be compared to a 'tradition'. In this reading, 'tradition' emerges in the aftermath of a primeval experience. At the same time, Freud admits that, on the model of 'the dream's navel [*der Nabel des Traums*]' (1900: 525), the binding of sense (or meaning) and its referent does not yield a complete representation of historical memory. Historical consciousness is subject to a mythical supplement at the origin. For Freud the ego, conceived as 'a precipitate of abandoned object cathexes' (1923b: 29), operates in conjunction with new myths and the spirits of the ancestors. The same applies to the mythical past as to mythological thought in general: one creates myths in order to render the 'unthinkable' thinkable, or the 'unimaginable' imaginable. This may also be seen as a way of keeping a memory of the 'unknowable'.

The structural disjuncture between sensory impressions and representational forms is a defining insight of Freudianism. Freud had already formulated a coherent account of memory along these lines by 1900; in the context of his self-analysis, he advanced the view (a) that the sense of the past *per se* is identified with 'screen memories' and (b) that the reach for meaning is modelled on the dream-work and its interpretation. On both counts, the theory of memory is a theory of psychic elaboration or redescription. It is clear that Freud did not simply underwrite the hermeneutics of reason (Derrida 1996: 4) any more than he committed analysis to a linear conception of time. He began with a model of resistance and interpretation in which representation is repressed, or 'forced out of consciousness and out of memory' (Breuer and Freud 1893–95: 269). Importantly, he maintained that while the 'psychical trace' of the idea appears to be lost, in fact it 'must be there'. The archaeological metaphor pertains on the grounds that there really is something there, a past to which we are accountable, and whose meanings (in principle, at least) are legible. Interpretation, in sum, applies (a) where (past) experience remains unthinkable; (b) where things or thing-presentations (*Sach-Vorstellung*) are manifest prior to words and resist translation; and (c) where past perceptions fail to acquire sufficient meaning, resulting in 'unlaid ghosts'. The Rat Man's recovery of his memories of being beaten by his father is a case in point.

Freud's notion of 'recollection' amounts to far more than a record of past events. Yet matters become significantly more complex when we pose the problem of the past beyond the model of repressed-retrievable memories. In order to address this complexity, one needs to trace the different meanings assigned to the past in Freudian metapsychology: following the thread from the 1895 *Project* through the archaeological model of the mature works to the late work in the 1930s. Broadly speaking, at the same time as the theory of psycho-neurosis assumed prominence – see the papers on metapsychology – the reach for meaning was specified increasingly in terms of the search after memories. The archaeological principle of unearthing or 'bringing to light' ties the question of sense yet more tightly to the economy of repression. This is a matter of historical record. In the theoretical and technical refinements of psychoanalytic treatment after 1910, the centrality of the archaeological analogy was consolidated in terms of transference and the 'transference neurosis' (*Übertagungsneurose*).

Freud remained committed to this model almost until the end, identifying the practice of psychoanalysis with the repression-recollection couple. The late works, however, open up a new line of inquiry, the radical import of which is discernible in Freud's attempt to rethink the reality of the past from the point of view of 'conviction' (*Überzeugung*). The past is redefined along these lines in 'Constructions in Analysis' (1937b), as well as key passages in *New Introductory Lectures* (1933). Preoccupied with the ordeal of interminable analysis – a sobering assessment of the therapeutic efficacy of analytic treatment – Freud (1937a, 1937b) effectively outlined a new theory of meaning. The theory was designed to account for the resistance of the id; hence the radical, albeit perturbing discovery of Freud's late work. On the grounds of the 'repetition compulsion' and up against the conservatism of the instincts, Freud posited 'conviction' as an active conception of remembering. The task of 'bringing to light' pertains where the conflictual dynamic between the pleasure principle and the reality principle results in repression. But as Freud (1937b: 258–59) eventually admits, the quest for memories is supplemented by the analyst's task 'to make out what has been forgotten from the traces which it has left behind or, more correctly, to *construct* it'.

Construction facilitates conviction by means of 'working-through' (*Durcharbeitung*). For example, in the case of Elizabeth von R., Freud (Breuer and Freud 1893–95) demonstrated the extent to which the construction of meaning, under conditions of deferral and delay, depends on the patient working through earlier impressions. Working through is a way of redescribing reality. It supports the unconscious process of retroactive elaboration and, thereby, invests the indefinite past with a potential depth of meaning. This applies not only to memory traces, but also to the somatic events and perceptual impressions of unassimilated or unthinkable experience (unlived life). Traces and impressions alike are subject to reframing as potential signs. At least as early as 1896, Freud (1985: 2017) emphasised that deferred revision, what he called a 're-arrangement' or 're-transcription', applies particularly to unthinkable or traumatic experience.

How does the redescription of the past differ from the interpretation of the repressed? Freud (1933: 29) reveals the extent to which the 'constructivist' emphasis goes beyond the measure of the archaeological analogy, with respect to the *attempted fulfilment* of wishes in dreams: 'While the sleeper is obliged to dream, because the relaxation of repression at night allows the upward pressure of the traumatic fixation to become active, there is a failure in the functioning of his dream-work, which would like to transform the memory-traces of the traumatic event into the fulfilment of a wish'. The 'failure' of the dreamwork reveals that further to wish-fulfilment, the more primitive function of the dream is one of binding. The dreamwork is thus aimed at unformulated experience or the not-yet-experienced, while conviction turns out to be something like a constitutive supplement. Freud continued to insist that memories can be lost but not abolished – and yet he came around to the view that there is more to the reality of the past than so many hidden meanings. The analyst brings about in the patient 'an assured conviction of the truth of the construction' which 'achieves the same therapeutic result as a recaptured memory' (1937b: 266). Again, the analyst 'lays before the subject of the analysis a piece of his early history that he has forgotten' (1937b: 261), but which he cannot recollect or recount. Taken together, the hypothesis of attempted fulfilment and the act of working-through account for constructions that compel convictions as memories.

In order fully to appreciate the problem of memory in Freud, one needs to differentiate between the perceptual testing of reality and the philosophical acceptance of reality. Freud associated the meaning of 'reality' not only with a principle (or criterion) but also with a worldview. Reality-testing denotes a particular 'mental function' – indeed, indicative of an adaptation to time as part of an overall orientation towards the object-world (Freud 1911b). On the other hand, acceptance involves the renunciation demanded by reality, or resignation to that which cannot be avoided – including, above all, 'the immutable law of death' (Freud 1913b: 299). It is possible, therefore, from a Freudian perspective, to pose the question of reality in two ways. What is the reality principle? How do we make meaningful contact with reality?

Acceptance adds an ethical dimension to the psychological notion of adaptation. The criterion of necessity (*Ananke*), as Freud developed it in his later writings, applies to the inevitable harshness of life in which our relation to death comes to the fore. For Freud (1927: 15) the very elements, the reality of natural forces, seem 'to mock at all human control'. Death assumes a central position here not only in Freud's theory of the drives, but also in his general attitude towards reality. The exteriority of reality, conceived as a necessity, is pitted against Eros and the love of life. As such, reality is construed as an 'assault' or 'interference', as Loewald (1951: 12) noted, 'directed against the strivings for gratification of the libidinal urges toward the mother'. The love of life and the hatred of external reality comprise yet one more example of Freudian dualism. However, leaving aside the question of Freud's philosophical temperament, it seems to me that reality and Eros are clearly reconcilable in Freudian terms

(Loewald's contribution is predicated on this assumption) and, moreover, that reality and Eros prove consistent as temporal phenomena. This applies not only to the envisioned future but also to the sense of the past, to the redescriptive power of memory and the belief it affords us.

The reality principle denotes an *activity* of mind that is consistent with the synthetic function of Eros. The sense of reality may be seen therefore as an integral part of the primordial function of psychic life, rather than a secondary elaboration. Indeed, Freudianism remains viable as a theory of libidinal investment (*Besetzung*) only so long as primary reality itself remains open to redescription. This includes the creation and binding of meaning in a backward as well as a forward direction. The constitutive reworking of reality presupposes that the reality of the past is coexistent with the retrogressive reach of meaning; that one's understanding of oneself and the world begins with a retrospective construction of appearance and, as such, extends beyond the perceptual testing of reality. The theory of regressive-retrogressive states as constitutive was available to Freud from at least as early as the *Traumdeutung*.

In addition to psychic redescription, our *belief in* (Winnicott 1963c) the reality of the past confirms the continuity of reality and Eros. The sense of the past is not reducible to true or false empirical beliefs; memory is not that kind of problem. In dynamic terms, belief may be seen as a subjective expression of the ontological structure of redescription. The two operate in tandem. The redescription of reality articulates the link between the principle of reality and the primal creative force of human life (our primordial belonging to a world) in conjunction with our capacity to believe. By identifying redescription and belief-in, I mean to draw attention to two fundamental aspects of living-there: (a) the all-pervasive nature of retroactive elaboration; and (b) the significance and validity of believing with conviction. The coherence of retroactivity and conviction reveals the semantic innovation inherent in statements about the past. This seems to me the best answer that psychoanalysis has come up with for the question of how experience *lives on* in memory. For example, in the Winnicottian tradition of post-Freudian thought, the imaginative sense of reality afforded by illusion realises the potentiality of the not-yet-conceived significance of the past. Most importantly, the relationship between retroactivity and conviction is one of *potential* meaning, in which hope animates historic consciousness by means of living metaphor. Looked at from the dynamic point of view of retroactive meaning, the past is always unfinished, while the primacy of illusion presupposes the ontological incompleteness of reality itself. We are always going forth into the past, summoned by a sense of reality the meaning of which, on condition of the average expectable environment (Winnicott 1965), remains within reach.

The realisation of potential does not amount simply to a quest for memories, but operates more profoundly throughout the realm of meaning along the related axes of retroactivity and conviction. Construed in terms of the structure of 'deferment' (*Nachträglichkeit*), Freud placed the reality of the past in the realm of meaning. We can retrace the Freudian interpretation, here, along the lines of indestructibility and believability. The proposition of indestructibility is based on the link between repression and recollection, a link underpinned by the idea that the unconscious is simultaneously timeless (*zeitlos*) and organised. The legible meanings of unconscious mentation comprise those memories about which, for conflictual reasons of one kind or another, one is no longer able to think. On the other hand, equivalent activities to remembering presuppose an alternative therapeutic arrangement – that is, where no memory-traces remain, even in the unconscious; where the primary object is lost, decathected, or subject to erasure rather than forgotten; and where links, far from being attacked, have not been created in the first place. This requires a revised theory of destruction and indestructibility, where the 'only real thing is the gap; that is to say, the death or the absence or the amnesia ... The amnesia is real, whereas what is forgotten has lost its reality' (Winnicott 1971a: 22).[15]

The notion of 'trauma' plays a decisive role here. Freud (1895: 347–59) began with the model of hysterical repression, the idea that a repressed memory only becomes traumatic by deferred action. The structure of deferment was set out, initially, alongside the theory of seduction (Freud 1896a, 1896b, 1896c). For example, in discussing the case of Emma in the *Project*, Freud accounts for the patient's phobia on the grounds that the child receives an impression to which she reacts, but without taking the *experience* fully into her mind. It is the memory of the event, rather than the event itself, that proves traumatic. That Freud consolidated the link between construction and conviction in his later writings is the burden of my argument. Meanwhile, the essential idea that traumatic after-effects necessitate the action of redescription is present in Freud from the late 1800s onwards.

In order to fully acknowledge the radical import of the constructive-reconstructive horizon of intelligibility, we need to differentiate between the proposition of deferred action and the accompanying explanation. In both the *Project* and *Studies on Hysteria*, Freud attempts to explain the deferred action of trauma from a genetic point of view. Considered in terms of the deferral of early scenes until the age of puberty, it is the child's premature state of sexual development that puts the event of molestation beyond her and, only in retrospect, causes it to become traumatic. The argument is that an instance of postpubertal seduction revives the memory of the early seduction, which had not previously been registered, that is to say, as a traumatic condition of hysteria: 'We invariably find that a memory is repressed which has only become a trauma by *deferred action* [*nur nachträglich*]' (1895: 356) The process of psychosexual maturation, that is the 'retardation' (*Verspätung*) of puberty, allows for the possibility of 'a different understanding of what was remembered' (1895: 356).

The explanation privileges genetics over semantics. Rather than our maturing through understanding in the Winnicottian sense, the assumption is that understandings come about as a consequence of our psychological and sexual development. The explanation threatens to reduce the dynamic conception of time to a teleological account of psychological growth. To the extent that it blurs the distinction between development and deferred action psychoanalysis is able to claim no greater explanatory value than developmental psychology. In this case, the sense of the past is reduced to the *telos* of autobiographical memory. The basic proposition of deferred action, on the other hand, rests on Freud's (1895: 350–51) initial hypotheses in the second part of the *Project*: (a) 'for every compulsion there is a corresponding *repression*'; and (b) the repressed idea may be remembered insofar as it is 'isolated' but not 'forgotten'.

Freud presented the indestructibility of the past as a founding principle of psychoanalysis, a principle to which he adhered unwaveringly from beginning to end, ruling out the possibility that 'any psychical structure can really be the victim of total destruction' (1937b: 260). As a theory of trauma, the proposition of deferred action rests on the link between repression and recollection. Furthermore, the proposition, if not the explanation, survives Freud's hasty dismissal of the seduction theory. This indicates the extent to which Freud never completely abandoned trauma and seduction as significant factors; that the pathogenic significance of seduction was retained, even if the seduction theory was more or less discarded (Blum 1994; Ahbel-Rappe 2006). More importantly, it also shows how far the *Project* set the parameters for a theory of memory, where the repressed becomes traumatic only in retrospect.

Überzeugung

Freud questioned the reality of the past, most vociferously, in the case-history of the 'Wolf Man', where he applied himself, 'in a way that can almost be described as an anguish, to the question – what is the first encounter, the real, that lies behind the phantasy?' (Lacan 1973: 54). The way in which he grappled with the problem of memory in this case-history is indeed revealing. Here, I shall focus in turn on the *object* and the *aim* of construction. The psychosomatic impressions of infantile life come to the fore in 'From the History of an Infantile Neurosis' (1918), as the object of construction. The observation of parental intercourse, described in the 'Wolf Man' as the 'primal scene' (*Urszene*), makes sense only in retrospect. In this case, Freud was intent on demonstrating, first, that neuroses in adult life are based on infantile neuroses, and, second, that sexuality is the main aetiological factor. For Freud, the very belatedness of trauma confirms the interpretation of castration anxiety, where the dream of a four-year-old child, a disturbing dream in which wolves appeared sitting in a tree, was reported some twenty-odd years later in the course of an adult analysis. Freud (1918: 38) treats the dream as a deferred reactivation of the primal scene, a 'deferred revision' of 'impressions' in want of appropriate meaning. Construction is integral to active repetition, where 'impressions' amount to so many fragments: 'A real occurrence – dating from a very early period – looking – immobility – sexual problems – castration – his father – something terrible' (1918: 34). It is clear from Freud's account that the fragmentary impressions constitute the object of construction.

The trauma, in this case, is understood as 'another instance of *deferred action [nachträglich]*' (1918: 45 n1), insofar as the repetition of the primal scene, during the night of the dream, marks the onset of the patient's illness. This raises fundamental questions about the relationship between reality and testimony. Did the scene actually take place? Was the scene witnessed by the 18-month-old child, or imagined as a retrospective fantasy (*Zurückphantasien*)? Freud (1918: 103 n1) assumed that this was *the* 'most delicate question in the whole domain of psychoanalysis', although he admitted that, in certain respects, it is 'a matter of indifference ... whether we choose to regard [the observation of parental intercourse] as a primal *scene* or as a primal *phantasy*' (1918: 120 n1). The reality of the past is not exhausted by the 'scene'. The important point is that 'something happened' prior to the presumption of meaning. Freud outlined a radically new theory of meaning on these grounds – a theory, that is, based on the idea that primal scenes 'are as a rule not reproduced as recollections, but have to be divined – constructed' (1918: 51). The dynamic repetition of the construct presupposes a past that has never been present. Looking backward in terms of the developmental sequence (from present to past) and forward from the point of view of 'potentially pathogenic developments' (from past to present), Freud employed a combined method of reconstruction and predicative psychopathology. The contrasting ways of making sense of the past – which is the theme under discussion in this chapter – are woven together in complicated ways under the heading of 'deferred reactivation'.

Here, as elsewhere, dream analysis provides the model of active repetition. Freud held that the analysis of the patient's dream revealed the extent to which his childhood disturbance – including, violent temper tantrums, obsessional symptoms, and phobia – came about through the identification of more mature sexual feelings with the primal scene. For Freud (1918: 121 n1) the patient retrospectively introduced a 'phantasy' of his parents copulating into the scene that he had witnessed at 18 months of age. What did the patient himself make of things? It seems he was convinced about the reality of the recollection of his seduction as a three-year-old by his precocious six-year-old sister. On the other hand, he remained unconvinced about having witnessed *a tergo* coitus between his parents as an infant. This is pivotal: for the patient, 'his seduction by his elder sister was an indisputable reality'; the question for Freud (1918: 97) is 'why should not the same have been true of

his observation of his parents' intercourse?' In raising the question of believability, Freud introduced a new way of thinking about repetition and the
reality of the past. A complex semantic arrangement is postulated on the
grounds that certain conditions are required if the patient is to establish a
sense of 'conviction' (*Überzeugung*) about the past. Freud's approach – in
this case, at least – is consistent with conclusions reached in an earlier paper,
'Remembering, Repeating, and Working-Through' (1914a: 149), which describes states of mind in which 'something is "remembered" which could
never have been "forgotten" because it was never at any time noticed – was
never conscious'.

Freud thus introduced the idea of 'remembering' something that has not
yet happened under the heading of conviction. Importantly, the conditions
of possibility pertaining in the case of conviction are different from
those required for 'recollection'. Freud (1914a: 149) made this clear on
three counts: (a) in the case of early childhood experiences, which cannot
be understood at the time, 'no memory as a rule can be recovered'; (b) 'the
conviction which the patient obtains in the course of his analysis' is therefore
irreducible to recollection; (c) the patient relies instead on 'quasi-
hallucinatory' images obtained from dreaming. Dream analysis provides the
model. The patient has to 'dream back', as it were, something of the past
that has yet to be experienced (lived). In this respect, the reality of the past is
believable, the patient is 'obliged' to accept the reality of the past, without
recourse to transference and remembering: 'we can ascertain for ourselves
that the patient, after his resistances have been overcome, no longer invokes
the absence of any memory of [early childhood experiences] (any sense of
familiarity with them) as a ground for refusing to accept them' (1914a: 149).
Dreaming is conceived as 'another kind of remembering' (1918: 51), where
the dream-memory (*Traumgedächtnis*) evokes unlived experiences of infancy
and early childhood.

The idea that mnemic experience relies on fragmentary impressions, which
continue to exert a pressure on the patient to make sense of the past, rests on a
distinction between truth-effects and truth-content. It requires a considerable
shift in thinking to link our sense of the past with 'quasi-hallucinatory'
images. The reference to 'another kind of remembering' is decisive.
Essentially, the idea of 'dreaming back' allows one to approach the problem
of memory in terms of the 'backward direction' or 'retrogressive movement'
(Freud 1900: 542–43), the formally retrogressive trajectory towards nonverbal
perception and nonrepresentation, characteristic of dreaming. To take Freud
(1918: 51) at his word, mnemic experience is 'divined' between the recollection
of historical truths and the construction of truth-effects. The 'profound
conviction of the reality' of the past that comes about in this way is considered
'in no respect inferior' to memories based on recollection.

The advances made in the case history of the 'Wolf Man' anticipate an
augmentation of the Freudian interpretation. The recollection of the past

based on a comprehensive lifting of infantile amnesia is supplemented by an alternative model of therapeutic action. Freud finally, if somewhat reluctantly, acknowledged the limitation regarding the lifting of infantile amnesia; in place of which he found more to say about construction as an essential aspect of the analyst's task. Further to his initial account of the deferred action of a trauma, Freud (1939: 74) confirmed in *Moses and Monotheism* that where traumas occur in early childhood they are 'not accessible to memory'. He arrived at this conclusion via the problem of interminability. On the one hand, he admits that, with respect to 'the earliest impressions of our childhood' (1900: 163–64), the traumatic situation may be redescribed on the model of dream-memoires. On the other hand, recollection cannot rely on access to intelligible memory-traces; instead, conviction adheres to the potential meanings of fragmentary impressions and their repetition.

Memory-traces do not stand as guarantors of sense under traumatic conditions, or at the deepest levels of psychic life. Further to this basic discovery, Freud (1937b: 266) maintained that where the attempt to complete a patient's fragmentary impressions of past perceptions fails, the analyst creates 'an assured conviction of the truth of the construction'. The inventiveness that goes into making the past believable may be seen as a spontaneous primitive phenomenon rooted in neonatal life. It is the immemorial past of early somatic experience, coupled with primary object-cathexis, that animates our deepest convictions. Freud (1918: 120) framed this basic supposition in terms of a phylogenetic hypothesis, indicating a type of preprimitive affective *a priori* that has no means of representation: 'some sort of hardly definable knowledge, something, as it were, preparatory to an understanding ... at work in the child at the time [of the primal scene]'. The hypothesis accounts for belief-in as 'a primitive kind of mental activity', believing as the doing of a certain kind of action at the beginning of life. In this respect, our capacity to believe, in large part, is directed towards the unrepresented 'sensory remains' of the past, prior to the fixation of memories.

Reclamation

Having discussed the object of construction in terms of the sensory impressions of the earliest relationship, I shall now turn to the aim of construction. And I shall discuss the latter in terms of the reclamation of something that has not yet happened. Once again, dream analysis provides the model. The dream of the burning child, from the final metapsychological chapter of *The Interpretation of Dreams*, demonstrates the extent to which the psychology of the dream-processes provides a model not only of wish-fulfilment but also of reclamation and psychic survival.[16]

At the beginning of chapter 7 of *The Interpretation of Dreams*, Freud recounts 'a moving dream' that he heard thirdhand from one of his female patients in which a dead child speaks to his father. The father dreamt that 'his child was standing beside his bed, caught him by the arm and whispered to him reproachfully: "Father, don't you see I'm burning?" [*Dass das Kind an seinem Bette stecht, ihn am Arme fasst und ihm, vorwurfsvoll zuraunt: "Vater, siehst du den nicht dass ich verbrenne?"*]' (1900: 509). Prior to the dream, the father had been keeping watch beside the child's bed in his final illness and, following his death, had gone into the adjacent room to rest. He left the door ajar so that he could see into the room where the child's body was laid out surrounded by burning candles; he also engaged an old 'watchman' (*Wächter*) to sit and keep watch over the dead child. Presently, the father awoke to 'a bright glare of light' and, rushing into the next room, discovered that the watchman had fallen asleep and that 'the wrappings and one of the arms of his beloved child's dead body had been burned by a lighted candle that had fallen on them' (1900: 509).

Freud admits the role of external factors in the creation of this dream, allowing that the 'glare of light shone through the open door into the sleeping man's eyes and led him to the conclusion ... that a candle had fallen over and set something alight in the neighbourhood of the [child's] body' (1900: 509). Nevertheless, there is a delay in the father's response to the reality of the situation; he does not immediately wake up and rush into the next room but incorporates the real perception into a dream. This poses an interesting question – why did the dream occur when a very different kind of response was called for? We can I think extend the meaning of this question, with respect to reclamation and the aim of construction: what does a response to 'unlived' experience entail? I shall come back to the question of survival in a moment. Meanwhile, Freud provides two explanations for why the father dreamt rather than woke. Initially, the dream is presented as yet another example of wish-fulfilment: 'The dream was preferred to a waking reflection because it was able to show the child as once more alive' (1900: 510). The theory of wish-fulfilment provides one explanation of reclamation. The father's wish to sleep makes a claim on life, more particularly, on the prolongation of the child's life, albeit by a brief 'moment of time'. The dream thus transforms the dead child into a living one.

The redescriptive power of the dream, its capacity to transform death into life, is carried in the child's address – *Vater, siehst du den nicht dass ich verbrenne?* The possibility of more life is inscribed in the statement that Freud (1900: 510) believes 'must have been made up of words which [the child] had actually spoken in his lifetime ... For instance, *"I'm burning"* may have been spoken during the fever of the child's last illness'. The claim on life issues from the repetition of a reality that the father cannot encounter awake but only when he is dreaming. The father prolongs his sleep on account of what he *can* see in the dream, but was unable to face in reality – the child's catching a fever that would result in his death. However, further to the father's wish to keep his child alive, Freud (1900: 571) defines the father's wish to sleep as an additional motive in the creation of the dream – 'the [conscious] wish to sleep lends its support to the unconscious wish [to see the child again]'.

Lacan (1973: 58) takes the interpretation of the dream in yet another direction by asking about 'the missed reality that caused the death of the child' – what is it that wakes the sleeper? The question concerns the theory of desire but (once again) not necessarily the fulfilment of a wish by unconscious fantasy. For Lacan (1973: 58) the father is awoken not by the sound of the candle falling on the child's body (the noise in the next room), but rather by the 'message' expressed in the child's words.[17] It would appear that the dream itself wakes the father; that the 'message' expresses a more profound, if not poignant sense of reality, an awakening or response to a call that can be heard only in a dream. Far from prolonging the wish to sleep, or the wish to keep the child alive by 'one moment', the dream wakes the father to the reality of the child's death. In this respect, the dream is seen as 'an act of homage to the missed reality – the reality that can no longer produce itself except by repeating itself endlessly' (1973: 58). Something makes itself heard in the dream: the child's call to be seen, the father's response to which, in awakening, testifies to the impossibility of responding.

How does the 'impossible' function as a referent? The father awakens to the stricture of the message; his eyes are open (*it can be seen*) to not knowing. Awakening thus repeats the predicament of failed witness, the necessity and impossibility of responding to a summons. Responsibility is called up as an excess of desire, which, as a response to the dead child, manifests itself in the dream by the loss expressed in an image, as Lacan (1973: 59) noted, 'at the cruellest point of the object'. The interpretation of desire thus accounts for the repetition of the mnemic act as a testimonial encounter – an encounter, that is, with the experience of *not* seeing: 'Only a rite, an endlessly repeated act, can commemorate this not very memorable encounter – for no one can say what the death of a child is, except the father *qua* father, that is to say, no conscious being' (1973: 59). In defiance of the wish to sleep, the father wakes up to reality – he responds to the summons by seeing what cannot be seen.

What does the father's predicament amount to? Can one speak of a trauma of awakening? Caruth reads Lacan from this point of view.[18] Essentially, she identifies an irreducible 'bond' between the father and the child predicated on 'the impossibility of a proper response' (2016: 103). According to Lacan (1973: 58) the 'bond' which I describe in terms of proximity, is revealed in the dream as an encounter with the real: 'What encounter can there be henceforth with that forever inert being – even now being devoured by the flames – if not the encounter that occurs precisely at the moment when, by accident, as if by chance, the flames come to meet him?' Determined by 'the impossible structure of response' (the repeated failure to see the child in its death), living-there may be seen not only as 'an accidental living beyond the child' but also as an awakening to one's own

survival in the aftermath of the traumatic accident. The event takes place
too soon for it to be experienced (lived); it cannot be grasped by consciousness as anything other than a 'gap' in the fabric of being.
Consequently, one always sees (wakes up) too late – in awakening, the father
'sees the child's death too late, and thus cannot truly or adequately respond'
(Caruth 2016: 106).

Lacan (1973: 55) contextualised the Freudian concept of 'trauma' in terms
of the function of the real as encounter, precisely an 'encounter insofar as it
may be missed, insofar as it is essentially the missed encounter'. He described
a situation in which the impossible meeting of the *tuché* determines the reality
of the past beyond the coming-back; hence 'an essential encounter – an ap-
pointment to which we are always called with a real that eludes us' (1973: 53).
How does this affect the meaning of *here is where we meet*? Two things follow
from the configuration of belatedness: firstly, the question of survival places
the encounter with death in the context of the earliest relationship; secondly,
the hypothesis of 'traumatic awakening' places reclamation and the ideal of
more life beyond the theory of wish-fulfilment. In short, the theory of trauma
is irreducible to the theory of wish-fulfilment. The fulfilment or frustration of
a wish presupposes the affective *a priori* of living-there; the reclamation of
unlived life operates on the principle that more life issues from the traumatic
origins of life itself.[19]

Lacan (1973: 55) confirms the extent to which awakening is a function of
belatedness, that is to say, insofar as the real presents itself 'in the form of
that which is *unassimilable* in it – in the form of the trauma'. The very *form*
of previously unformulated experience presupposes a link between trauma
and survival, between the child's death and the father's living-on. For
Caruth (2016: 106) Lacan's interpretation of the dream, as an instantiation
of 'an *ethical* relation to the real', rests on this link between the father's
survival and the call of a dead child – that is, on a responsibility towards the
'the nakedness of the face and its mortality'. The impossible responsibility of
consciousness – the 'impossible demand at the heart of human consciousness' (Caruth 2016: 108) – is construed along psychoanalytic lines as an
ethical relation to the real and, by the same token, as an ethical determination of trauma. The latter covers not only a failure of seeing and responding but also a reclamation in the form of an awakening to life – 'It is
precisely the dead child, the child in its irreducible inaccessibility and
otherness, who says to the father: *wake up, leave me, survive; survive to tell
the story of my burning*' (Caruth 2016: 109). The mnemic act is henceforth
inscribed in the constitutive opening between death and life. It operates
between the words of the dying child and a father who is capable of
transmitting the vital message of more life – indeed, in the form of a reenactment of the child's dying. It is not possible, under traumatic conditions,
to say what really happened in the past. Rather, as a reenacted on the site of
a trauma, the act of seeing *too late* becomes a redescription, an act of

remembering, in which the sense of the past is constructed and, thereby, reclaimed beyond the devitalised affect and general lifelessness of the repetition compulsion.

Unlived life

The criterion of action allows us to draw out aspects of memory and the experience of time that remain implicit in Freud's account. At the same time, we can retrace the conceptual trajectory of Freud's more explicit images of memory: from the neurological metaphor in the 1895 *Project* through the redescriptive nature of memory in 'Screen Memories' (1899) to the scriptural analogy in 'A Note upon the "Mystic Writing-Pad"' (1925a). Freud raised the problem of memory in the 1895 *Project* in terms of receptivity and retention. How does the mind store memories while, at the same time, making fresh additions possible? The initial solution that Freud came up with rests on the $Q\eta$ theory, the hypothesis of contact-barriers, and two kinds of neurones. Together, these foundational conceptual hypotheses describe the breaking open of a 'path' (*Bahn*) and the possible accumulation of $Q\eta$. Freud (1895: 298) noted that the latter 'is made possible by the assumption of resistances which oppose discharge; and the structure of neurones makes it probable that the resistances are all to be located in the *contacts* [between one neurone and another], which in this way assume the value of *barriers*'.

Freud (1895: 300) expanded on the basic distinction, with regards to '*permeable* neurones (offering no resistance and retaining nothing), which serve for perception [without memory], and *impermeable* ones (loaded with resistance, and holding back $Q\eta$), which are the vehicles of memory'. In the case of the former, $Q\eta$ passes through a neurone or from one neurone to another ('Q flow'), with the result that 'the passage of excitation' leaves no trace or impression. The 'current' passes through as though the neurones possess no contact-barriers; they appear to offer no resistance of any kind to Q flow. By contrast, where contact-barriers oppose the quantity of excitation, where they make themselves felt, $Q\eta$ therefore passes only 'with difficulty or partially'; hence 'a cathected neurone filled with a certain $Q\eta$' (1895: 298). In this case, neurones may, 'after each excitation, be in a different state from before and they thus afford a *possibility of representing memory*' (1895: 299: emphasis in the original).

It is the difference between breaches that accounts for the origin of memory in the $Q\eta$ theory: 'in relation to the passage of an excitation, memory is evidently one of the powers which determine and direct its pathway, and, if facilitation were everywhere equal, it would not be possible to see why one pathway should be preferred [*Wegbevorzugung*] ... *memory is represented by the differences in the facilitation between the neurones*' (1895: 300). Breaching (*Bahung*) operates as the pivotal concept here. The problem of memory reveals the extent to which psyche may be seen as a relationship of forces manifest as the difference between breaches.

I shall come back in a moment to Freud's revision of the $Q\eta$ theory. But first I want to draw attention to another key concept in Freud's analysis of memory, namely, the concept of 'screen memories'. Freud first introduced this idea in 1899; having embarked on his self-analysis in the summer of 1897, he was engaged in a series of problems concerning the nature of memory *per se*, as well as normal and pathological types of amnesia, particularly the amnesia covering the early years of childhood and its relation to infantile sexuality. The 1899 paper is based on a 'recollection' that Freud attributes to one of his patients; it is in fact a thinly disguised autobiographical memory. Starting with a general theoretical overview, Freud rehearses the repression-recollection model of memory. This is followed by a detailed analysis of an autobiographical screen memory, which takes things in the alternative direction of construction-conviction.

The role of repression in the formation of memories is set out, with respect to the 'remarkable choice' that memory makes among the elements of early childhood experience – namely, the retention of seemingly 'trivial' or 'indifferent' elements and the repression of what is most significant or 'noteworthy'. The summary account proceeds with the idea that the repressed aspects of the event are '*omitted* rather than forgotten'. Accordingly, Freud (1899: 306) construes analytic treatment as a means of 'uncovering the missing portions' of childhood memories. The assumption is that when the seemingly indifferent 'impression' is 'restored to completeness', it thereby reveals the true significance of our recollections. Freud completes the summary by furnishing the clinical description with a theoretical explanation based on the notion of unconscious conflict.

A screen memory is seen as the result of a 'compromise' between 'two psychical forces', one of which retains the 'indifferent' event in memory while the other resists what is unacceptable to consciousness. The explanation rests on the idea of a substitutive compromise, whereby the unacceptable is 'displaced' (transferred, transported) onto the retrievable. Through the psychical mechanism of 'condensation' the retentive work of the mnemic image holds the psychic tension between the memorable and the unacceptable, between its own innocuous content and a repressed sexual content. We are familiar with this account of sexual repression and neurotic conflict, an account in which the defence is set against the internal processes of drives, affects, and representations. But there is more to the paper on 'screen memories' than a reiteration of the repression-recollection model. In fact, it demonstrates the extent to which Freud had already laid the conceptual ground for a 'constructivist' theory of memory.

The more radical import of Freud's account is evident in the second half of the paper, where an autobiographical memory is presented in support of the main thesis. The memory itself dates from Freud's early childhood, before the age of three and a half years, and includes a bucolic scene in which he recalls playing in a meadow with his nephew and niece, John and Pauline, before the family moved from Freiberg to Manchester, and before Freud's own family relocated from Freiberg to Leopoldstadt. We are offered something of a fairy-tale, 'an uncontaminated state of pristine nature prior to the Fall' (Whitebook 2017: 79). The details of the memory need not concern us here. It is what Freud had to say about the *formation* of memory that proves decisive.

It would appear that the scene did not recur periodically in Freud's memory, but was stirred up only when, at the age of 16 (a year younger than reported in the paper), Freud returned to Freiberg for the first time to spend his summer holidays with the Fluss family. One of the daughters of this family, Gisela, who was three years younger than Freud, came to his attention: 'I fell immediately in love ... I kept it completely secret. After a few days the girl went off to her school ... and it was this separation after such a short acquaintance that brought my longings to a really high pitch. I passed many hours in solitary walks through the lovely woods that I had found once more and spent my time building castles in the air. These, strangely enough, were not concerned with the future but sought to improve the past' (1899: 313). His fantasies and longings, on this occasion, encapsulate the retrospective-prospective movement of psychic time, in which the unlived life ('to improve the past') comes to the fore as a fictional construct of autobiographical memory. It is the fictional narrative, the creative imperative to relive the past in accordance with a primordial sense of hopefulness, that renders the 'recollection' meaningful as a memory.[20]

The 'recollection' has yet to emerge as a fully formed memory; in fact, Freud recounts a second occasion which shapes the 'impressions' of the Alpine scene. At the age of 19 (again, a year younger than reported in the paper) Freud visited his half-brother, Emanuel, and his family in Manchester, where they had settled after leaving Freiberg. During the visit, he was reacquainted with the two children who appear alongside him in the screen memory. And while on this occasion he does not fall in love (with Pauline), nonetheless, he learns that his father and his uncle 'had concocted a plan by which I was to exchange the abstruse subject of my [university] studies for one of more practical value, settle down, after my studies were completed, in the place where my uncle lived, and marry my cousin' (1899: 314). With the passage of time, the affective threads of memory and hope move closer together under the verdict of longing. Jones (1954: 28–29) describes how Freud, '[w]hen faced with the difficulty of finding a livelihood in Vienna ... often reflected on this second, lost opportunity of an easier life and thought that there had been much to be said for his father's plan'.

Jones gives us a key to the formation of Freud's early childhood memory by referring to the *repetition* of a 'lost opportunity'. Our attention is directed to the act of temporal recovery as a repeated response to primordial loss.

For Freud, Gisela Fluss and his niece Pauline are identified with each other in a construction that rests on the impression of an 'unlived life'. The construction reveals the not unfamiliar fantasy that had one married this or that person, one's life 'would have become much pleasanter' (Freud 1899: 317). But there is more to the thought than wistful regret. The 'unlived life' is also an 'internal image' of the archaic, preoedipal past, the reclamation of which provides our memories with increasing depth and meaning. On the one hand, Freud's adolescent love for Gisela reveals an unconscious longing for the 'primary love' of the earliest relationship. A myth of origins is inscribed in the screen memory: 'On looking back [Freud] attributed his infatuation to Gisela's black hair and eyes and to the deeply moved state of mind that this visit to his birthplace had induced. It was evidently not the girl's charms themselves, since he commented on his lack of taste; he also said that he never exchanged a single word with her. So it was love of some internal image of his own plainly derived from far deeper sources but associated with his early home' (Jones 1954: 38 n 3). On the other hand, the childhood memory is constructed by an imaginative projection of two longed-for fantasies of marriage and prosperity – 'deflowering a girl' and 'material comfort' (1899: 318) – on to one another. Freud (1899: 315) himself attests to the fictional quality of his construction: 'people often construct such things unconsciously – almost like works of fiction'.

Is the qualification of memory's fictional nature warranted? It would appear that Freud believed so. The authenticity of the remembered past is maintained on the grounds that while we 'select' a given memory as homologous to subsequent experiences and fantasies, the memories themselves are nonetheless perfectly genuine. Freud (1899: 316) duly arrived at his definition of a 'screen memory' – namely, a 'recollection whose value lies in the fact that it represents in the memory impressions and thoughts of a later date whose content is connected with its own by symbolic or similar links'. Presented in the form of childhood memories, fantasy thereby extends the reach for meaning to unconscious thoughts; in particular, it disguises the explicit sexual element ('gross sexual aggression') by means of more acceptable content. Freud believed that it was possible for repressed fantasies to 'slip away into a childhood scene' only insofar as the impressions left by the original event resonated with the fantasies. In this respect, the mnemic trace provides a surface of emergence for the disguised fantasy, which, in turn, subjects the original scene to a degree of distortion. The subjective nature of the latter does not cast the objectivity of the scene itself into doubt. The past remains real in its effects.

Let us take stock. Based on the notion of 'screen memories', remembering may be broken down into its component parts – namely, (a) the mnemic trace, (b) the mnemic act, and (c) the mnemic image. Firstly, while insisting on the authenticity of the original scene, Freud (1899: 322) adds that 'the raw material of memory-traces ... remains unknown to us in its original form'. The primal form of mnemic-experience is accessible only in its effects. Secondly, the transformation from primary impression (the unconscious mnemic trace) to representational image involves the doing of a certain kind of action. For Freud the mnemic act results in 'falsifications of memory'. He believed that this was due largely to the logic of repression, although he admitted other motives with no greater regard for 'historical accuracy'. The important point is that the groundwork of memory consists in the imaginative elaboration of the mnemic act. Thirdly, the mnemic image is a repetition, but not 'an exact repetition of the impression that was originally received'. The mnemic image does not correspond to the actual facts of early childhood distinct from imaginative elaboration; the so-called original impression is already 'worked over' by the productive imagination.

The scriptural analogy

Let me now pick up the threads of the $Q\eta$ theory. In a letter to Fliess, written three years before the publication of 'Screen Memories', Freud (1985, 207-8) announced a momentous shift in his thinking, a shift that redefined memory not only as a structure of delay (*Nachträglichkeit*) but also as a type of 'writing'. The letter effectively cleared the ground for a reformulation of the entire system of the *Project* under the heading of a 'new psychology' – including, a theory of perception and (at least) three modes of registration. Recourse to the vocabulary of 'registration' (*Niederschrift*), 'transcription' (*Umschrift*), and 'sign' (*Zeichen*) placed the psychoanalytic theory of memory on a new footing.

This brings us to another key text. Further to the theoretical advance achieved in the 1895 *Project*, Freud sought to consolidate the analogy of 'psyche' and 'apparatus' in his 1925 paper 'A Note upon the "Mystic Writing-Pad"'. Its brevity notwithstanding, the paper is among Freud's most important contributions to the psychoanalysis of time. The Mystic Writing-Pad (*der Wunderblock*) is a children's toy, a writing machine, consisting of a slab of dark resin or wax with a paper edging, on top of which rests a thin transparent sheet comprising two layers, an upper layer of transparent celluloid and a lower layer of thin translucent waxed paper. While the upper sheet is fixed in place, the lower layer can be moved. It requires two hands to operate the device, which consists in scratching or scoring the surface layer of celluloid with a stylus, writing without ink, and thus pressing the lower surface of the waxed paper onto the wax slab. This produces legible marks ('dark writing') on the otherwise smooth whitish-grey sheet of celluloid. In order to 'destroy' what has been rendered visible, to make the legible illegible, one need only lift the double covering-sheet from the wax slab; the impressions now disappear and, indeed, do not reappear when the two surfaces come together once more.

Freud (1925a: 230) was intrigued by a further aspect of the device – the fact that, even though the surface of the Mystic Pad may be clear, 'it is easy to discover that the permanent trace of what was written is retained upon the wax slab itself and is legible in suitable lights'. We can see how the Mystic Pad articulates the basic problem of memory. The mechanical device provided Freud (1925a: 230) with a perfect analogy of 'two separate but interrelated component parts or systems' – including, a 'receptive surface' together with a 'protective shield' (the layer of celluloid) and 'permanent traces' comprising legible meanings. The analogy allowed Freud to posit a radically new theory of meaning. In particular, further to the intentional horizon of reference, which Husserl treated as a pattern of recollections and expectations ('retention' and 'protentions'), Freud conceived the problem of memory increasingly in scriptural terms.[21] In effect, the 1925 paper carried the Freudian interpretation beyond the phenomenological notion of horizon – including, the past-oriented and future-oriented parts of the horizon of the act of perception.

Freud (1925a: 228) continued to remodel what he saw as the essential problem of memory, namely, how to account for an 'unlimited receptive capacity for new perceptions' and, at the same time, for the retention of 'permeant memory-traces' of those perceptions. In the 1925 paper, he explicitly ruled out forms of supplementary memory, or substitutes for memory (paper, slate), where one or other of the basic criteria (receptivity, retention) is not met. Further to which he presented the Mystic Pad as analogous to his conception of the perceptual apparatus (the system *Pcpt.-Cs.*); most importantly, the model allows for the idea that perceptions are received but not retained. At the same time, Freud (1925a: 228) observed that 'the permanent traces of the excitations which have been received are preserved in "mnemic systems" [the *Ucs.*] lying behind the perceptual system'. The work of memory takes places in 'adjoining systems' alongside the receptive surface; the impressions left in the mnemic systems are not susceptible to erasure. The Pad thus offers an image of indestructibility pertaining below the surface play of appearance and disappearance – operating, that is, at a deeper level than 'the flickering-up [*Aufleuchten*] and passing-away [*Vergehen*] of consciousness in the process of perception' (1925a: 231).

What does this mean for our understanding of time and memory? The radical significance of the scriptural analogy is the topic of Derrida's celebrated commentary on Freud's paper.[22] Derrida demonstrates the extent to which 'A Note Upon the "Mystic Writing-Pad"' consolidates a major conceptual trajectory in the Freudian science. The emphasis on 'dark writing' clarifies the link between meaning and memory. More particularly, Derrida (1966: 228) described a definitive shift in Freud's discourse from the 'neurological tales of the *Project*' to the fraught 'ground' of metapsychology. The important point is that having once located himself on 'psychological ground' (1900: 536), Freud steadfastly remained put. In doing so he demonstrated a combination of tenacity and consistency that is sorely lacking in the repeated attempts, on the part of his successors, to reinstate a redundant neurological problematic in the hermeneutic field of psychoanalysis.

Derrida shows how Freud approached the problem of memory in three progressive stages, with increasing 'rigour, inwardness, and differentiation'. I alluded to these stages in my initial description of the Mystic Pad, starting with the consideration of writing as 'a technique subservient to memory, an external, auxiliary technique of psychical memory which is not memory itself' (Derrida 1966: 221). Freud did not fully explore the implications of the 'exteriority' of memory. Nevertheless, the initial reference to auxiliary apparatuses (*Hilfsapparate*) raises the question of artificial or prosthetic memory, and as such recalls the distinction between *hypomnēsis* and *mnēmē* in the *Phaedrus*. Derrida (1968b: 108) noted that Plato's attack is levelled not at memory *per se* so much as 'the substitution of the mnemonic device for live memory', the substitution of 'the passive, mechanical "by-heart" for the active reanimation of knowledge, for its reproduction in the present'. Writing enters the fray at this point: 'The space of writing, space *as* writing, is opened up in the violent movement of this surrogation, in the difference between the *mnēmē* and *hypomnēsis*. The outside is already *within* the work of memory. The evil slips in within the relation of memory to itself, in the general organisation of the mnesic activity' (1968b: 109). In a classical play of purity and danger, the metaphysical endorsement of 'living memory' casts the whole idea of metaphorical memory under the heading of defilement: 'Memory is ... contaminated by its first substitution: *hypomnēsis*. But what Plato *dreams* of is a memory with no sign. That is, with no supplement. A *mnēmē* with no *hypomnēsis*, no *pharmakon*' (1968b: 109).

In the first place, it is simply a question of considering the conditions which more or less conventional 'writing surfaces impose on the operation of mnemic supplementation' (Derrida 1966: 222). In this respect, the model does not address the essential problem of memory that carries over from the *Project*: weighing the different properties of a sheet of paper and a slate, Freud (1925a: 227–28) came to the conclusion that 'an unlimited receptive capacity and a retention of permanent traces seem to be mutually exclusive properties in the apparatus which we use for our memory: either the receptive surface must be renewed or the note must be destroyed'. The critical evaluation of 'customary writings surfaces' reveals the extent to which 'Freud, like Plato ... continues to oppose hypomnemic writing and writing *en tei psychei*, itself woven of traces, empirical memories of a present truth outside of time' (Derrida 1966: 227).

The Freudian interpretation remains limited by the opposition of 'interiority' and 'exteriority'; hence the 'Platonic' closure of Freudianism. There is nonetheless an inherent tension in Freud between recollective and productive memory. This is the theme under discussion in this chapter. In this respect, the second analogy goes further than a mere acknowledgement of an *aide-mémoire*. The contradictory criteria dating from the *Project*, namely, 'a receptive surface that can be used over and over again' (like a slate) and the retention or 'permanent traces of what has been written' (like a sheet of paper), are met by a double system. The Mystic Pad thus 'solves the problem of combining two functions *by dividing them between two separate but interrelated component parts of systems*' (1925a: 230; emphasis in the original). Despite the persistent underlying opposition between psychical and metaphorical memory, the whole of psyche, and not just the perceptual layer, can be modelled according to the second analogy.

The scriptural model comprises a third and final analogy, which points to the most far-reaching aspect of Freud's theory of memory. It is also a defining example of his metaphorical thinking *per se*. As we have seen, Freud (1925a: 230–31) compared 'the celluloid and waxed paper cover with the system *Pcpt. Cs.* and its protective shield, the wax slab with the unconscious behind them'. Furthermore, he (1925a: 231) went on to admit the *temporality* of the wax slab ('the appearance and disappearance of the writing'), which he compared to 'the flickering-up [*Aufleuchten*] and passing-away [*Vergehen*] of consciousness in the process of perception'. The alternating of the visible and the invisible – the legible and illegible determinations of meaning – admits the phenomenon of active, psychic time in conjunction with 'the multiplicity of sensitive layers'. Consequently, the 'heterogenous temporal fabric of psychical work itself', what Derrida (1966: 225) described as the discontinuous hypothesis of temporality, appears distinct from 'the continuity of a line' or 'the homogeneity of a volume'.[23]

It remains for us to explore the many and varied possibilities that Freud brought into view by means of the scriptural analogy. How far does the resemblance of artificial memory to human memory extend? It is hard to think of any aspect of contemporary life to which this question does not apply. Freud (1925a: 231) himself pressed the analogy yet further: 'On the Mystic Pad the writing vanishes every time the close contact is broken between the paper which receives the stimulus and the wax slab which preserves the impression. This agrees with a notion which I have long had about the method by which the perceptual apparatus of our mind functions, but which I have hitherto kept to myself'. Freud draws attention to the role of periodic erasure in the experience of time, the idea that consciousness fades each time the cathexis is withdrawn and the contact is broken. The basic intuition of 'discontinuity' extends from the 1895 *Project* and Freud's letters to Flies through *Beyond the Pleasure Principle* (1920) to the paper under consideration, as well as the comparably brief contemporaneous paper 'Negation' (1925c).

There are various ways of reconstructing this line of thinking. I shall limit myself to three propositions:

a Freud simultaneously announced and resisted the rule of metaphor
On the one hand, he (1925a: 230) relied on the authority of tradition for his resistance to the idea of a supplement at the origin: 'There must come a point at which the analogy between an auxiliary apparatus [*Hilfsapparate*] of this kind [the Mystic Pad] and the organ which is its prototype will cease to apply. It is true, too, that once the writing has been erased, the Mystic Pad cannot "reproduce" it from within; it would be a mystic pad indeed if, like our memory, it could accomplish that'. On the other hand, the possibility of undoing its own binary oppositions is integral to the Freudian interpretation, which, in this case, means that the sense of the past cannot be exhausted by psychology alone. The analysis of memory has to take cognisance of the exteriority of mechanical models and archival apparatuses (metaphorical memory) as well as the 'natural wax' (so to speak) of physical memory. Freud went further than even his most radical successors in treating 'spontaneity' as metaphorical as well as gestural.

b The mnemic-trace operates through the registration of its own erasure
Freud (1925a: 232) advanced this proposition at the level of representation (*die Vorstellung*): 'If we imagine one hand writing upon the surface of the Mystic Writing-Pad while another periodically raises its covering-sheet from the wax slab, we shall have a concrete representation of the way in which I tried to picture the functioning of the perceptual apparatus of our mind'. The work of remembering registers that which it represses and disavows. Accordingly, Derrida (1966: 226) underlined the extent to which mnemic-traces, 'in the "present" of their first impression' (the 'original' impression of the senses, living-there at the beginning), are determined and formed by 'the double force of repetition and erasure'.

c Metaphor constitutes a past that has never been present
The recourse to the metaphor of 'dark writing' raises a question which 'despite his premises, and for reasons which are no doubt essential ... [Freud] failed to make explicit, at the very moment when he had brought this question to the threshold of being thematic and urgent' (Derrida 1966: 228). The question of nonpsychical mnemic iteration – the reproducibility of fragmentary impressions of the senses (sensible impression) – presents us with the most rigorous, uncompromising expression of possibility in Freud's discourse: 'Writing, here, is *technē* as the relation between life and death, between present and representation, between the two apparatuses" (1966: 228).[24]

Mnemic experience

Pressing the scriptural analogy towards the 'discontinuous' hypothesis of 'temporality as spacing', Freud placed the work of remembering according to the metaphors of trace, breach, and path. Derrida insists on the centrality of this hypothesis in Freud's analysis of time. I propose, in turn, that Freud continued to view conscious recollections relating to our childhood as distortions ('screens') that allow us to conceal what actually happened, or what we wished for, in childhood. But rather than a static reproduction of something that occurred in the past, childhood memories are viewed as so many fantasy-based confabulations, the disturbing aspects of which are disguised by more acceptable wishes.

Freud set the scene for this more active conception of 'recollective' experience not only in 'Screen Memoires' but also in his *agon* with 'aesthetics' in 'The "Uncanny"' (1919). Memory is played out in disturbing but vital ways in uncanny experience; but before turning to the relationship between memory and the uncanny, let me first retrace my steps. When Freud (1899: 318) proposed that 'the childhood scene itself ... undergoes changes' in the *act* of remembering; that the retrieval situation actively contributes to the meaning of time past; and that 'falsifications of memory may be brought about in this way' – when advancing these propositions, he drew attention to the fundamental paradox pertaining to autobiographical memory. The past (the childhood scene) is not necessarily fictitious but it exists in memory only by fictional means. The point is not that 'historical truth' is inimical to the actualities pertaining to the past, but rather, that our sense of the past is grounded in impressions that are already 'worked over' by 'an initial metaphorical impulse' (Ricoeur 1978: 23). Fiction thus presents the '*not I*' self of the remembered past. The distinction between 'screen memories' and 'other memories derived from our childhood' breaks down, at this point, in dramatic terms: 'It may indeed be questioned whether we have any memories at all *from* our childhood: memories *relating to* our childhood may be all that we possess' (1899: 322; emphasis in the original). This surely counts among Freud's most searching observations.

The mediation of memory and reality by fiction – the 'falsification of memory' – is acknowledged as an inevitable but perturbing phenomenon of psychic life. Screen memories confirm the extent to which past events are routinely subject to imaginative elaboration. The suspended relation between imagination and reality comes to the fore in the link between memory and the uncanny (*das Unheimliche*): 'an uncanny effect is often and easily produced when the distinction between imagination and reality is effaced' (Freud 1919: 244). Paradoxically, the uncanny is understood as something strangely familiar that cannot be remembered.

Freud (1901: 265) presented a clear formulation of the perturbation of memory in *The Psychopathology of Everyday Life*, insisting that 'what is looked for is never remembered'. The connection between memory and the uncanny accounts for a disquieting sense of strangeness – including, a 'feeling of derealisation' (*Entfremdungsgefühl*) – that extends from one's sense of the past to the sense of oneself as another. In a late but important contribution to the conceptual itinerary under discussion, Freud (1936: 246) describes 'a disturbance of memory and a falsification of the past' from his own experience. The experience itself dates from 1904: standing on the

Acropolis and surveying the surrounding landscape, Freud was surprised by the thought that suddenly entered his mind: 'So all this really *does* exist'. The 'disturbance' demonstrates the extent to which derangement plays a decisive role in the innovation of the mnemic act. Freud (1936: 246–47) went on to explain that he had not previously 'doubted the real existence of Athens. I only doubted whether I should ever see Athens. It seemed to me beyond the realms of possibility that I should travel so far ... there was something about it that was wrong, that from the earliest times had been forbidden ... the essence of success was to have got further than one's father'.

We can summarise the 'disturbance of memory' on three counts. Firstly, imagination and reality exert themselves equiprimordially in the 'uncanny effect' (Freud 1919: 244): the blurred relationship between imagination and reality is less important for our sense of the past than the codetermining function of imagination and reality. 'Even in its caprices', Freud (1921: 111) noted in a more or less contemporaneous work, 'language remains true to some kind of reality'. Secondly, as Freud's experience on the Acropolis demonstrates, remembering our past is invariably disturbing; the act of remembering and the act of perturbing are inextricably linked in the 'uncanny effect' of temporality. Thirdly, the creative imperative of recollective experience is driven by the very perturbation of the latter; we repeatedly translate (redescribe) the *unheimlich* in and through the stories that we tell ourselves about our past. It is precisely in our efforts to ward off the more disturbing feelings of derealisation, to settle things in our mind, that 'false pronouncements about the past' (Freud 1936: 244) come into being.

Freud's analysis of the uncanny mnemic-trace is a radical contribution to the psychoanalysis of memory. Importantly, for our purposes, it draws attention to a significant exchange in the scientific controversies of the British Society. During the first series of discussions, Brierley (1943) summarised the problem in her attempt to show: (a) that Klein's theory of 'internalised object phantasies' was consistent with Freud's general conception of mental functioning; and (b) that 'memory' and 'phantasy' are linked in terms of a 'common foundation in memory-traces'. Brierley was keen to distance herself from Klein's 'expansion' of the definition of 'phantasy'; she did not accept the idea that 'phantasy' is the primary content of unconscious mental processes or the expression of thinking *per se*. At the same time, she maintained that it was possible to accommodate the concepts of 'internalised objects' and 'memory images' in a coherent theory of human experience. The accommodation of both concepts in a consistent theory rests on the classic Freudian notion of 'wish', understood as an imaginary substitute gratification in the presence of frustration. Accordingly, Brierley (1943; quoted in King and Steiner 1991: 401) held that the concept of 'internalised object' refers to 'an unconscious phantasy gratifying the wish to have the mother constantly present in the form of a belief that she is literally inside the child's body'.

Brierley assumed that Klein's notion of 'internalised object phantasies' represented a special class of unconscious phantasy, rather than an entirely new psychic phenomenon without precedent in the Freudian interpretation. Starting from this basic assumption, she proposed that both 'memory' and 'phantasy' are grounded in 'memory-images'. What does she mean by 'memory'? For Brierley, as for Freud, the problem of memory consists in the articulation of receptivity and retention. She accepted Freud's idea that experiences are registered in the psyche as mnemic traces, indeed, in such a way that they can be revived either in hallucination or in imaginative elaboration. Memory-images thus comprise images derived from memory-traces laid down, in the first instance, by perceptual experience, the remnants of which form the basis of mnemic constructs. This much is consistent with Freud's account of the way in which events are registered in different systems, stored permanently, and reactivated once they have been cathected.

Brierley, however, went on to make two further observations about memory-traces, the first brings the notion of 'experience' more sharply into focus, the second posits grounds for the creation of meaning through the 'activation' of the trace. On the one hand, she claimed that it made more sense to think of mnemic traces as 'experience-traces' or 'reaction-traces', rather than isolated sensory traces: 'The unit of experience is not an isolated element, a separate impulse, feeling or image, but always a definite relationship of impulse, and feeling to presentation' (1943; quoted in King and Steiner 1991: 402). Based on Freud's dynamic concept of mental life, she pointed out that it is not the sensory image alone that is subject to revival but the image combined with its associated affects and impulses. Reactivation and revival are seen as integral parts of the overall structure of the feeling intellect. On the other hand, given the fact that imaginary experiences are psychologically real experiences, Brierley considered ways in which images and the imaginary contribute to the orientation and organisation of 'trace systems' – including, what she called the child's unconscious 'mother-system'. Most importantly, she proposed that the activation of mnemic traces not only 'permits past experience to be revived' but also 'modifies subsequent experience'. For Brierley, the act of memory discloses new meaning through the affective force of the trace coupled with the restorative capacity of reactivation. Here, as elsewhere, Brierley established the grounds for contemporary Independent perspectives on memory.

Redescriptive memory

Mnemic experience is not a given. In the most far-reaching contribution of the English school to the psychoanalysis of time and memory, Winnicott extended the Freudian concept of *Nachträglichkeit* in terms of unlived experience. The affective basis of the not-yet-conceived past was central to Winnicott's late discovery of the 'fear of breakdown', although it is worth noting that there are certain inconsistencies in Winnicott's original formulation. In stating his main theme, Winnicott (1974: 104; emphasis in the original) proposed that 'clinical fear of breakdown is *the fear of a breakdown that has already been experienced*'. One of Winnicott's patient's, Margaret Little (1990: 62), testified to this interpretation of 'memory in the future tense' – '[Winnicott] told me that such fear of annihilation as I felt belonged to "annihilation" that had already happened'. Based on her own account, it would appear the patient 'experienced' something that happened in the past and, as such, explained her current state of persecutory anxiety. Like Winnicott, Margaret Little refers to 'reliving the past experience', which presupposes the retention of mnemic experience as a causal factor in the reenactment of early trauma.

Ogden (2014: 55; emphasis in the original) draws our attention to the inconsistencies in Winnicott's original formulation: 'Winnicott has mis-stated his main theme. What I think he means ... is that the fear of breakdown is a fear of a breakdown that has *already happened*, but has *not yet been experienced*'. Ogden, in turn, provides an illuminating discussion of the 'fear of breakdown', emphasising the analytic task of 'reclaiming' a life the full extent of which proved too much to bear in infancy and childhood. For Ogden the mnemic activity of reclamation is directed upon an 'event' that, due to the immaturity of the ego, was never fully experienced or symbolised. To restate the Winnicottian paradox from Ogden's point of view: the fear of happenings' breaking down is symptomatic of what *has* happened – namely, the not-yet-experienced breakdown in 'the mother-infant tie'.

Ogden's commentary serves as a corrective to Winnicott's original statement, although he acknowledged that Winnicott corrected himself by admitting the not-yet-experienced past in several passages of 'Fear of Breakdown'. In fact, the original formulation is yet more radical than Ogden's revision suggests. Winnicott (1974: 105) refers not only to 'a past event that has not yet been experienced' but also to a past that has 'not happened yet'. The full import of Winnicott's discovery only becomes apparent with his analysis of the negative aspects of object-relationships based on 'what didn't happen' (Pontalis 2003: 45). The negative, broadly defined, provides the context for the not-yet-conceived. This is evident in Winnicott's most influential paper, 'Transitional Objects and Transitional Phenomena', where a coherent theory of the negative is set out along both developmental and clinical lines.

The developmental argument is predicated on the idea that experience relies for its integrity on certain conditions. For Winnicott, the possibility of the infant's transition from 'dependence' to 'relative dependence' rests on the mother's 'special capacity' in making allowances for the 'illusion' that what the infant creates actually exists. The 'intermediary' status of the object, between inner and external (shared) reality, is seen as 'the basis of initiation of experience' (1971a: 14). In particular, the developmental aspects of the negative are presented in terms of 'the normality of transitional phenomena' (Winnicott 1971a: 15) – including (a) the infant's use of transitional objects as the first 'not-me' possession (1971a: 1) and (b) the movement 'towards experience' from the purely subjective to objectivity and the object-world. On both counts, Winnicott emphasised the actuality, rather than the symbolic significance, of transitional objects. The negative quality of transitional objects is seen as integral to the paradox of invention/ discovery; the object's 'not being the breast (or the mother), although real, is as important as the fact it stands for the breast (or mother)' (1971a: 6).

In addition to the identification of the negative with normal development and the formation of self-experience, Winnicott also addressed the psychopathology of the negative in terms of separation and loss. Although in the original version of the paper, which dates from 1951, he focused on the circumstances of the healthy infant, he (1971a: 9–10) nonetheless pointed out that 'a persistence of inadequacy of the external object ... leads to deadness or to a persecutory quality of the internal object'. The idea that the internal object becomes 'meaningless' due to a lack of 'aliveness' in the external object was part of the original hypothesis of transitional objects. It was only in the final version of the paper, however, published posthumously in *Playing and Reality* (1971) with two new clinical sections, that the psychopathology of the transitional or intermediary area was fully elaborated, with direct implications for the analysis of psychic temporality.

The clinical material from an adult female patient, presented for the first time in the final version of the paper, was used 'to show how the sense of loss itself can become a way of integrating one's self-experience' (1971a: 20). In effect, Winnicott put forward a new model of psychic pain based on the not-yet-conceived object and its catastrophic impact. In his account of a single analytic session, he drew attention to what he called 'the negative side of relationships' – including, the traumatic situation of catastrophic disillusionment brought about by the mother's inexplicable absence. When the knowledge of understanding is not yet available to the child, 'then when the mother is away ... she is dead from the point of view of the child' (1971a: 21–22). The unavailability of the mother results in a decathexis of the object: 'If the mother is away over a period of time which is beyond a certain limit measured in minutes, hours, or days, then the memory of the internal representation fades' (1971a: 15). It is the fading of the 'internal representation' that proves catastrophic, insofar as it interrupts the primordial movement 'towards experience'. Essentially, the disaster consists in an interruption of the experience of the transitional area, which, according to Winnicott, becomes gradually 'meaningless'. The reality that the transitional objects convey gives way to something lifeless and unreal that amounts to a break in the continuity of being. A child who has yet to experience the vitality of the object internally, that is to say, apart from the 'reassurance' of perceptual reality, cannot revive the 'dead mother' but is left only with the *remains* of not-yet-conceived the object.

In what amounts to a past that has never been present one 'remembers' at best something that might have been; or as Winnicott (1971a: 22) puts it, 'the only real thing is the gap ... the important communication for me to get [from the patient] was that there could be a blotting out, and that this blank could be the only fact and the only thing that was real'. In this case, what is 'forgotten' loses its reality; it is only the 'amnesia' that is real. Again, the 'real thing is the thing that is not there' (1971a: 23); indeed, what *is* 'not there' is more real than either the forgotten-retrievable object or the existing objects that are presently available. Winnicott's patient reveals this mnemic situation at its most profound by comparing him to the last of her former analysts, for whom she believes she will always be searching amidst the prevailing sense of absence and negativity. She acknowledges the greater good that Winnicott provides, while at the same time stating that 'The negative of him is more real than the positive of you' (1971a: 23).

Unavailability, decathexis, and unlived experience may be seen as the constituent elements of a negative configuration, the essential meaning of which was set out in Winnicott's theory of the transitional area and its vicissitudes. The urge to reclaim experience under these conditions may become a compulsive activity, something that is repeated without being integrated, resulting in a narcissistic withdrawal. Repetition issues in this case not from the repressed unconscious; but rather, from an unconscious that is formed where 'the ego integration is not able to encompass something' (Winnicott 1974: 104). Whether one can actually alter the patient's past is a moot point. Meanwhile, the analytic task consists in helping the patient gather the negative of blank pain ('primitive agony') into his or her 'present time experience'. This means meeting the patient's urgent need to lay claim to more life. The mnemic activity of reclamation thus presses for a new semantic pertinence. Memory manifests its objects. This, at least, is my thesis: that for the reclamation of unlived experience to mean anything at all there must be something essentially innovative about the mnemic act. Thinking aloud in the company of someone who is listening remains the *sine qua non* of Freudian therapy. Together with our patients, we 'remember' by *talking about* a past that has never been present; metaphors of the past elaborate on the remains of something that did not happen.

Winnicott's theory of not-yet-conceived objects provides the groundwork for the idea of redescriptive memory: 'it is not possible to remember something that has *not yet happened*, and this thing of the past has *not happened yet* because the patient was *not there* for it to happen to' (1974: 105; emphasis added). The sense of the past is occluded by the deficiency of the environment combined with the immaturity of the ego. The 'event' itself admits only a negative value. In the aftermath of negated happenings, the act of remembering is directed towards something that has *not* happened. There is nothing to remember. The unavailability of the mother at the beginning leaves its mark and, without being remembered *as such*, is manifest as a 'gap'. There is not always sufficient acknowledgement, on the part of his commentators, of Winnicott's insistence on the 'not yet happened'. César and Sára Botella

(2005: 116), for instance, miss the essential negativity in Winnicott's account. Their own work is nonetheless consistent with Winnicott's findings and, as such, provides a further elaboration on the 'not yet happened' from the point of view of the negative of the trauma: '*Something fundamentally evident for the subject that should have happened did not happen, even though he is not aware of it and*, a fortiori, *cannot form an idea of what this negative is*' (2005: 116; emphasis in the original).

Redescriptive memory may be defined as 'memory without recollection', where there is neither a distortion of reality testing, nor a recovery of the 'forgotten' object. In this case, as the Botellas (2005: 117) note, the mnemic situation consists in neither a 'return from the outside, like the *Verwerfung* [repudiation], for it is not an abolition [*Aufheben*]'; nor a 'return from the inside, as is the case of the repressed, for it is not a memory-trace'. Rather, the mnemic act is directed upon the 'psychical holes' (Green 1983: 146) that remain in the unconscious as a result of the decathexis of the object. Reclamation works along these lines on condition that the negative simultaneously shows that something should have happened (or might have happened) and presses for an augmentation of available reality. I have addressed this process throughout the chapter from the point of view of semantic innovation. The latter complements what the Botellas (2005: 117) describe as the work of 'figurability', the analyst's ability to grasp the irrepresentable by an involuntary suspension of comprehension coupled with a retrogressive movement of imaginative elaboration: 'the negative of the trauma is only discernible in the regression of the analytic situation, in the retrogressive encounter of two psyches'.[25] Finally, an augmented field of clinical action aimed at meeting the needs of this or that patient, is rooted in the tradition of Independent psychoanalysis but, as we have seen, extends more widely, which consists in enabling the patient to find or invent a narrative path in which time becomes human time.

Notes

1 See Heidegger (1992: 22) for the shift from *Was ist die Zeit?* to *Bin ich meine Zeit?*
2 Heideggerian ontology 'cannot assume the privilege of opposing all other ontologies by confining them inside the bounds of "the" metaphysical. Its unacceptable claim is that it puts an end to the history of being, as if "being disappeared in *Ereignis*" [the "thing itself"]' (Ricoeur 1978: 312).
3 See Loewald (1972a) on memory.
4 For further commentaries on Heidegger and the question of how we 'repeat' our predecessors see Wood (2002) and Sheehan (1999).
5 See Parsons (2009a; 2009b; 2011; 2014a) for a sustained engagement with the psychoanalysis of memory.
6 The figure of the 'unlaid ghost' casts a long shadow over the problem of memory in psychoanalysis. Loewald (1960: 249) discerned the deep meaning of Freud's metaphor of the ghost: 'Those who know ghosts tell us that they long to be released from their ghost life and led to rest as ancestors. As ancestors they live

forth in the present generation, while as ghosts they are compelled to haunt the present generation with their shadow life'.

7 The Freudian term and concept 'transference' recalls the Aristotelean notion of *epiphora*, a definition of metaphor in terms of movement: the transfer of meaning 'from (*apo*) … to (*epi*)'. The following well-known definition is taken from *De Poetica* (1457b 6–9): 'Metaphor consists in giving the thing a name that belongs to something else; the transference being either from genus to species, or from species to genus, or from species to species, or on grounds of analogy'.

8 The theory of 'construction' forms part of the new perspectives emergent in Freud's (1924b; 1925c; 1940b) late work. And see Freud (1900: 343–44) for 'considerations of representability' – essentially, representability in visual images – as a condition of the transformation of dream-thoughts into the dream content.

9 See Rapaport (1947) and Novey (1957) for the confluence of Kantian and Freudian thought.

10 See Richards (1926: 108–11) for the distinction between 'tied images' and 'free imagery'. Hester (1976) also differentiates between the 'free image' of the theory of association and the 'bound image' of poetic diction.

11 *The Rule of Metaphor* does not address the problem of memory; nor is Ricoeur's approach to the phenomenology of memory my topic. Rather, I draw on the hermeneutic conception of metaphor in support of my own analysis of re-descriptive memory. As regards Ricoeur's approach to the phenomenon of memory, it remains something of a lacuna in the problematic of *Time and Narrative* (1984–88) and in *Oneself as Another* (1992). It was taken up only belatedly, in the first part of *Memory, History, Forgetting* 2004) as a 'median level' between time and narrative.

12 See Lacan (1957: 421) for the designation of metonymy (displacement) as 'the first aspect of the actual field the signifier constitutes', and metaphor (condensation) as the other aspect. Ricoeur's (1978: 171–87) critique of Jakobson is pertinent, here, although it should be noted that in elaborating on the bipolarity of metaphor and metonymy, Lacan substantially alters Jakobson's work on aphasic disturbance.

13 See Ricoeur (1978: 247; Study 7, *et passim*) for the referential relationship of language to reality, namely, 'the claim of the metaphorical statement to reach reality in some particular manner'.

14 Ricoeur (1978: Study 4) traces structural linguistics and the Saussurean definition of the sign back to the beginnings of modern structural semantics – including, an emphasis on changes in the meaning of words in the work of Michel Bréal and Arsène Darmesteter. Moreover, he demonstrates that the semantics of the word takes up the most explicit aspect of the Aristotelian definition of metaphor as *epiphora* of the name.

15 See Winnicott (1971d) for a reconceptualisation of the destructive element from the point of view of object-use. Ogden (2016b) provides a useful gloss on Winnicott's paper.

16 For further commentaries on this dream, see Felman (1985), Gallop (1985), Shengold (1991), and Caruth (2016).

17 Lacan, in a telling deviation from Freud's text, insists on seeing the child in the dream as a son – one is entitled to read the statement '*I, too, have seen with my own eyes …*' (1973: 63) from the standpoint of 'the most anguishing mystery, that which links a father to the corpse of his son close by, of his dead son' (1973: 34). It is 'some secret or other shared by the father and the son' (1973: 34) that continues to exert a pressure in Lacan's reading of Freud's text.

18 See Caruth (2016) for Lacan's interpretation of the dream as an extension of Freud's late work on trauma.

19 See chapter 5 of *Beyond the Pleasure Principle* (1920) for trauma – an 'awakening' from death – as the origins of life under the auspices of Eros.

20 Jones (1954: 28) provides the requisite oedipal interpretation: 'The love episode with [Gisela], and the unconscious erotic phantasy that accompanied it, must have re-animated the infantile rape phantasy [defloration] concerning Pauline (and, doubtless, ultimately his mother also)'.

21 The terms 'retention' and 'protention' are used by Husserl in his account of our experience of time: 'retention' refers to the past-oriented aspect of the horizon of the act of perception, and 'protention' to the future-oriented aspect of the horizon. Husserl (1973: 111) maintained that 'an ego-act is subject in each of its phases to the law of retention and protention'. The extent to which psychoanalysis itself provides new perspectives on the *horizon* of the acting person is my topic in chapters 3 and 4.

22 The text, which is taken from a lecture delivered at the *Institut de psychanalyse* as part of André Green's seminar, and published initially in *Tel Quel*, represents a significant early contribution to Derrida's oeuvre; nor does the problematic set out in this text become any less urgent in Derrida's later works.

23 Compare Green's (2002) notion of *le temps éclaté* ('shattered time').

24 Derrida (1995: 25) elaborates at greater length on this possibility in *Archive Fever*, with respect to the 'hypomnesic and prosthetic experience of the technical substrate', or the 'moment *proper* to the archive'. The distinction between 'memory' and 'archive' underwrites the defining possibility of Freudianism in terms of the 'substrates of traces', the transference of affect, and the temporalisation of the unconscious. Derrida announced the *trajection* – crossing, transmission, transference – of this possibility in '*Différance*'. The potential of psychoanalysis itself amounts to yet one more elaboration on *Nachträglichkeit* and its two structural moments – deferral and construction: 'The alterity of the "unconscious" makes us concerned not with horizons of modified – past or future – presents, but with a "past" that has never been present, and which never will be, whose future to come will never be a production or a reproduction in the form of presence' (1968a: 21).

25 Compare Winnicott's (1954b) theory of regression in the analytic setting.

Bibliography

Abraham, K. (1911) 'Notes on the psycho-analytical investigation and treatment of manic-depressive insanity and allied conditions', in *Selected Papers on Psycho-analysis*, London: Hogarth Press, 1927, pp. 137–156.

Abraham, K. (1916) 'The first pregenital stage of the libido', in *Selected Papers on Psycho-analysis*, London: Hogarth Press, 1927, pp. 248–279.

Abraham, K. (1924) 'A short study of the development of the libido, viewed in the light of mental disorders', in *Selected Papers on Psycho-analysis*, London: Hogarth Press, 1927, pp. 418–501.

Abram, J. (2008) 'The evolution of Winnicott's theoretical matrix: A brief outline', in *Donald Winnicott Today*, J. Abram (ed.), Hove: Routledge, 2013, pp. 73–112.

Ahbel-Rappe, K. (2006) '"I no longer believe": Did Freud abandon the seduction theory?' *Journal of the American Psychoanalytic Association*, 54: 171–199.

Alvarez, A. (1992) *Live Company: Psychoanalytic Psychotherapy with Autistic, Borderline, Deprived and Abused Children*, London and New York: Routledge.

Amacher, P. (1965) *Freud's Neurological Education and Its Influence on Psychoanalytic Theory*, New York: International Universities Press.

Anzieu, D. (1975) 'La psychanalyse encore', *Revue française de psychanalyse*, 39: 135–146.

Anzieu, D. (1989) *The Skin Ego: A Psychological Approach to the Self*, trans. Chris Turner, New Haven: Yale University Press.

Aristotle (2001) *The Basic Works of Aristotle*, edited by Richard McKeon with an Introduction by C. D. C. Reeve, New York: Modern Library.

Aron, L. (1996) *A Meeting of Minds*, Hillsdale, NJ: Analytic Press.

Ayer, A. J. (1936) *Language, Truth and Logic*, London: Gollancz.

Balint, A. (1939) 'Love for the mother and mother love', in *Michael Balint Primacy Love and Psycho-Analytic Technique*, London: Maresfield, 1985, pp. 109–127.

Bass, A. (2000) *Difference and Disavowal: The Trauma of Eros*, Stanford, CA: Stanford University Press.

Beattie, H. J. (2003) 'The repression and the return of bad objects: W. R. D. Fairbairn and the historical roots of theory', *International Journal of Psychoanalysis*, 84: 1171–1187.

Bennington, G. (1991) 'Derridabase', in *Jacques Derrida, Geoffrey Bennington and Jacques Derrida*, trans. Geoffrey Bennington, Chicago: University of Chicago Press.

Beres, D. (1958) 'Vicissitudes of superego functions and superego precursors in childhood', *Psychoanalytic Study of the Child*, 13: 324–351.

Bick, E. (1968) 'The experience of the skin in early object relations', in *Surviving Space: Papers on Infant Observation*, A. Briggs (ed.), London: Karnac, 2002, pp. 55–59.

Bick, E. (1986) 'Further considerations on the function of the skin in early object relations', in *Surviving Space: Papers on Infant Observation*, A. Briggs (ed.), London: Karnac, 2002, pp. 60–71.

Blattner, W. D. (1999) *Heidegger's Temporal Idealism*, Cambridge: Cambridge University Press.

Blum, H. P. (1994) *Reconstruction in Psychoanalysis: Childhood Revisited and Recreated*, New York: International Universities Press.

Bollas, C. (1999) *The Mystery of Things*, London and New York: Routledge.

Bollas, C. (2007) *The Freudian Moment*, London: Karnac Books.

Bollas, C. (2009) *The Evocative Object World*, London and New York: Routledge.

Botella, C. and Botella, S. (2005) *The Work of Figurability: Mental States without Representation*, trans. Andrew Weller with the collaboration of Monique Zerbib. Hove and New York: Routledge.

Bouvet, M. (1967) *Oeuvres Psychanalytiques I. La Relation d'Objet*. Paris: Payot.

Breuer, J. and Freud, S. (1893–1895) 'Studies on Hysteria', *SE*, 2: 1–305.

Brierley, M. (1943) 'Third discussion of scientific controversies', in *The Freud-Klein Controversies 1941-45*, P. King and R. Steiner (eds.), London: Routledge, 1991, pp. 385–414.

Brusset, B. (1988) *Psychoanalyse du Lein, la Relation d'Objet*, Paris: Cenurion.

Buber, M. (1959) *I and Thou*, second edition, trans. Ronald G. Smith, Edinburg: T and T Clark.

Caruth, C. (2016) *Unclaimed Experience: Trauma, Narrative, and History*, 20th Anniversary Edition, Baltimore, MD: Johns Hopkins University Press.

Chabert, C. (2003) *Féminin mélancolique*, Paris: PUF.

Chodorow, N. (2003) 'The psychoanalytic vision of Hans Loewald', *International Journal of Psychoanalysis*, 84: 897–913.

Chodorow, N. (2008) 'Introduction: The Loewaldian legacy', *Journal of the American Psychoanalytic Association*, 56: 1089–1096.

Chodorow, N. (2020) *The Psychoanalytic Ear and the Sociological Eye: Toward an American Independent Tradition*, New York: Routledge.

Chrétien, J-L. (2004) *The Call and the Response*, trans. Anne A. Davenport, New York: Fordham University Press.

Colarusso, C. A. (2006) 'The absence of a future: The effect of past experience and current developmental conflicts on a midlife analysis', *Journal of the American Psychoanalytic Association*, 54 (3): 919–943.

Dastur, F. (1999) *Heidegger and the Question of Time*, trans. F. Raffoul and D. Pettigrew, Amherst, NY: Humanity Books.

Demske, J. M. (1970) *Being, Man, and Death: A Key to Heidegger*, Kentucky: University Press of Kentucky.

Derrida, J. (1964) 'Violence and metaphysics: An essay on the thought of Emmanuel Levinas', in *Writing and Difference*, trans. Alan Bass, London and Henley: Routledge and Kegan Paul, 1978, pp. 79–153.

Derrida, J. (1966) 'Freud and the scene of writing', in *Writing and Difference*, trans. Alan Bass, London and Henley: Routledge and Kegan Paul, 1978, pp. 196–231.

Derrida, J. (1968a) 'Différance', in *Margins of Philosophy*, trans. Alan Bass, Brighton: Harvester Press, 1982, pp. 3–27.

Derrida, J. (1968b) 'Plato's pharmacy', in *Dissemination*, trans. Barbara Johnson, London: Athlone Press, 1981, pp. 61–172.

Derrida, J. (1991) *Given Time: 1. Counterfeit Money*, trans. Peggy Kamuf, Chicago: University of Chicago Press, 1992.

Derrida, J. (1996) *Resistances of Psychoanalysis*, trans. Peggy Kamuf, Pascale-Anne Brault, and Michael Naas, Stanford, CA: Stanford University Press, 1998.

Donnet, J.-L. (2016) *Dire ce qui vient. Association libre et transfert*, Paris: Presses Universitaires de France.

Dreyfus, H. L. (1991) *Being-in-the-World: A Commentary on Heidegger's* Being and Time, *Division I*, Cambridge, MA: MIT Press.

Fairbairn, W. R. D. (1930) 'Libido theory re-evaluated', in *From Instinct to Self: Selected Papers of W. R. D. Fairbairn, Vol. II, Applications and Early Contributions*, E. F. Birtles and D. E. Scharff (eds.), New Jersey: Jason Aronson, 1994, pp. 115–156.

Fairbairn, W. R. D. (1940) 'Schizoid factors in the personality', in *Psychoanalytic Studies of the Personality*, London: Tavistock, 1952, pp. 3–27.

Fairbairn, W. R. D. (1941) 'A revised psychopathology of the psychoses and psychoneuroses', in *Psychoanalytic Studies of the Personality*, London: Tavistock, 1952, pp. 28–58.

Fairbairn, W. R. D. (1943) 'The repression and the return of bad objects (with special reference to the "war neuroses")', in *Psychoanalytic Studies of the Personality*, London: Tavistock, 1952, pp. 59–81.

Fairbairn, W. R. D. (1944) 'Endopsychic structure considered in terms of object-relationships', in *Psychoanalytic Studies of the Personality*, London: Tavistock, 1952, pp. 82–136.

Fairbairn, W. R. D. (1946) 'Object-relationships and dynamic structure', in *Psychoanalytic Studies of the Personality*, London: Tavistock, 1952, pp. 137–151.

Fairbairn, W. R. D. (1952) *Psychoanalytic Studies of the Personality*, London: Tavistock.

Fairbairn, W. R. D. (1954) 'The nature of hysterical states', in *From Instinct to Self: Selected Papers of W. R. D. Fairbairn, Vol. I, Clinical and Theorectical Papers*, E. F. Birtles and D. E. Scharff (eds.), New Jersey: Jason Aronson, 1994, pp. 13–40.

Fairbairn, W. R. D. (1958) 'On the nature and aims of psychoanalytical treatment', in *From Instinct to Self: Selected Papers of W. R. D. Fairbairn, Vol. I, Clinical and Theoretical Papers*, E. F. Birtles and D. E. Scharff (eds.), New Jersey: Jason Aronson, 1994, pp. 74–92.

Falzeder, E., Barabant, E. and Giampieri-Deutsch, P. (eds.) (1996) *The Correspondence of Sigmund Freud and Sándor Ferenczi, Vol. 2*, transl. Peter T. Hoffer, Cambridge, MA: Beknap Press.

Falzeder, E. (ed.) (2002) *The Complete Correspondence of Sigmund Freud and Karl Abraham 1907-1925*, transl. Caroline Schwarzacher, London: Karnac.

Felman, S. (1985) '"Don't you see I'm burning?" Or Lacan and philosophy', in *Writing and Madness: Literature/Philosophy/Psychoanalysis*, Ithaca, NY: Cornell University Press, pp. 134–140.

Fenichel, O. (1926) 'Identification', in *The Collected Papers of Otto Fenichel*, First Series, H. Fenichel and D. Rapaport (eds.), New York: W. W. Norton, 1953, pp. 97–112.

Ferenczi, S. (1913) 'Stages in the development of the sense of reality', in *First Contributions to Psycho-Analysis*, London: Hogarth, reprinted by Karnac Books, 1980, pp. 213–239.

Ferenczi, S. (1925) 'Psycho-analysis of sexual habits', in *Further Contributions to the Theory and Technique of Psycho-Analysis*, London: Hogarth, reprinted by Karnac Books, 1980, pp. 259–297.

Fogel, G. I. (1991) 'Loewald's integrate and integrative approach', in G. I. Fogel (ed.), *The Work of Hans Loewald: An Introduction and Commentary*, Northvale, NJ: Jason Aronson, 1991, pp. 3–11.

Forrester, J. and Cameron, L. (2017) *Freud in Cambridge*, Cambridge: Cambridge University Press.

Fraiberg, S. (1952) 'A critical neurosis in a 2½-year-old girl', *Psychoanalytic Study of the Child*, 7: 173–215.

Freud, S. (1895) 'Project for a scientific psychology', *SE*, 1: 295–397.

Freud, S. (1896a) 'The aetiology of hysteria', *SE*, 3: 191–221.

Freud, S. (1896b) 'Further remarks on the neuro-psychoses of defence', *SE*, 3: 159–188.

Freud, S. (1896c) 'Heredity and the aetiology of the neuroses', *SE*, 3: 143–156.

Freud, S. (1899) 'Screen memories', *SE*, 3: 299–322.

Freud, S. (1900) 'The interpretation of dreams', *First Part. SE*, 4: 23–338.

Freud, S. (1900–1901) 'The interpretation of dreams', *Second Part. SE*, 5: 339–621.

Freud, S. (1901) 'The psychopathology of everyday life', *SE*, 6: 1–310.

Freud, S. (1905) 'Three essays on the theory of sexuality', *SE*, 7: 123–245.

Freud, S. (1908 [1907]) 'Creative writers and day-dreaming', *SE*, 9: 143–153.

Freud, S. (1909a) 'Analysis of a phobia in a five-year-old boy', *SE*, 10: 1–149.

Freud, S. (1909b) 'Notes upon a case of obsessional neurosis', *SE*, 10: 155–318.

Freud, S. (1910a) 'Leonardo da Vinci and a memory of his childhood', *SE*, 11: 63–137.

Freud, S. (1910b) 'The future prospects of psychoanalytic therapy', *SE*, 11: 141–151.

Freud, S. (1910c) 'The psychoanalytic view of psychogenic disturbance of vision', *SE*, 11: 211–218.

Freud, S. (1911a) 'Psycho-analytical notes on an autobiographical account of a case of paranoia (Dementia Paranoides)', *SE*, 12, 12–82.

Freud, S. (1911b) 'Formulations on the two principles of mental functioning', *SE*, 12: 218–226.

Freud, S. (1912) 'Recommendations to physicians practising psycho-analysis', *SE*, 12: 111–121.

Freud, S. (1913a) 'On beginning the treatment (Further recommendations on the technique of psycho-analysis I)', *SE*, 12: 123–144.

Freud, S. (1913b) 'The theme of the three caskets', *SE*, 12: 289–301.

Freud, S. (1913c [1912–13]). 'Totem and Taboo', *SE*, 13: 1–162.

Freud, S. (1914a) 'Remembering, repeating and working-through (Further recommendations on the technique of psycho-analysis II)', *SE*, 12: 147–156.

Freud, S. (1914b) 'On narcissism: An introduction', *SE*, 14: 67–102.

Freud, S. (1915a) 'Instincts and their vicissitudes', *SE*, 14: 117–140.

Freud, S. (1915b) 'The unconscious', *SE*, 14: 166–215.

Freud, S. (1915c) 'Thoughts for the times on war and death', SE, 14: 275–302.

Freud, S. (1915d [1914]) 'Observations on transference-love (Further recommendations on the technique of psycho-analysis II)', *SE*, 12: 159–171.

Freud, S. (1917a [1915]) 'A metapsychological supplement to the theory of dreams', *SE*, 14: 222–235.

Freud, S. (1917b [1915]) 'Mourning and melancholia', *SE*, 14, 237–258.

Freud, S. (1918 [1914]) 'From the history of an infantile neurosis', *SE*, 17: 7–122.

Freud, S. (1919) 'The "uncanny"', *SE*, 17: 219–256.

Freud, S. (1920) 'Beyond the pleasure principle', *SE*, 18: 1–64.

Freud. S. (1921) 'Group psychology and the analysis of the ego', *SE*, 18: 65–143.

Freud, S. (1923a [1922]) 'Two encyclopaedia articles', *SE*, 18: 235–259.

Freud, S. (1923b) 'The Ego and Id', *SE*, 19: 1–66.

Freud, S. (1924a [1923]) 'Neurosis and psychosis', *SE*, 19: 147–153.

Freud, S. (1924b) 'The economic problem of masochism', *SE*, 19: 159–170.

Freud, S. (1925a [1924]) 'A note upon the "Mystic Writing-Pad"', *SE*, 19: 227–232.

Freud, S. (1925b) 'Some additional notes on dream-interpretation as a whole', *SE*, 19: 127–138.

Freud, S. (1925c) 'Negation', *SE*, 19: 233–239.

Freud, S. (1926 [1925]) 'Inhibitions, symptoms and anxiety', *SE*, 20: 87–175.

Freud, S. (1927) 'The future of an illusion', *S.E.*, 21: 5–56.

Freud, S. (1930 [1929]) 'Civilization and its discontents', *SE*, 21: 57–145.

Freud, S. (1933 [1932]) 'New introductory lectures on psycho-analysis', *SE*, 22: 5–182.

Freud, S. (1936) 'A disturbance of memory on the Acropolis', *SE*, 22: 239–248.

Freud, S. (1937a) 'Analysis terminable and interminable', *SE*, 23: 216–253.

Freud, S. (1937b) 'Constructions in analysis', *SE*, 23: 257–269.

Freud, S. (1939 [1934–38]) 'Moses and monotheism: Three essays', *SE*, 23: 7–137.

Freud, S. (1940a [1938]) 'An outline of psycho-analysis', *SE*, 23: 144–207.

Freud, S. (1940b [1938]) 'Splitting of the ego in the process of defence', *SE* 23: 275–278.

Freud, S. (1985) *The Complete Letters of Sigmund Freud to Wilhelm Fliess 1887–1904*, translated and edited by J. Masson, Cambridge, MA: Harvard University Press.

Freud, S. (1987) *A Phylogenetic Fantasy: Overview of the Transference Neuroses*, transl. Hoffer and Hoffer, Cambridge, MA: Harvard University Press.

Gallop, J. (1985) *Reading Lacan*, Ithaca, NY: Cornell University Press.

Gay, P. (1988) *Freud: A Life for Our Time*, London: Dent.

Giannakoulas, A. (2010) *La tradizione psicoanalitica britannica Indipendente tradition*, Rome: Borla.

Glover, E. (1956) *On the Early Development of the Mind, Vol. I, Selected Papers on Psychoanalysis*, London: Imago.

Green, A. (1983) 'The dead mother', in *On Private Madness*, London: Hogarth Press, 1986, pp. 142–173.

Green, A. (2002) *Time in Psychoanalysis: Some Contradictory Aspects*, trans. A. Weller, London: Free Association Books.

Green, A. (2005) *Key Ideas for a Contemporary Psychoanalysis: Misrecognition and Recognition of the Unconscious*, trans. A. Weller, London and New York.

Greenberg, J. R. (1991) *Oedipus and Beyond: A Clinical Theory*, Cambridge, MA: Harvard University Press.

Greenberg, J. R. and Mitchell, S. A. (1983) *Object Relations in Psychoanalytic Theory*, Cambridge, MA: Harvard University Press.

Grosskurth, P. (1985) *Melanie Klein: Her World and Her Work*, London: Hodder and Stoughton.

Grotstein, J. S. (1980) 'Primitive mental states', *Contemporary Psychoanalysis*, 16: 479–546.

Grotstein, J. S. (1981) *Splitting and Projective Identification*, New York: Jason Aronson.

Guntrip, H. (1961) *Personality Structure and Human Interaction*, London: Hogarth Press.

Hamilton, E. and H. Cairns (eds.) (1961) *The Collected Dialogues of Plato*, Princeton, NJ: Princeton University Press.

Harrison, R. P. (2003) *The Dominion of the Dead*, Chicago: Chicago University Press.

Hanley, C. (1994) 'Clinical advantages and disadvantages of multiple models', *Psychoanalytical Inquiry*, 14: 164–184.

Hartmann, H. (1948) 'Comments on the psychoanalytic theory of instinctual drives', in *Essays on Ego Psychology*, New York: International Universities Press, 1964, pp. 69–89.

Hartocollis, P. (1972) 'Time as a dimension of affects'. *Journal of the American Psychoanalytic Association*, 20: 92–108.

Hartocollis, P. (1976) 'On the experience of time and its dynamics, with special reference to affects'. *Journal of the American Psychoanalytic Association*, 24: 363–375.

Haugeland, J. (2002) 'Temporality', in John Haugeland, *Dasein Disclosed: John Haugeland's Heidegger*, J. Rouse (ed.), Cambridge, MA: Harvard University Press, 2013, pp. 221–240.

Haugeland, J. (2007a) 'Letting be', in John Haugeland, *Dasein Disclosed: John Haugeland's Heidegger*, J. Rouse (ed.), Cambridge, MA: Harvard University Press, 2013, pp. 167–178.

Haugeland, J. (2007b) 'Death and Dasein', in John Haugeland, *Dasein Disclosed: John Haugeland's Heidegger*, J. Rouse (ed.), Cambridge, MA: Harvard University Press, 2013, pp. 179–186.

Haugeland, J. (2013) *Dasein Disclosed: John Haugeland's Heidegger*, J. Rouse (ed.), Cambridge, MA: Harvard University Press.

Hayman, A. (2013) *What Do Our Terms Means? Explorations Using Psychoanalytic Theories and Concepts*, London: Karnac.

Haynal, A. and Falzeder, E. (2002) 'Introduction' to *The Complete Correspondence of Sigmund Freud and Karl Abraham 1907–1925*, E. Falzeder (ed.), transl. Caroline Schwarzacher, London: Karnac, pp. xix–xxx.

Heidegger, M. (1962) *What is a Thing?* trans. W. B. Barton, Jr.and V. Deutsch, South Bend, Indiana: Regnery/Gateway, 1967.

Heidegger, M. (1962 [1927]) *Being and Time*, trans. J. Macquarrie and E. Robinson, Oxford: Basil Blackwell.

Heidegger, M. (1973) *Kant and the Problem of Metaphysics*, trans. Richard Taft, Bloomington and Indianapolis: Indiana University Press, 1990.

Heidegger, M. (1992) *The Concept of Time*, trans. William McNeill, Oxford: Blackwell.

Hermann, I. (1976) 'Clinging-going-in-search: A contrasting pair of instincts and their relation to sadism and masochism'. *Psychoanalytic Quarterly*, 45: 5–36.

Hester, M. B. (1967) *The Meaning of Poetic Language*, The Hague: Mouton.

Hughes, J. M. (1989) *Reshaping the Psycho-Analytic Doman: The Work of Melanie Klein, W. R. D. Fairbairn, and D. W. Winnicott*, Berkley and Los Angeles, CA: University of California Press.

Husserl, E. (1950) *Cartesian Meditations: An Introduction to Phenomenology*, trans. Dorion Cairns, Dordrecht: Kluwer Academic Publishers.

Husserl, E. (1970a) *Logical Investigations*, Volumes 1 and 2, trans, J. N. Findlay, London: Routledge.

Husserl, E. (1970b) *The Crisis of European Sciences and Transcendental Phenomenology*, trans. David Carr, Evanston: Northwestern University Press.

Husserl, E. (1973) *Experience and Judgement: Investigations in a Genealogy of Logic*, trans. James S. Churchill and Karl Ameriks, Evanston: Northwestern University Press.

Hutchinson, B. (2016) *Lateness in Modern European Literature*, Oxford: Oxford University Press.

Isaacs, S. (1943) 'The nature and function of phantasy', in P. King and R. Steiner (eds.) *The Freud-Klein Controversies 1941–1945*, London: Routledge, 1991, pp. 265–314.

Jacobson, E. (1964) *The Self and the Object World*, London: Hogarth Press.

Jones, D. (1959) *Free Associations: Memories of a Psycho-Analyst*, London: The Hogarth Press.

Jones, E. (1954) *Sigmund Freud: Life and Work, Volume 1, The Young Freud 1856-1900*, London: Hogarth Press.

Kant, I. (1798/1978) *Anthropology from a Pragmatic Point of View*, trans. Victor Lyle Dowdell, Carbondale and Edwardsville: Southern Illinois University Press.

Kant, I. (1781/1998) *Critique of Pure Reason*, trans. Paul Guyer and Allen W. Wood, Cambridge: Cambridge University Press.

Keene, J. (2012) 'Reflections on the evolution of Independent psychoanalytic thought', in P. Williams, J. Keene and S. Dermen (eds.) *Independent Psychoanalysis Today*, London, Karnac Books, pp. 3–61.

Kernberg, O. F. (1976) *Object Relations Theory and Clinical Psycho-Analysis*, New York: Jason Aronson.

Kernberg, O. F. (1980) *Internal World and External Reality*, New York: Jason Aronson.

King, P. (1989) 'Paula Heimann's quest for her own identity as a psychoanalyst: An introductory memoir', in M. Tonnesmann (ed.), *About Children and Children-No-Longer: Collected Papers 1942–80*. London: Routledge, pp. 1–9.

King, P. and Steiner, R. (eds.) (1991) *The Freud-Klein Controversies: 1941–45*, London: Routledge.

Klein, M. (1928) 'Early stages of the Oedipus conflict', in *Love, Guilt and Reparation and Other Works 1921–1945*, London: Hogarth Press, 1981, pp. 186–198.

Klein, M. (1930) 'The importance of symbol-formation in the development of the ego', in *Love, Guilt and Reparation and Other Works 1921–1945*, London: Hogarth Press, 1981, pp. 219–232.

Klein, M. (1935) 'A contribution to the psychogenesis of manic-depressive states', in *Love, Guilt and Reparation and Other Works 1921–1945*, London: Hogarth Press, 1981, pp. 262–289.

Klein, M. (1940) 'Mourning and its relation to manic-depressive states', in *Love, Guilt and Reparation and Other Works 1921–1945*, London: Hogarth Press, 1981, pp. 344–369.

Klein, M. (1946) 'Notes on some schizoid mechanism', in R. Money-Kyrle (ed.) *Envy and Gratitude and Other Works 1946–1963*, London: Hogarth Press, 1980, pp. 1–24.

Klein, M. (1952a) 'The origins of transference', in R. Money-Kyrle (ed.) *Envy and Gratitude and Other Works 1946–1963*, London: Hogarth Press, 1980, pp. 48–56.

Klein, M. (1952b) 'Some theoretical conclusions regarding the emotional life of the infant', in R. Money-Kyrle (ed.) *Envy and Gratitude and Other Works 1946–1963*, London: Hogarth Press, 1980, pp. 61–93.

Klein, M. (1957) 'Envy and gratitude', in R. Money-Kyrle (ed.) *Envy and Gratitude and Other Works 1946–1963*, London: Hogarth Press, 1980, pp. 176–235.

Klein, M. (1963) 'On the sense of loneliness', in R. Money-Kyrle (ed.) *Envy and Gratitude and Other Works 1946–1963*, London: Hogarth Press, 1980, pp. 300–313.

Kohon, G. (ed.) (1986) *The British School of Psychoanalysis: The Independent Tradition*, London: Karnac Books.

Kohon, G. (ed.) (2018) *British Psychoanalysis: New Perspectives in the Independent Tradition*, Oxford and New York: Routledge.

Krell, D. F. (2015) *Ecstasy, Catastrophe: Heidegger from* Being and Time *to the* Black Notebooks, New York: State University of New York Press.

Lacan, J. (1957) 'The instance of the letter in the unconscious or reason since Freud', in *Écrits*, trans. Bruce Fink, New York: Norton, 2006, pp. 412–441.

Lacan, J. (1973) *The Seminar of Jacques Lacan. Book XI: The Four Fundamental Concepts of Psycho-Analysis*, trans. Alan Sheridan, New York: Norton, 1978.

Lacan, J. (1975) *The Seminar of Jacques Lacan. Book I: Freud's Papers on Technique 1953-1954*, trans. John Forrester, Cambridge: Cambridge University Press, 1988.

Lacan, J. (1978) *The Seminar of Jacques Lacan. Book II: The Ego in Freud's Theory and in the Technique of Psychoanalysis 1954–1955*, trans. Sylvana Tomaselli, Cambridge: Cambridge University Press, 1988.

Lacan, J. (1994) *The Seminar of Jacques Lacan. Book IV: The Object Relation*, trans. A. R. Price, Cambridge: Polity Press, 2020.

Lacan, J. (2004) *The Seminar of Jacques Lacan. Book X: Anxiety*, trans. A. R. Price, Cambridge: Polity Press, 2014.

Lagache, D. (1961) 'La psychanalyse et la structure de la personnalité', *La Psychanalyse 6, Société psychoanalytique de Paris*, Presses universitaires de France.

Laplanche, J. (2015) *Between Seduction and Inspiration: Man*, New York: The Unconscious in Translation.

Lear, J. (1996) 'The introduction of Eros: reflections on the work of Hans Loewald', in *Open Minded: Working Out the Logic of the Soul*, Cambridge, MA: Harvard University Press, 1998, pp. 121–147.

Lear, J. (2006) *Radical Hope: Ethics in the Face of Cultural Devastation*, Cambridge, MA: Harvard University Press.

Levinas, E. (1964) 'Meaning and sense', in *Basic Philosophical Writings*, trans. Adriaan T. Peperzak, Simon Critchley and Robert Bernasconi, Bloomington and Indianapolis: Indiana University Press, 1996, pp. 33–64.

Levinas, E. (1969) *Totality and Infinity: An Essay on Exteriority*, trans. Alphonso Lingis, Dordrecht: Kluwer Academic Publishers.

Levinas, E. (1974) *En découvrant l'existence avec Husserl and Heidegger*, second edition, Paris: Vrin.

Levinas, E. (1976) 'The ethical relationship as a departure from ontology', in *God, Death, and Time*, W. Hamacher and D. E. Wellbery (eds.), Stanford, CA: Stanford University Press, 2000, pp. 180–184.

Levinas, E. (1981) *Otherwise than Being or Beyond Essence*, trans. Alphonso Lingis, The Hague: Martinus Nijhoff Publishers.

Levinas, E. (1986) 'The proximity of the other', in *Is it Righteous to Be? Interviews with Emmanuel Levinas*, J. Robbins (ed.), Stanford, CA: Stanford University Press, 2001, pp. 211–218.

Levinas, E. (1988) 'Dying for...', in *Entre Nous: On Thinking-of-the-Other*, trans. Michael B. Smith and Barbara Harshav, London: Athlone Press, 1998, pp. 207–217.

Little, M. I. (1990) *Psychotic Anxieties and Containment: A Personal Record of an Analysis with Winnicott*, Northvale, NJ: Jason Aronson.

Loewald, H. (1949) 'Ego and reality', in *Papers on Psycho-Analysis*, New Haven: Yale University Press, 1980, pp. 3–20.

Loewald, H. (1951) 'The problem of defense and the neurotic interpretation of reality', in *Papers on Psycho-Analysis*, New Haven: Yale University Press, 1980, pp. 21–32.

Loewald, H. (1960) 'On the therapeutic action of psychoanalysis', in *Papers on Psycho-Analysis*, New Haven: Yale University Press, 1980, pp. 221–256.

Loewald, H. (1962a) 'Internalization, separation, mourning, and the superego', in *Papers on Psycho-Analysis*, New Haven: Yale University Press, 1980, pp. 257–276.

Loewald, H. (1962b) 'Superego and time', in *Papers on Psycho-Analysis*, New Haven: Yale University Press, 1980, pp. 43–52.

Loewald, H. (1969) 'Freud's conception of the negative therapeutic reaction, with comments on instinct theory', in *Papers on Psycho-Analysis*, New Haven: Yale University Press, 1980, pp. 315–325.

Loewald, H. (1970) 'Psychoanalytic theory and the psychoanalytic process', in *Papers on Psycho-Analysis*, New Haven: Yale University Press, 1980, pp. 277–301.

Loewald, H. (1971a) 'On motivation and instinct theory', in *Papers on Psycho-Analysis*, New Haven: Yale University Press, 1980, pp. 102–137.

Loewald, H. (1971b) 'The experience of time', in *Papers on Psycho-Analysis*, New Haven: Yale University Press, 1980, pp. 138–147.

Loewald, H. (1972a) 'Perspectives on memory', in *Papers on Psycho-Analysis*, New Haven: Yale University Press, 1980, pp. 148–173.

Loewald, H. (1972b) 'Freud's conception of the negative therapeutic reaction, with comments on instinct theory', in *Papers on Psycho-Analysis*, New Haven: Yale University Press, 1980, pp. 315–325.

Loewald, H. (1973) 'On internalization', in *Papers on Psycho-Analysis*, New Haven: Yale University Press, 1980, pp. 69–86.

Loewald, H. (1974) 'Psychoanalysis as an art and the fantasy character of the psychoanalytic situation' in *Papers on Psycho-Analysis*, New Haven: Yale University Press, 1980, pp. 352–371.

Loewald, H. (1977) 'Reflections on the psychoanalytic process and its therapeutic potential', in *Papers on Psycho-Analysis*, New Haven: Yale University Press, 1980, pp. 372–383.

Loewald, H. (1978a) 'Primary process, secondary process, and language', in *Papers on Psycho-Analysis*, New Haven: Yale University Press, 1980, pp. 178–206.

Loewald, H. (1978b) 'Instinct theory, object relations, and psychic structure formation', in *Papers on Psycho-Analysis*, New Haven: Yale University Press, 1980, pp. 207–218.

Loewald, H. (1988) *Sublimation: Inquires into Theoretical Psychoanalysis*, New Haven: Yale University Press.

Lyotard, J.-F. (1984) *The Postmodern Condition: A Report on Knowledge* (trans. G. Bennington and B. Massumi). Manchester: Manchester University Press.

Masterman, M. (1957) 'Metaphysical and ideographic language', in C. A. Mace (ed.) *British Philosophy in the Mid-Century*, London: Allen and Unwin, 1957, pp. 283–357.

Marty, P. (1976) *Les mouvements individuels de vie et de mort*, Paris: Payot.

Mauss, M. (1950) *The Gift: The Form and Reason for Exchange in Archaic Societies*, trans. W. D. Halls, London: Routledge, 1990.

May, U. (2019) 'In conversation: Freud, Abraham and Ferenczi on "Mourning and Melancholia" (1915–1918)', *International Journal of Psychoanalysis*, 100 (1): 77–98.

Meltzer, D. (1966) 'The relation of anal masturbation to projective identification', in *Melanie Klein Today: Developments in Theory and Practice*, Vol. 1, Mainly Theory, London: Routledge, pp. 102–116.

Merleau-Ponty, M. (1964) *Signs*, trans. Richard C. McCleary, Evanston, IL: Northwestern University Press.

Merleau-Ponty, M. (1968) *The Visible and the Invisible*, trans. Alponso Lingis, Evanston, IL: Northwestern University Press.

Milner, M. (1969) *The Hands of the Living God: An Account of a Psycho-analytic Treatment*, London: Hogarth Press.

Milner, M. (1977) 'Winnicott and overlapping circles', in *The Suppressed Madness of Sane Men: Forty-Four Years of Exploring Psychoanalysis*, London and New York: Tavistock, 1987, pp. 279–286.

Mitchell, S. (1981) 'The origin and the nature of the "object" in the theories of Klein and Fairbairn', *Contemporary Psychoanalysis*, 17: 374–398

Mitchell, S. (1988) *Relational Concepts in Psychoanalysis: An Integration*, Cambridge, MA: Harvard University Press.

Mitchell, S. (1997) *Influence and Autonomy in Psychoanalysis*, Hillside, New York: Analytic Press.

Mitchell, S. (1998) 'From ghosts to ancestors: The psychoanalytic vision of Hans Loewald', *Psychoanalytic Dialogues*, 8 (6): 825–855.

Mitchell, S. (2000) *Relationality: From Attachment to Intersubjectivity*, London and New York: Routledge.

Mitchell, S. and Aron, L. (1999) *Relational Psychoanalysis: The Emergence of a Tradition*, London and New York: Routledge.

Mitchell, S. and Black, M. J. (2016) *Freud and Beyond: A History of Modern Psychoanalytic Thought*, second edition, New York: Basic Books.

Novey, S. (1957) 'A re-revaluation of certain aspects of the theory of instinctual drives in the light of modern ego psychology', *International Journal of Psychoanalysis*, 38: 137–145.

Nunberg, H. (1955) *Principles of Psycho-Analysis: Their Application to the Neuroses*, New York: International Universities Press.

Ogden, T. H. (1997) 'Reverie and metaphor: Some thoughts on how I work as a psychoanalyst', in *Conversations at the Frontier of Dreaming*, London: Karnac, 2002, pp. 17–46.

Ogden, T. H. (2001) 'Reading Winnicott', *Psychoanalytic Quarterly*, 70: 299–323.

Ogden, T. H. (2002) 'A new reading on the origins of object-relations theory', *International Journal of Psychoanalysis*, 83: 767–782.

Ogden, T. H. (2010) 'Why read Fairbairn?', *International Journal of Psychoanalysis*, 91: 101–118.

Ogden, T. H. (2014) 'Fear of breakdown and the unlived life', *International Journal of Psychoanalysis*, 91: 205–224.

Ogden, T. H. (2015) *This Art of Psychoanalysis: Dreaming Undreamt Dreams and Interrupted Cries*, London and New York: Routledge.

Ogden, T. H. (2016a) *Reclaiming Unlived Life: Experiences in Psychoanalysis*, London and New York: Routledge.

Ogden, T. H. (2016b) 'Destruction reconceived: On Winnicott's "The Use of an Object and Relating through Identification', *International Journal of Psychoanalysis*, 97(5): 1243–1262.

Paris, M. L. (2000) '"Mourning and melancholia": The genesis of a text and of a concept', *International Journal of Psychoanalysis*, 82: 283–305.

Parsons, M. (2009a) 'Keeping death alive', in *Living Psychoanalysis: From Theory to Experience*, Hove: Routledge, 2014, pp. 3–16.

Parsons, M. (2009b) 'Why did Orpheus look back. *Après-coup, avant-coup*', in *Living Psychoanalysis: From Theory to Experience*, Hove: Routledge, 2014, pp. 17–34.

Parsons, M. (2011) 'In defence of the uncanny', in *Living Psychoanalysis: From Theory to Experience*, Hove: Routledge, 2014, pp. 48–61.

Parsons, M. (2014a) 'More about memory', in *Living Psychoanalysis: From Theory to Experience*, Hove: Routledge, 2014, pp. 35–47.

Parsons, M. (2014b) 'An Independent theory of clinical technique', in *Living Psychoanalysis: From Theory to Experience*, Hove: Routledge, 2014, pp. 184–204.

Parsons, M. (2017) 'Free association and the death drive: The solemn freedom of psychoanalysis', *Bulletin of the British Psycho-Analytical Society*, 53 (1): 3–11.

Pine, F. (1985) *Developmental Theory and Clinical Process*, New Haven: Yale University Press.

Pine, F. (1988) 'The four psychologies of psychoanalysis and their place in clinical work', *Journal of the American Psychoanalytic Association*, 36: 571–596.

Pine, F. (1989) 'Motivation, personality organization, and the four psychologies of psychoanalysis', *Journal of the American Psychoanalytic Association*, 37: 31–64.

Pine, F. (1990) *Drive, Ego, Object, Self: A Synthesis for Clinical Work*, New York: Basic Books.

Pontalis, J.-B. (1974) 'A propos de Fairbairn: Le psychisme comme double métaphore du corps', *Nouvelle Revue de Psychanalyse*, 10: 56–59.

Pontalis, J.B. (1993) *Love of Beginnings*, trans. James Green with Marie-Christine Réguis, London: Free Association Books.

Pontalis, J-B. (2003) *Windows*, trans. Anne Quinney. Lincoln: University of Nebraska Press.

Pribram, K. H. (1969) 'Freud's project: An open biologically based model of psychoanalysis', in N. S. Greenfield and W. C. Lewis (eds.), *Psychoanalysis and Current Biological Thought*, Madison and Milwaukee: University of Wisconsin Press, 1965, pp. 93–124.

Pribram, K. H. and Gill, M. M. (1976) *Freud's 'Project' Reassessed: Preface to Contemporary Cognitive Theory and Neuropsychology*, New York: Basic Books.

Rapaport, D. (1947) 'Dynamic psychology and Kantian epistemology', in M. Gill (ed.), *The Collected Papers of David Rapaport*, New York: Basic Books, 1967, pp. 289–298.

Rapaport, D. (1960) 'On the psychoanalytic theory of motivation', in M. R. Jones (ed.), *Nebraska Symposium on Motivation*, Lincoln: University Nebraska Press, 1960, pp. 173–247.

Rayner, E. (1990) *The Independent Mind in British Psychoanalysis*, London: Free Association Books; republished by Routledge in 2020 with a new foreword from Maurice Whelan.

Reich, A. (1954) 'Early identification as archaic elements in the superego', *Journal of the American Psychoanalytic Association*, 2: 218–238.

Richards, I. A. (1926) *Principles of Literary Criticism*, second edition, London: Routledge and Kegan Paul.

Richards, I. A. (1936) *The Philosophy of Rhetoric*, Oxford: Oxford University Press.

Richards, I. A. (1955) 'Towards a more synoptic view', in *Richards on Rhetoric. I. A. Richards: Selected Essays (1929–1974)*, Oxford: Oxford University Press, 1991, pp. 222–229.

Ricoeur, P. (1970) *Freud and Philosophy: An Essay on Interpretation*. New Haven and London: Yale University Press.

Ricoeur, P. (1978) *The Rule of Metaphor: Multi-disciplinary studies of the creation of meaning in language*, trans. Robert Czerny, London and Henley: Routledge and Kegan Paul.

Ricoeur, P. (1984) *Time and Narrative*, volume 1, trans. Kathleen McLaughlin and David Pellauer, Chicago: Chicago University Press.

Ricoeur, P. (1985) *Time and Narrative*, volume 2, trans. Kathleen McLaughlin and David Pellauer, Chicago: Chicago University Press.

Ricoeur, P. (1988) *Time and Narrative*, volume 3, trans. Kathleen McLaughlin and David Pellauer, Chicago: Chicago University Press.

Ricoeur, P. (1991a) *From Text to Action: Essays in Hermeneutics*, II, trans. Kathleen Blamey and John B. Thompson, Evanston, IL: Northwestern University Press.

Ricoeur, P. (1991b) 'Imagination in discourse and in action', in *From Text to Action: Essays in Hermeneutics*, II, trans. Kathleen Blamey and John B. Thompson, Evanston, IL.: Northwestern University Press, 1991, pp. 168–187.

Ricoeur, P. (1992) *Oneself as Another*, trans. Kathleen Blamey, Chicago: University of Chicago Press.

Ricoeur, P. (1997) 'Otherwise: A reading of Emmanuel Levinas's Otherwise Than Being or Beyond Essence', in *Yale French Studies* 104, *Encounters with Levinas*, T. Trezise (ed.), New Haven, CT: Yale University Press, 2004, pp. 82–99.

Ricoeur, P. (2004) *Memory, History, Forgetting*, trans. Kathleen Blamey and David Pellauer, Chicago: University of Chicago Press.

Rorty, R. (1980) *Philosophy and the Mirror of Nature*, Oxford: Basil Blackwell.

Rosenfeld, H. (1962) 'The superego and the ego-ideal', in *Psychotic States: A Psychoanalytical Approach*, London: Karnac Books, 1982, pp. 144–154.

Roussillon, R. (2011) *Primitive Agony and Symbolization*, London: Karnac.

Rubens, R. L. (1984) 'The meaning of structure in Fairbairn', *International Review of Psychoanalysis*, 11: 429–440.

Rubens, R. L. (1994) 'Fairbairn's structural theory', in *Fairbairn and the Origins of Object Relations*, J. S. Grotstein and D. B. Rinsley (eds.), London: Free Association Books, 1994, pp. 151–173.

Rycroft, C. (1995) *A Critical Dictionary of Psychoanalysis*, second edition, Harmondsworth: Penguin Books.

Sandler, J. (1960) 'The background of safety', in *From Safety to Superego: Selected Papers of Joseph Sandler*, New York: Guilford, 1987, pp. 1–8.

Sandler, J. (1972) 'The role of affects in psychoanalytic theory', in *From Safety to Superego: Selected Papers of Joseph Sandler*, New York: Guilford, 1987, pp. 285–297.

Schafer, R. (1976) *A New Language for Psychoanalysis*, New Haven: Yale University Press.

Schmitz, K. L. (1994) *At the Centre of the Human Drama: The Philosophical Anthropology of Karol Wojtyla/Pope John Paul II*, Washington, DC: Catholic University America Press.

Sharpe, E. F. (1940) 'Psycho-physical problems revealed in language: an examination of metaphor', in *Collected Papers on Psycho-Analysis*, London: Hogarth Press, 1950, pp. 155–169.

Sharpe, E. F. (1943) 'Memorandum on her technique', in P. King and R. Steiner (eds.) *The Freud-Klein Controversies 1941–45*, London: Routledge, 1991, pp. 639–645.

Sheehan, T. (1999) 'Choosing one's fate: A re-reading of *Sein und Zeit*, § 74', *Research in Phenomenology*, 29: 63–83.

Shengold, L. (1991) *"Father, Don't You See I'm Burning?" Reflections on Sex, Narcissism, Symbolism, and Murder: From Everything to Nothing*, New Haven: Yale University Press.

Skolnick, N. J. (1998) 'The good, the bad, and the ambivalent: Fairbairn's difficulty locating the good object in the endopsychic structure', in N. J. Skolnick and D. E. Scharff (eds.) *Fairbairn, Then and Now*, Hillsdale, NJ.: Analytic Press, 1998, pp. 137–159.

Solms, M. and Saling, M. (1987) 'On psychoanalysis and neuroscience: Freud's attitude to the localizationist tradition', *International Journal of Psychoanalysis*, 67: 397–416.

Spinoza, B. (1985) *The Collected Works of Spinoza*, Vol. I, edited and translated by E. Curley, Princeton, NJ: Princeton University Press.

Spitz, R. A. (1955) 'The primal cavity: A contribution to the genesis of perception and its role for psychoanalytic theory', *Psychoanalytic Study of the Child*, 10: 215–240.

Spitz, R. A. (1957) *No and Yes: On the Genesis of Human Communication*, New York: International University Press.

Spitz, R. A. (1958) 'On the genesis of super-ego components', *Psychoanalytic Study of the Child*, 13: 375–404.

Spitz, R. A. (1972) 'Bridges – on anticipation, duration, and meaning', *Journal of the American Psychoanalytic Association*, 20: 721–735.

Strachey, J. (1943) 'Discussion Memorandum by James Strachey, Member of the Training Committee, February 24th, 1943', in P. King and R. Steiner (eds.) *The Freud-Klein Controversies: 1941–45*, London: Routledge, 1991, pp. 602–610.

Sullivan, H. S. (1953) *The Interpersonal Theory of Psychiatry*, New York: Norton.

Symington, N. (1983) 'The analyst's act of freedom as agent of therapeutic change', in *Becoming a Person through Psychoanalysis*, London: Karnac Books, 2007, pp. 51–68.

Symington, N. (1987) 'John Klauber – Independent clinician', in *Illusion and Spontaneity in Psychoanalysis*, London: Free Association Books, 1987, pp. 46–65.

Symington, N. (1996) 'The origins of rage and aggression', in *Becoming a Person through Psychoanalysis*, London: Karnac Books, 2007, pp. 115–121.

Symington, N. (2002) *A Pattern of Madness*, London: Karnac.

Symington, N. (2007) *Becoming a Person through Psychoanalysis*, London: Karnac Books.

Tustin, F. (1985) 'The rhythm of safety', in *Autistic Barriers in Neurotic Patients*, London: Karnac, 1986, pp. 268–285.

Vermorel, H. (2005) 'Fairbairn in France', in J. S. Scharff and D. E. Scharff (eds.) *The Legacy of Fairbairn and Sutherland: Psychotherapeutic Applications*, London: Routledge, 2005, pp. 50–60.

Weissman, P. (1954) 'Ego and superego in obsessional character and neuroses', *Psychoanalytic Quarterly*, 32: 529–543.

Whitebook, J. (2017) *Freud: An Intellectual Biography*, Cambridge: Cambridge University Press.

Widlöcher, D. ([2006] 2012) 'Winnicott and the acquisition of a freedom of thought', in J. Abram (ed.) *Donald Winnicott Today*, Hove: Routledge, 2013. pp. 235–249.

Williams, P., Keene, J. and Dermen, S. (eds.) (2012) *Independent Psychoanalysis Today*, London: Karnac.

Williams, R. (2014) *The Edge of Words: God and the Habits of Language*, London: Bloomsbury.

Winnicott, D. W. (1939) 'Aggression', in C. Winnicott, R. Shepherd and M. Davis (eds.) *Deprivation and Delinquency*, London and New York: Tavistock Publications, 1984, pp. 84–92.

Winnicott, D. W. (1945) 'Primitive emotional development', in M. Khan (ed.), *Through Paediatrics to Psychoanalysis*, London: Hogarth Press, 1978, pp. 145–156.

Winnicott, D. W. (1949) 'Mind and its relation to the psyche-soma', in M. Khan (ed.), *Through Paediatrics to Psychoanalysis*, London: Hogarth Press, 1978, pp. 243–254.

Winnicott, D. W. (1950–55) 'Aggression in relation to emotional development', in Khan, M. (ed.), *Through Paediatrics to Psychoanalysis*, London: Hogarth Press, 1978, pp. 204–218.

Winnicott, D. W. (1952) 'Anxiety associated with insecurity', in *Through Paediatrics to Psycho-Analysis*, London: Hogarth Press, 1978, pp. 97–100.

Winnicott, D. W. (1954a) 'Withdrawal and regression', in *Through Paediatrics to Psycho-Analysis*, London: Hogarth Press, 1978, pp. 255–261.

Winnicott, D. W. (1954b) 'Metapsychological and clinical aspects of regression within the psycho-analytical set-up', in *Through Paediatrics to Psycho-Analysis*, London: Hogarth Press, 1978, pp. 278–294.

Winnicott, D. W. (1954–55) 'The depressive position in normal emotional development', in *Through Paediatrics to Psycho-Analysis*, London: Hogarth Press, 1978, pp. 262–277.

Winnicott, D. W. (1956a) 'Primary maternal preoccupation', in *Through Paediatrics to Psycho-Analysis*, London: Hogarth Press, 1978, pp. 300–305.

Winnicott, D. W. (1956b) 'The antisocial tendency', in C. Winnicott, R. Shepherd and M. Davis (eds.) *Deprivation and Delinquency*, London and New York: Tavistock Publications, 1984, pp. 120–131.

Winnicott, D. W. (1957) 'Integrative and disruptive factors in family life', in *The Family and Individual Development*, London: Tavistock Publications, pp. 40–49.

Winnicott, D. W. (1960a) 'Ego distortion in terms of true and false self', in *The Maturational Processes and the Facilitating Environment*, London: Hogarth Press, 1985, pp. 140–152.

Winnicott, D. W. (1960b) 'The theory of the parent-infant relationship', in *The Maturational Processes and the Facilitating Environment*, London: Hogarth Press, 1985, pp. 37–55.

Winnicott, D. W. (1962) 'Ego integration in child development', in *The Maturational Processes and the Facilitating Environment*, London: Hogarth Press, 1985, pp. 56–63.

Winnicott, D. W. (1963a) 'The development of the capacity for concern', in *The Maturational Processes and the Facilitating Environment*, London: Hogarth Press, 1985, pp. 73–82.

Winnicott, D. W. (1963b) 'From dependence towards independence in the development of the individual', in *The Maturational Processes and the Facilitating Environment*, London: Hogarth Press, 1985, pp. 83–92.

Winnicott, D. W. (1963c) 'Morals and education', in *The Maturational Processes and the Facilitating Environment*, London: Hogarth Press, 1985, pp. 93–105.

Winnicott, D. W. (1964) *The Child, the Family, and the Outside World*, Harmondsworth: Penguin Books.

Winnicott, D. W. (1965) 'A clinical study of the effect of a failure of the average expectable environment on a child's mental functioning', *International Journal of Psychoanalysis*, 46: 81–87.

Winnicott, D. W. (1967) 'The location of cultural experience', in *Playing and Reality*, London: Tavistock Publications, 1971, pp. 95–103.

Winnicott, D. W. (1968a) 'Communication between infant and mother, and mother and infant, compared and contrasted', in *Babies and their Mothers*, edited by Clare Winnicott, Ray Shepherd, and Madeleine Davis, Reading, Mass.: Addison-Wesley Publishing Company, 1987, pp. 89–103.

Winnicott, D. W. (1968b) 'Comments on my paper "The Use of an Object"', in *Psychoanalytic Explorations*, edited by Clare Winnicott, Ray Shepherd, and Madeleine Davis, London: Karnac Books, 1989, pp. 238–240.

Winnicott, D. W. (1969) 'The use of an object in the context of *Moses and Monotheism*', in *Psychoanalytic Explorations*, edited by Clare Winnicott, Ray Shepherd, and Madeleine Davis, London: Karnac Books, 1989, pp. 240–246.

Winnicott, D. W. (1970) 'On the basis for self in body', in *Psychoanalytic Explorations*, edited by Clare Winnicott, Ray Shepherd, and Madeleine Davis, London: Karnac Books, 1989, pp. 261–283.

Winnicott, D. W. (1971a) 'Transitional objects and transitional phenomena', in *Playing and Reality*, London: Tavistock Publications, 1971, pp. 1–25.

Winnicott, D. W. (1971b) 'Playing: A theoretical statement', in *Playing and Reality*, London: Tavistock Publications, 1971, pp. 38–52.

Winnicott, D. W. (1971c) 'Playing: Creative activity and the search for the self', in *Playing and Reality*, London: Tavistock Publications, 1971, pp. 53–64.

Winnicott, D. W. (1971d) 'The use of an object and relating through identifications', in *Playing and Reality*, London: Tavistock Publications, 1971, pp. 86–94.

Winnicott, D. W. (1971e) 'The place where we live', in *Playing and Reality*, London: Tavistock Publications, 1971, pp. 104–110.

Winnicott, D. W. (1974) 'Fear of breakdown', *International Review of Psychoanalysis*, 1: 103–107.

Winnicott, D. W. (1987) *The Spontaneous Gesture: Selected Letters of D. W. Winnicott*, F. R. Rodman (ed.), Cambridge, MA: Harvard University Press.

Winnicott, D. W. (1988) *Human Nature*. London: Free Association Books.

Winnicott, D. W. and Khan, M. (1953) 'A review of Fairbairn's *psychoanalytic studies in personality*', *International Journal of Psychoanalysis*, 34: 329–333.

Wojtyła, K. (1979) *The Acting Person, Analecta Husserliana, the Yearbook of Phenomenological Research*, Vol. X, A.-T. Tymieniecka (ed.), trans. Andrzej Potocki. Dordrecht: D. Reidel Publishing Company.

Wojtyła, K. (2013) *Love and Responsibility*, trans. and foreword Grzegorz Ignatik, Boston: Pauline Books.

Wood, D. (2002) *Thinking after Heidegger*, Cambridge: Polity Press.

Zahavi, D. (2003) *Husserl's Phenomenology*, Stanford, CA: Stanford University Press.

Zucket, R. (2007) 'Projection and purposiveness: Heidegger's Kant and the temporalization of judgement', in S. Crowell and J. Malpas (eds.) *Transcendental Heidegger*, Stanford, CA: Stanford University Press, pp. 213–231.

Index

For Product Safety Concerns and Information please contact our EU
representative GPSR@taylorandfrancis.com
Taylor & Francis Verlag GmbH, Kaufingerstraße 24, 80331 München, Germany

9 781138 241237